Old-Age Income Support in the 21st Century

An International Perspective
on Pension Systems and Reform

Robert Holzmann and Richard Hinz

together with

Hermann von Gersdorff, Indermit Gill, Gregorio Impavido,
Alberto R. Musalem, Robert Palacios, David Robolino,
Michal Rutkowski, Anita Schwarz, Yvonne Sin,
Kalanidhi Subbarao

THE WORLD BANK
WASHINGTON, D.C.

ISBN 0-8213-6040-X
eISBN 0-8213-6168-6
EAN 978-0-8213-6040-8

Library of Congress Cataloging-in-Publication Data
Holzman, Robert, 1949–
    Old-age income support in the 21st century : an international perspective on pension systems and reform / Robert Holzman, Richard Hinz.
    p. cm.
    Includes bibliographical references.
    ISBN 0-8213-6040-X (pbk.)
    1. Old age pensions—Government policy. 2. Aging—Economic aspects—Government policy. 3. Income maintenance programs. 4. Social security. I. Hinz, Richard P. II. Title.

HD7105.3.H65 2005
331.25'2—dc22

                                                                2005043404

The cover photos are from the World Bank Photo Library.

Contents

iii

FIGURES

TABLES

Preface

THIS REPORT WAS INITIATED BY THE OFFICE of the Chief Economist of the World Bank, which wanted the key staff involved in pension issues to explain the Bank's perspective on pension reforms to other Bank staff and the outside world. The result constitutes a joint cross-sectoral effort, much of which was undertaken outside of regular working hours. The cross-sectoral and cross-regional Bank team includes staff from three sectors or networks (Social Protection, Financial Sector, and Poverty Reduction and Economic Management) and four Bank regions (Europe and Central Asia, Latin America and the Caribbean, Middle East and North Africa, and East Asia and the Pacific). The biographical information of lead and collaborating authors appear at the end of the report.

The team's work benefited from presentations and comprehensive discussions with the pension community inside and outside the Bank, from consultations at the General Assembly of the International Social Security Association (Beijing, September 12–18, 2004) and at the International Labour Organization during the General Assembly (Geneva, November 8, 2004), from comments by the international trade union movement, and from quite tough but extremely valuable reviews and guidance from five outside experts: Mukul Asher (University of Singapore), Nicholas Barr (London School of Economics), Axel Boersch-Supan (University of Mannheim), Peter Diamond (Massachusetts Institute of Technology), and Salvador Valdés-Prieto (Catholic University of Santiago, Chile). We are grateful for all the feedback and suggestions we have received, many of which are reflected in the revised version, and we appreciate the interest of so many pension experts in the pension work of the Bank. All remaining errors are, of course, our own.

This report has not undergone the review accorded to official World Bank publications. The findings, interpretations, and conclusions expressed herein are those of the authors and do not necessarily reflect the views of the World Bank and its affiliated organizations or those of the executive directors of the World Bank or the governments they represent.

Acronyms and Abbreviations

AFAP	Administradora de Fondos de Ahorro Provisional (Uruguay)
AFJP	Administradora de Fondos de Jubilaciones y Pensiones (Argentina)
AFORE	Administradora de Fondos para el Retiro (Mexico)
AFP	Administradora de Fondos de Pensiones (Bolivia, Chile, Colombia, Dominican Republic, El Salvador, Nicaragua, Peru)
EDAP	Entidades Depositarias del Ahorro Provisional (Ecuador)
EET	Exempt-exempt-tax (treatment of contributions, returns, and benefits)
ERISA	Employee Retirement Income Security Act (United States)
EU	European Union
GDP	Gross domestic product
HIV/AIDS	Human immunodeficiency virus/acquired immune deficiency syndrome
ILO	International Labour Organization (Geneva)
IMF	International Monetary Fund (Washington, D.C.)
IOPS	International Organization of Pension Supervisors
IPD	Implicit pension debt
ISSA	International Social Security Association (Geneva)
OECD	Organization for Economic Co-operation and Development (Paris)
OED	Operations Evaluation Department (World Bank)
OPC	Operadora de Pensiones Complementarios (Costa Rica)
PROST	Pension Reform Options Simulation Toolkit
TEE	Tax-exempt-exempt (treatment of contributions, returns, and benefits)

Introduction and Executive Summary

THE PAST DECADE HAS BROUGHT BROAD RECOGNITION of the importance of pension systems to the economic stability of nations and the security of their aging populations. For the past 10 years, the World Bank has taken a leading role in addressing this challenge through its support for pension reform around the world.

The Bank has been involved in pension reform in more than 80 countries and provided financial support for reform to more than 60 countries, and the demand for such support continues to grow. This experience has significantly expanded the knowledge and insights of Bank staff and stimulated an ongoing process of evaluation and refinement of the policies and priorities that guide the work in this area.

What emerges from these interactions with policymakers, pension experts, and representatives from civil society in client and donor countries is the continued relevance of the main objectives of pension systems—poverty alleviation and consumption smoothing—and of the broader goal of social protection. The Bank continues to perceive advantages in multipillar designs that contain some funded element when conditions are appropriate but increasingly recognizes that a range of choices can help policymakers to achieve effective old-age protection in a fiscally responsible manner.

The suggested multipillar pension system is composed of some combination of five basic elements: (a) a noncontributory or "zero pillar" (in the form of a demogrant or social pension) that provides a minimal level of protection;[1] (b) a "first-pillar" contributory system that is linked to varying degrees to earnings and seeks to replace some portion of income; (c) a mandatory "second pillar" that is essentially an individual savings account but can be constructed in a variety of ways; (d) voluntary "third-pillar" arrangements that can take many forms (individual, employer sponsored, defined benefit, defined contribution) but are essentially flexible and discretionary in

1

nature; and (e) informal intrafamily or intergenerational sources of both financial and nonfinancial support to the elderly, including access to health care and housing. For a variety of reasons, a system that incorporates as many of these elements as possible, depending on the preferences of individual countries as well as the level and incidence of transaction costs, can, through diversification, deliver retirement income more effectively and efficiently.

The main changes to the Bank's perspective concern the enhanced focus on basic income provision for all vulnerable elderly as well as the enhanced role for market-based, consumption-smoothing instruments for individuals both within and outside mandated pension schemes. The Bank increasingly recognizes the importance of initial conditions and the extent to which conditions in a particular country necessitate a tailored or tactically sequenced implementation of the multipillar model.

This policy report was written to clarify and update the World Bank's perspective on pension reform, incorporating the lessons learned from recent experience and research that has advanced the understanding of how best to proceed in the future. It has been developed as a policy note, not as a research paper. As such, it is intended to conceptualize and explain current policy thinking within the Bank rather than to announce a new policy approach.

This articulation of policies and priorities is intended to assist Bank clients and the broader international public to understand and appreciate the Bank's framework for pension reform and to facilitate its ability to work effectively with clients in meeting the challenges ahead. This report provides a guide to the criteria and standards that the World Bank will apply in deciding when and where to provide financial and technical support for pension reforms.

The report has two main parts. Part 1 presents the framework for the Bank's thinking on pension reform, including its origins and scope, and the structure of Bank lending in this area. Part 2 highlights key issues pertaining to design and implementation. This introduction summarizes the main messages and outlines the structure of the report.

A Framework for Pension Reform

The evolution of the Bank's perspective on pension reform over the past decade reflects the extensive experience with reform in client countries, an ongoing dialogue with academics and partner organizations, and intensive internal discussion and evaluation of pension reforms worldwide. As a result, the original concept of a specific three-pillar structure—(a) a mandated, unfunded, and publicly managed defined-benefit system, (b) a mandated, funded, and privately managed defined-contribution scheme, and (c) voluntary retirement savings—has been extended to include two additional pillars: (d) a basic (zero) pillar to deal more explicitly with the poverty objective and (e) a nonfinancial (fourth) pillar to include the broader context of social policy, such as family support, access to health care, and housing.

The past decade of experience, while contributing considerable depth to the understanding of the nuances and challenges of pension reform, has reinforced the need in nearly every circumstance to move away from the single-pillar design. Experience has demonstrated that the multipillar design is better able to deal with the multiple objectives of pension systems—the most important being poverty reduction and income smoothing—and to address more effectively the kinds of economic, political, and demographic risks facing any pension system. The proposed multipillar design is much more flexible and better addresses the main target groups in the population. Advance funding is still considered useful, but the limits of funding in some circumstances are also seen much more sharply. The main motivation for the Bank to support pension reform has not changed. Instead it has been strengthened by the past decade of experience: most pension systems in the world do not deliver on their social objectives, they create significant distortions in the operation of market economies, and they are not financially sustainable when faced with an aging population.

Review and Extension of the Original Concept

The extensive experience in implementing pension reforms in a range of settings since the early 1990s has motivated Bank staff to review and refine the Bank's framework to guide the appropriate objectives and path of a reform effort. The evolution of policy is characterized by five main additions to the Bank's perspective:

- *A better understanding of reform needs and measures.* This includes (a) assessing the need for reform beyond fiscal pressure and demographic challenges to address issues such as socioeconomic changes and the risks as well as opportunities of globalization; (b) understanding the limits and other consequences of mandating participation in pension systems, particularly for low-income groups, for which risks other than old age may be more immediate and much stronger; and (c) reassessing the continued importance, but also the limitations, of prefunding for dealing with population aging in recognition of the importance of associated behavioral changes, including enhanced labor supply and later retirement.
- *The extension of the multipillar model beyond the three-pillar structure to encompass as many as five pillars and to move beyond the conventional concentration on the first and second pillars.* Experience with low-income countries has brought into focus the need for a basic or zero

(or noncontributory) pillar that is distinguished from the first pillar in its primary focus on poverty alleviation in order to extend old-age security to all of the elderly. Experience in low- to middle-income countries has heightened awareness of the importance of the design and implementation of the third and voluntary pillar, which can effectively supplement the basic elements of a pension system to provide reasonable replacement rates for higher-income groups, while constraining the fiscal costs of the basic components. Last, but not least, is recognition of the importance of a fourth pillar for retirement consumption, which consists of a mixture of access to informal support (such as family support), other formal social programs (such as health care), and other individual financial and nonfinancial assets (such as home ownership) and the need to incorporate their existence or absence explicitly into the design of the pension system.

- *An appreciation of the diversity of effective approaches, including the number of pillars, the appropriate balance among the various pillars, and the way in which each pillar is formulated in response to particular circumstances or needs.* Some pension systems function effectively with only a zero pillar (in the form of a universal social pension) and a third pillar of voluntary savings. In some countries, the introduction of a mandatory second pillar is required to gain popular acceptance for a reform of the first pillar, while the political economy of other countries makes a reformed (first-pillar) public system in conjunction with voluntary schemes the only realistic alternative.

- *A better understanding of the importance of initial conditions in establishing the potential for and limitations within which reforms are feasible.* There is now greater awareness of the extent to which the inherited pension system as well as the economic, institutional, financial, and political environment of a country dictate the options available for reform. This is particularly important in establishing the pace and scope of a viable reform.

- *A strong interest in, and support of, country-led innovations in pension design and implementation.* These innovations include (a) the nonfinancial or notional defined-contribution system as a promising approach to reforming or implementing an unfunded first pillar; (b) the clearinghouse and similar concepts as a means to reduce transaction costs for funded and privately managed pillars; (c) the transformation of severance payments into combined unemployment and retirement-benefit savings accounts; and (d) public prefunding under an improved governance structure as introduced in a number of high-income countries. While each of these innovations is promising, they require close monitoring and evaluation, as transferability to other countries cannot be assumed.

Statement of Key Principles

Although the essential policy formulation explicitly recognizes country-specific conditions and leads to implementation of the multipillar model in a variety of ways, the Bank's perspective incorporates several principles that are deemed essential to any successful reform.

First, all pension systems should, in principle, have elements that provide basic income security and poverty alleviation across the full breadth of the income distribution. Fiscal conditions permitting, this suggests that each country should have provisions for a basic pillar, which ensures that people with low lifetime incomes or who only participate marginally in the formal economy are provided with basic protections in old age. This may take the form of a social assistance program, a small means-tested social pension, or a universal demogrant available at higher ages (for example, age 70 and up). Whether this is viable—and the specific form, level, eligibility, and disbursement of benefits—will depend on the prevalence of other vulnerable groups, availability of budgetary resources, and design of the complementary elements of the pension system.

Second, if the conditions are right, prefunding for future pension commitments is advantageous for both economic and political reasons and may, in principle, be undertaken for any pillar. Economically, prefunding requires the commitment of resources in the current period to improve the future budget constraints of government and may contribute to economic growth and development. A key issue in determining whether advance funding is advantageous is the extent to which it results in net additions to national savings. Politically, prefunding may better guarantee the capacity of society to fulfill pension commitments because it ensures that pension liabilities are backed by assets protected by legal property rights, regardless of whether the funding is through government debt or other types of assets. The decision to prefund, however, requires careful consideration of benefits and costs, as net benefits are not automatically assured and political manipulation can make prefunding illusory. This decision also requires a close look at the implementation capacity of a country.

Third, in countries where prefunding promises to be beneficial, a mandated and fully funded second pillar provides a useful benchmark (but not a blueprint) against which the design of a reform should be evaluated. As a benchmark, it serves as a reference point for the policy discussion and a means to evaluate crucial questions about welfare improvement and the capacity to finance the transition from pay-as-you-go to funded regimes. The efficiency and equity of alternative approaches to retirement savings, such as a significant reliance on voluntary individual or occupational systems, should be evaluated in relation to this benchmark.

Goals of a Pension System and Reform

This policy framework considers pension systems and their reform in terms of adherence to core principles and the capacity to achieve a flexible and context-specific set of social and economic outcomes. It does not narrowly prescribe the structure, implementing institutions, or operations of a system. On a practical level, the application of such a standard requires the articulation of goals and criteria against which a proposed reform can be evaluated.

The primary goals of a pension system should be to provide adequate, affordable, sustainable, and robust retirement income, while seeking to implement welfare-improving schemes in a manner appropriate to the individual country:

- An *adequate* system is one that provides benefits to the full breadth of the population that are sufficient to prevent old-age poverty on a country-specific absolute level in addition to providing a reliable means to smooth lifetime consumption for the vast majority of the population.
- An *affordable* system is one that is within the financing capacity of individuals and the society and does not unduly displace other social or economic imperatives or have untenable fiscal consequences.
- A *sustainable* system is one that is financially sound and can be maintained over a foreseeable horizon under a broad set of reasonable assumptions.
- A *robust* system is one that has the capacity to withstand major shocks, including those coming from economic, demographic, and political volatility.

The design of a pension system or its reform must explicitly recognize that pension benefits are claims against future economic output. To fulfill their primary goals, pension systems must contribute to future economic output. Reforms should, therefore, be designed and implemented in a manner that supports growth and development and diminishes possible distortions in capital and labor markets. This requires the inclusion of secondary developmental goals, which seek to create positive developmental outcomes by minimizing the potential negative impacts that pension systems may have on labor markets and macroeconomic stability while leveraging positive impacts through increased national saving and financial market development.

Criteria for Evaluation

The application of a goal-oriented and context-specific flexible policy framework also necessitates the formulation of criteria against which a reform proposal is evaluated in comparison with the existing arrangements. These include criteria directed to the content of the reform and others directed to the process of reform.

The Bank uses four primary content criteria to judge the soundness of a proposal:

- *Does the reform make sufficient progress toward the goals of a pension system?* Will the reform provide reasonable protections against the risks of poverty in old age by efficiently allocating resources to the elderly? Does it provide the capacity to sustain consumption levels and provide social stability across the full range of socioeconomic conditions that are prevalent in the country? Does the reform meet distributive concerns? Does it offer access to retirement savings and poverty protection on an equivalent basis to all people with significant economic participation, including informal sector workers and those performing mainly noneconomic work? Is the burden of transition financing equitably distributed between and within generations?
- *Is the macro and fiscal environment capable of supporting the reform?* Have financial projections been thoroughly evaluated over the long-term periods appropriate to pension systems and rigorously tested across the range of likely variations in economic conditions over these time periods? Is the proposed financing of the reform within the limits reasonably imposed on both public and private sources? Is the reform consistent with the macroeconomic objectives and available instruments of government?
- *Can the public and private structure operate the new (multipillar) pension scheme efficiently?* Does the government have the institutional infrastructure and capacity to implement and operate publicly managed elements of the reform? Is the private sector sufficiently developed to operate the financial institutions required for any privately managed elements?
- *Are regulatory and supervisory arrangements and institutions established and prepared to operate the funded pillar(s) with acceptable risks?* Is the government able to put in place sustainable and effective regulatory and supervisory systems to oversee and control the governance, accountability, and investment practices of publicly and privately managed components?

Experience also dictates that major emphasis must be given to the process of pension reform. Three process criteria are, therefore, also relevant:

- *Is there a long-term, credible commitment by the government?* Is the reform effectively aligned with the political economy of the country? Are the political conditions under which the reform will be implemented sufficiently stable to provide a reasonable likelihood for a full implementation and maturation of the reform?

- *Is there local buy-in and leadership?* Even the best technically prepared pension reform is bound to fail if it does not reflect the preferences of a country and is not credible to the population at large. To achieve this goal, the pension reform has to be prepared primarily by the country itself, by its politicians and technicians, and be communicated effectively to, and accepted by, the population. Outsiders, such as the Bank, can assist with advice and technical support, but ownership and public support must come from the client country.
- *Does it include sufficient capacity building and implementation?* Pension reform is not simply a change of laws, but a change in how retirement income is provided. Accomplishing this typically requires major reforms in governance, the collection of contributions, record keeping, client information, asset management, regulation and supervision, and benefit disbursement. With the passage of legislation providing for reform, only a small part of the task has been achieved. A major emphasis on and investment in local capacity building and implementation as well as continued work with the client and other international and bilateral institutions beyond reform projects or adjustment loans are required.

World Bank Financial Support for Pension Reform

From 1984 through 2004, the World Bank made 204 loans involving 68 countries that had some type of pension component. Analysis of these loans demonstrates the Bank's support for a diverse range of pension reforms within the broader, multipillar framework. Within the group of multipillar loans, the majority of lending followed the enactment of a reform rather than coming in the analysis and design phase. The lending related to pension reforms confirms the application of the policy framework set forth in this report. It indicates that the Bank has provided financial support for a diverse array of pension system designs and that only a small proportion of Bank lending has been directed toward reforms characterized by a dominant mandatory second pillar.

In addition to its lending activities, the World Bank provides technical assistance and analytical support to pension reforms undertaken by its clients and to this end relies on internal and external expertise. The vast majority of this support is associated directly with the lending activities of the Bank and is, therefore, aligned with the distribution of reforms outlined above. An effort to evaluate the scope and quality of this advice is currently under way within the Bank, and the distribution of reforms was derived from the initial data gathering associated with this undertaking. This project should yield additional insights into the nature of the World Bank's activities associated with pension reforms.

Design and Implementation Issues

Through its pension reform activities in client countries and the work of other institutions and analysts, the Bank has developed a clear understanding of good and best practices—of what works and what does not— in an increasing number of design and implementation areas. In a variety of other areas, however, open issues remain, and the search for good solutions continues.

Feasible Reform Options

The relevant subset from among the full scope of general options includes (a) parametric reforms that keep the structure of benefits, public administration, and unfunded nature of the system but change key elements of the parameters; (b) a nonfinancial or notional defined-contribution (or similar) reform that changes the structure of benefits but keeps public administration and the unfunded nature of the system; (c) a market-based approach that provides fully funded (defined-benefit or defined-contribution) benefits under private management; (d) public prefunding that provides defined benefits or defined contributions that are publicly administered; and (e) multipillar reforms that diversify the structure of benefits, administration, and funding of the pension system.

Each of these main options embodies pros and cons in pursuit of the primary and secondary goals of pension systems. The Bank-favored multipillar pension system (especially the inclusion of a zero pillar and an appropriate combination of mandatory and voluntary savings arrangements), with or without a notional defined-contribution reformed first pillar, is perceived as best directed to the needs of the main target groups in client countries: the lifetime poor, informal sector workers, and formal sector workers (see table 1).

The relevant options for reform depend on country-specific considerations, especially the existing pension scheme (and other related public programs); the special reform need(s) of these schemes; and the (enabling or disabling) environment, such as administrative capacity and development of financial markets. These considerations are broadly linked with the development status or income level of a country, which suggests a policy progression from mere focus on poverty-oriented systems in low-income countries through systems that support limited consumption smoothing under a public and unfunded, earnings-related scheme to the full breadth of all pillars that is feasible in high-income countries. While there is, indeed, a link between capacity and reform potential, the relationship is not linear with income level. Feasible reform options and actual choices are (co)determined by the inherited system and the transition costs of moving from unfunded to funded pillars, which in many cases are prohibitive. This path dependency implies that middle-income

Table 1. Multipillar Pension Taxonomy

	Target group			Main criteria		
Pillar	Lifetime poor	Informal sector	Formal sector	Characteristics	Participation	Funding or collateral
0	X	X	x	"Basic" or "social pension," at least social assistance (universal or means tested)	Universal or residual	Budget or general revenues
1			X	Public pension plan, publicly managed (defined benefit or notional defined contribution)	Mandated	Contributions, perhaps with some financial reserves
2			X	Occupational or personal pension plans (fully funded defined benefit or fully funded defined contribution)	Mandated	Financial assets
3	x	X	X	Occupational or personal pension plans (partially or fully funded defined benefit or funded defined contribution)	Voluntary	Financial assets
4	X	X	X	Access to informal support (family), other formal social programs (health care), and other individual financial and nonfinancial assets (homeownership)	Voluntary	Financial and nonfinancial assets

Note: The size and appearance of x reflect the importance of each pillar for each target group in the following increasing order of importance: x, X, **X**.

countries need to assess carefully their choice of reform and work diligently on their capacity to undertake reform if they want the full range of options to be available in the future.

Pillar Design, Poverty Alleviation, and Redistribution

The role and capacity of each pillar to provide poverty relief, consumption smoothing, and redistribution from the (lifetime) rich to those at risk of old-age poverty depend not only on the design and associated incentives and disincentives but also on administrative capacity. For each of the pillars, choices need to be made and coordinated among the pillars to avoid counterproductive outcomes. In more developed countries, all or any subset of the pillars may be directed toward the primary and secondary goals of a pension system, although the inherited system typically imposes constraints on the available choices. In contrast, developing countries are usually far less constrained, or even entirely unconstrained, by an inherited pension system but, lacking financial markets as well as the capacity to implement and administer new systems, face constraints on the available choices, at least in the short run. For old-age pensions, three main suggestions stand out. First, basic income support (a zero pillar) to alleviate old-age poverty should be part of any complete retirement system. While financing in low-income countries will be a challenge and needs to be assessed against the competing demands of other vulnerable groups, such as children, youth, and the disabled, the challenges of implementation are equally strong and require close attention. These include administering eligibility criteria and efficiently paying small amounts to a largely rural population that has little involvement with financial systems or institutions.

Second, mandated systems should be kept small and manageable. In many low-income countries, this may be a basic (zero) pillar that can be supplemented by a voluntary third pillar. If a mandated contributory (unfunded or funded) system can be effectively implemented, it should be aimed at modest replacement rates and require only moderate contribution rates.

Third, low-coverage, earnings-related systems should minimize redistribution, be self-financing, and not rely on budgetary transfers. Any redistribution to low-income groups should be financed by resources obtained from the group already within the system and not rely on budget resources financed in part by the less fortunate outside the system. In high-coverage situations, redistribution, especially for funded systems, can and should be provided by budgetary transfers, but this must be done in a transparent manner at the time the liability is created.

For the reform of disability and survivor pensions, best practices are less obvious and therefore require much more attention. For disability pensions, it appears that severing linkages with old-age pensions may be the best way to secure appropriate benefits, while keeping the potential for abuse low. Spousal and survivor pension rights compete with more redistributive and traditional approaches of compensating gender discrimination via the pension system and require more consideration to formulate best practices as well.

Mandated systems separated along professional and occupational lines should be avoided because they impede labor mobility and can lead to expensive and unsustainable pensions for some subgroups of the population. Civil servant pensions, often the oldest scheme in a country, should be integrated into a general and harmonized scheme for all sectors. Supplementary schemes should be established strictly on a funded basis.

Financial Sustainability

One of the main goals of pension reform is to achieve financial sustainability, meaning the payment of current and future benefits according to an announced path of contribution rates without unannounced hikes in contribution rates, cuts in benefits, or deficits that need to be covered by budgetary resources. To be credible, a pension reform requires, above all, credible financial projections that include both short-term and long-term flows and an assessment of the status and utilization of stocks of accumulated assets. For funded pillars, this requires a reasonable assessment of anticipated rates of return, including the role of foreign investment in diversification and management of returns. To this end, three main suggestions stand out.

First, a pension reform proposal that is not accompanied by credible cost estimates comparing it with the current scheme should not be undertaken (and will not be supported by the World Bank). For the projections, alternative models (in addition to the Bank's Pension Reform Options Simulation Toolkit—PROST—model) can, and should, be used. Differences in projections need to be understood and fully considered. Differences arising from alternative analytical methods provide valuable insights into the sensitivity of results to modeling assumptions and the degree of uncertainty and risk associated with the outcomes of reform.

Second, assessing the financial sustainability (in particular, of unfunded schemes) requires taking a long-term view and considering flows as well as stocks. For typical pay-as-you-go schemes, the stock is reflected in the implicit pension debt, which, for conceptual and data reasons, generally should be measured as the accrued-to-date liability. Defined-contribution systems need to recognize explicitly the volatility of benefit levels associated with variations in both asset returns as well as interest rates at the time account balances are converted to annuities. They require funding rates appropriate to benefit targets in consideration of these risks and need to communicate the degree of variation in anticipated benefit outcomes. Similarly, adjustments based on demographic and economic outcomes may need to be incorporated into some designs to ensure their long-term sustainability.

Finally, for partially and fully funded systems, the correct assessment of available assets and sustainable risk-adjusted rates of return is important. Publicly managed (central) pension funds have a poor track record to date in sustaining reasonable investment returns, which leaves three main options: (a) moving to an unfunded system if financial instruments, the capacity to keep the political pressure at bay, or both do not exist; (b) keeping the funding approach but moving to a privately managed and decentralized system; and (c) improving the governance structure of the centralized system. There is growing empirical evidence that governance is crucial for investment strategies that are the primary determinant of performance. Some countries and international organizations have developed guidelines for governance and investment process design. Part 2 of this report presents the key principles of good investment process design that may also be introduced in advanced client countries.

Administrative Preparedness and Implementation Constraints

There remains a broad range of implementation issues for which good answers are still required. Simply enumerating and summarizing them would be a challenge. This subsection presents some of the highlights, main messages, and suggestions.

The key issues in administrative preparedness of the new pension system, especially a defined-contribution one, are the introduction of personal identification systems and accounts (personification) and the unified collection of contributions. The greatest difficulties appear to be in integrating the flow of funds and data at the national level. From the point of view of social security institutions, the flow of money could remain decentralized, while the flow of data could be partially or fully centralized. Whatever the selected solution, the institutions need to be technically ready prior to implementation. Otherwise the reform may fail, and the approach to reform will be discredited for the wrong reason.

The recommended centralization of the flow of data calls for the creation of a clearinghouse to consolidate some aspects of second-pillar operations with operations of a first-pillar agency or tax authority. The phrase "clearinghouse" has come to encompass a variety of options along a spectrum that includes using a state or quasi-public agency to collect second-pillar contributions and allocate them among second-pillar funds, to be an alternative record keeper, or to be an exclusive record keeper and information agent for fund participants.

A related issue concerns the coexistence of tax collection and social insurance collection units. Although there are many good arguments for having only one collection agency over the long run (the national tax authority), experience in some regions suggests that the speed and preparedness to undertake such a merger need to be well considered.

The tax treatment of pension schemes is also critical to establishing appropriate and affordable incentives for retirement savings, while avoiding unintended subsidies to the wealthy or opportunities for tax evasion unrelated to pension savings. In quite a number of client countries, contributions, investment income, and benefits are essentially untaxed, providing windfall gains for the richer part of the population and leading to the substitution of tax-favored savings for savings that otherwise would have occurred. A better approach is to accord mandated pensions consumption-type income-tax treatment that exempts contributions and earned interest, while taxing benefit payments as ordinary income. A similar tax treatment of voluntary pension schemes, in view of their concentration in the upper-income strata, is less clear but should be considered only if reasonable limitations are imposed and there is some likelihood of positive externalities (such as enhanced savings or contributions to financial sector development).

However, the provision of subsidies should be considered as a means of enhancing the distributional equity of pension systems and expanding coverage. The establishment of tax credits or matching contributions to pension savings can provide significant incentives for lower-income workers, who typically remain outside the tax system, to participate. It may also alleviate the degree of redistribution in favor of higher-wage earners associated with a consumption-tax treatment in low-tax-coverage environments. The positive externality may include—besides increasing pension coverage—an increase in the national savings rate.

The level of fees or charges levied on financial retirement products is an area of considerable debate and research as well as an area of major concern for both critics and supporters of funded pensions. Although more research on this topic is needed, three approaches are promising. First, limit overall costs by saving on administrative expenses (for example, the collection of contributions and the administration of accounts) through the use of a central clearinghouse. Second, limit marketing expenditures by pension funds through blind accounts or constraints on switching among investment funds by individuals. Last, but not least, limit asset management fees by restricting the choice of individuals, including the use of passively managed investment products, employers' choice of financial provider, or competitive bidding for a restricted number of asset managers.

Finally, the provision of annuities by the private sector in funded retirement-income systems creates major challenges and constraints that may significantly influence the design and sequencing of the overall reform. While the conceptual and implementation issues during the accumulation phase of funded schemes are relatively well understood and manageable in most circumstances, the design and operation of the disbursement phase require more development. Some of the issues, such as the types of providers (whether to limit these to insurance companies or to include other financial institutions as well) and the products permitted to be offered, seem relatively settled. Issues related to the degree of mandating and, most important, the question of allocating and managing risks—in particular, rising life expectancy—remain quite open.

Financial Market Readiness, Regulatory, and Supervisory Issues

The question of what conditions are required for the introduction of a mandatory funded pillar has given rise to considerable debate that will take a few more years to resolve. Five issues are at the core of the debate: (a) Can funded pensions be introduced in a rudimentary financial market environment? (b) What are the regulatory standards and practices needed to ensure effective operation and security? (c) What supervisory practices and institutions need to be developed? (d) What level of costs is acceptable in the operation of a system, and at what threshold do operating costs mitigate the potential advantages of funding? (e) What are the options for countries with small open systems?

Not all countries are ready to introduce a funded pillar, and consequently some should not do so. However, the introduction of a funded pillar does not require perfect conditions, with all financial institutions and products available at the outset. Funded pillars ideally should be introduced gradually to enable them to facilitate financial market development. Nevertheless, minimum conditions need to be satisfied for the successful introduction of a funded pillar, including (a) a solid core of sound banks and other financial institutions capable of offering reliable administrative and asset management services; (b) a long-term commitment by government to pursue sound macroeconomic policies and related financial sector reforms; and (c) the establishment of core regulatory and supervisory systems concurrent with the implementation of a funded system and a long-term commitment for the support and continued development of a sound regulatory framework.

The extensive recent experience with pension reforms in Latin America and Central and Eastern Europe in addition to the much longer experience in the economies of the member countries of the Organization for Economic Co-operation and Development (OECD) has advanced the understanding of issues of financial market regulation. This experience indicates that certain basic (and less controversial) regulations should be applied to mandated funded schemes from the very beginning. These include appropriate licensing and capital requirements for providers, full segregation of pension assets from the other activities of sponsors and management firms, the use of external custodians, and the required application of broadly accepted and transparent asset valuation rules and rate-of-return calculations. There remains uncertainty regarding how and when a number of more controversial regulations should be applied. These include controls on market structure and choice of portfolio by members, minimum funding standards for defined benefits, investment requirements or specific limitations on particular types of assets, portability rules, profitability or minimum rate-of-return requirements, and guarantees.

Similarly, in financial market supervision, many rules are not controversial and should be applied early on. The less controversial rules and tasks for the supervisory body include (a) the need for an operationally independent, proactive, well-financed, and professional staff; (b) the vetting of the application for licensing; and (c) collaboration with other regulators. The more controversial rules and questions for supervision include choosing between a single-purpose or dedicated supervisory agency (such as pioneered in Chile) or integrating various supervisory authorities (such as insurance, securities markets, banking, or mutual funds) into a single agency; choosing the range of institutions permitted to offer retirement-income products; establishing effective collaboration among regulators and supervisors; and creating effective oversight and accountability of the supervisor.

Various small and open economies, such as in Central America and Central Europe, but also in Africa (Mauritius and Senegal), are starting pension reforms that include the development of a funded pillar. Undertaking such a reform in an environment with a limited financial sector creates both opportunities and challenges. The challenges include the resource-intensive development of country-specific regulations and the buildup of supervisory capacity; a potentially small number of pension funds given the small size of the country and the existence of significant economies of scale; and a limited range of financial instruments through which to diversify investment portfolios. The opportunities include full integration into the world economy, with much better opportunities to share and manage risks for retirees and the economy as a whole. The way forward is not easy, and the potential options include regional development of funded pension systems (which is a promising approach that, so far, has never been adopted), the application of practices of other countries, such as centralized public management (which is possible, but not fully convincing), and a mixture of importing knowledge by opening the financial sector up to foreign investment and keeping the government out of investment decisions, while undergoing cost-intensive buildup of institutions, regulations, and supervision. This capacity building may have positive overall developmental effects because reliable domestic financial markets are needed in any economy that wants to participate in and profit from globalization.

The Importance of Political Economy

Undertaking a successful and sustainable pension reform requires a deep understanding of the political economy of reform. While no dominant paradigm has emerged, experience with pension reforms in a variety of settings has advanced the understanding of effective approaches to the organization and process of reform. A conceptualization borrowed from political science that distinguishes three main phases of pension reform—commitment building, coalition building, and implementation—has proved useful in client countries.

The *commitment-building phase* is commonly the longest of the three phases. In this phase, it is desirable to include many actors in the debate, even at the expense of consensus. It also is important to expose to, and share with, the general public and key policy players the relevant reform experience of other countries. Key players include parliamentarians, trade unions, and the national press. The duration and coverage of the debate should not be limited in order to reach a quick but artificial agreement. Open disagreements at this stage help everyone to reach agreement in subsequent phases.

The *coalition-building phase* starts when the government decides to put forward a reform concept. Crucial for the move from the commitment-building to the coalition-building phase is the emergence of a champion who believes in the need for reform and links his or her political fate with the cause. During the coalition-building phase, the government remains open to modifications of the reform concept, but not necessarily to wholesale changes. The quality of the concept is of critical importance: the concept should be based on tried and tested knowledge and should bring in the experience of other countries. It should have strong long-term projections, including sensitivity analysis. It is essential to link the concept with opinion polls and focus groups showing that the concept responds to genuine concerns of the population with the existing system. Presentation of the concept requires a focus on key messages. This stage concludes with dissemination of the concept and its translation into a specific legislative proposal.

The passage of legislation marks the start of the most critical phase: *implementation.* Almost invariably, the administrative capacity to support the new system is lower than expected, and knowledge of best practices is in the early stages of development. Experience indicates that tension between political readiness and administrative preparation is inevitable, making it necessary to enact the reform law when the political opportunity emerges and expectations for continued commitment are sufficiently secure but to implement the reform only when the administrative preparation is sufficiently advanced and problems are expected to be manageable. Continued, active political support must continue throughout implementation for any reform to be successful.

Regional Reform Experience

Since the beginning of the 1990s, two regions—Latin America and Europe and Central Asia—have undertaken most of the reform activities and thus invite a first assessment. While the transition economies in Europe and Central Asia were somewhat influenced by the early experience in Latin America, reform developed quite differently in the two regions, including some innovative approaches to design and implementation of multipillar pension reform. In the four other Bank regions—South Asia, Sub-Saharan Africa, the Middle East and North Africa, and East Asia and the Pacific—actual and comprehensive country reforms are still limited, but not unknown. In these regions, it is encouraging to see that the policy discussion about the need for reform and its direction is taking place in many more countries.

LATIN AMERICA

Through the first half of 2004, 12 Latin American countries had passed legislation stipulating multipillar reforms, with implementation begun in 10 of the 12. Each of these countries has introduced a mandatory funded pillar, but the extent of the mandatory pillar relative to the pay-as-you-go system, as well as many other features, is unique to each of the reforms. In addition, all countries except Mexico and, partially, Colombia unified previously fragmented pension systems into a single system covering the whole formal labor market. Unifying the civil servant system with the national systems has been a significant achievement for both labor market flexibility and fiscal sustainability.

How have the Latin American reforms achieved the goals of a pension system, and what are the remaining issues? The greatest gains have been achieved in the area of fiscal sustainability. In some cases, full sustainability has yet to be achieved, but substantial progress has been made toward this objective. When well designed, the reforms have also been a positive catalyst, stimulating economic growth, which has helped to achieve robustness and to diversify the sources of pension income in old age. The experience with adequacy and affordability is somewhat more mixed, with reforms facing constraints imposed by the original systems. Systems that had high and unaffordable contribution rates typically had generous benefits. Since the generous benefits were acquired rights, it was politically feasible to reduce them prospectively rather than immediately, which meant that lowering contribution rates to affordable levels would jeopardize the objective of fiscal sustainability. As a result, the least affordable systems have remained unaffordable. Similarly, the record on providing adequate pensions for all of the elderly is also mixed. The reforms generally focused on the contributory system, which was nearing, or already in, deficit prior to the reform. After a transition period, the reforms should free up fiscal resources that can then be devoted to other social benefits, including noncontributory pensions. However, because the countries are still in the early phase of the transition, this positive result has not yet been achieved.

EUROPE AND CENTRAL ASIA

By early 2004, 10 out of 28 countries in the region had introduced multipillar pension systems. These reforms shifted a portion of the mandatory pension contributions to private institutions that have established individual defined-contribution accounts for each eligible worker. Some of these countries reformed the public first pillar through the introduction of individual and nonfinancial defined-contribution accounts. Their willing embrace of reforms may be explained by the need to reap the benefits of a funded pillar relatively quickly to increase savings and economic growth and by their willingness, after a profound ideological crisis, to emphasize personal accountability and private savings.

Reforms ran into some implementation problems, including the accurate transfer of contributions to pension funds and inefficient regulatory institutions. Old pension systems (still operating, as reforms have a long phase-in period) continue to constitute a serious fiscal burden, especially with the reform policy reversals that have occurred in several countries, although the old systems clearly constitute an even greater burden in countries that have not adopted the multipillar approach. After initial enthusiasm, there is some skepticism about the new systems because administrative costs are high, current pensions have declined as a part of fiscal adjustment, and the benefits of the new system are not yet visible. Although rates of return are high compared with investment funds or other reasonable benchmarks, it is doubtful whether these high returns can be maintained without a greater diversification of domestic private and foreign assets. The willingness of governments in the region to allow this is not fully in place, however. In addition, Maastricht criteria that are binding for European Union (EU) accession countries count explicit debt, but not the reduction in the implicit pension debt, which means that reforms adversely affect countries' position vis-à-vis the criteria.

The way forward for pension reforms, although clear, remains difficult to implement. Second pillars will continue to grow and consequently reduce net unit costs (although commissions remain high), but fiscal constraints on this growth are a serious issue. There remains a need to continue to reduce the administrative costs of the systems, preferably through more group contracting and less individual marketing. This may be hard to achieve in systems based on competition among pension funds for individual contributions, and thus far caps on expenses have not been very effective. International diversification of funds' investment is essential to optimize risk and returns; however, political opposition continues to be strong. The pension debate is nearing the end of the beginning rather than the beginning of the end.

On balance, however, pension reforms in Central and Eastern Europe have already led to systems that are more adequate, affordable, sustainable, and robust than the old ones. As far as adequacy is concerned, the target replacement rate remains quite high, usually above 50 percent (and much more for less-affluent individuals), given the prevalence of a minimum pension in the reformed systems. Also, with the expansion of voluntary third-pillar arrangements, the total replacement rate can easily reach 60–70 percent. Changes in retirement ages and the reduction of special privileges and overall benefit levels have substantially improved affordability and sustainability. From actuarially bankrupt systems that require year-to-year budget subsidies, countries in the region have moved to systems that are within the capacity of individuals and governments to finance and that are financially sound in both the short and long run. Finally, the new systems are much more robust, as they are diversified (including public and private provision and a combination of defined-benefit and defined-contribution arrangements) and somewhat immune to political shocks as a result of their market-oriented nature.

Structure of the Report

The articulation of the World Bank's perspective on pension reform that follows is organized into two parts. The first part presents the economic and social policy rationale for pension reform and outlines essential foundations of World Bank policy. This part is divided into four chapters. Chapter 1 discusses the impetus and justification for reform. This is followed by a presentation in chapter 2 of the conceptual foundation of the Bank's view of reform, which discusses the social risk management framework and rationale for public intervention in providing for old-age income security, the multipillar model, and the rationale for funding. Chapter 3 articulates more fully the goals and criteria against which reforms are assessed, followed by chapter 4, which summarizes the lending activities of the Bank from 1984 through 2004 to demonstrate the consistency of financing for pension reform with the policy framework. The second part of the report provides an overview of implementation issues and is divided into four chapters. Chapter 5 provides an in-depth discussion of the range of reform options that countries typically face and discusses how these might fulfill the goals and criteria set forth in the first part. Chapter 6 provides a brief but still voluminous overview of design and implementation issues and options that will arise in the reform process. Chapter 7 sketches the recent experience with reform in two regions—Latin America and Europe and Central Asia—and highlights the development of recent reforms in other regions. Chapter 8 provides a few concluding comments.

PART 1

CONCEPTUAL UNDERPINNINGS

The introduction cum executive summary outlines the Bank's perspective on pension systems and reforms. It is based on the deep conviction that every individual should have access to retirement-income support in one form or another and that the current provisions are in most cases inadequate, function poorly, and need reform. In nearly every circumstance, there are alternatives that promise better results. Consideration of these reform choices leads to a number of design and implementation issues, which are discussed in more depth in part 2.

This first part highlights the conceptual underpinnings of the World Bank's perspective on pension systems and their reform, including the central elements of the perceived need for reform in client countries, the conceptual basis for the perspective, the goals and criteria that define the perspective, and information about the World Bank's lending and technical assistance. The sequence and structure of these sections should explain the motivation for and clarify the World Bank's thinking, including the differentiated approach and its implementation in client countries.

Chapter 1

The Need for Reform

THIS CHAPTER DETAILS THE NEED FOR REFORM ALONG FOUR LINES. First, it describes the short-term fiscal pressures that typically dictate the need to take immediate action. However, often these reforms fail to address adequately the much larger problems looming as a result of population aging.[2] Second, it examines the inadequacy of current systems in most countries that, independent of population aging, promise much but often deliver very little. Third, it describes the socioeconomic changes that necessitate a rethinking of the original design of pension systems, some dating back more than 100 years. Fourth, it looks at the challenges and opportunities of globalization that require countries to pay more attention to the economic effects of pension schemes but also make possible a larger risk pool and more diversification. These four considerations outline the contours of promising directions for reform derived from recent experiences throughout the world.

Fiscal Pressure:
Short-Term Urgencies and Long-Term Needs

Pension reforms in most countries of the world initially are driven by short-term budgetary pressures resulting from fiscally unsustainable public systems. The more important longer-term problems of sustainability due to population aging typically figure less prominently in the initial debate.

The short-term fiscal pressure for pension reform, often in the face of economic crisis, is a common form of engagement by the Bank in client countries. It is generally not the result of population aging and the associated deterioration in demographic dependency ratios (the share of elderly to working population) but instead is linked to exploding expenditures

23

resulting from deteriorating system dependency ratios (the share of beneficiaries to contributors). High benefit levels, dwindling revenues due to
informalization of the labor force, problems with the collection of contributions, and a low rate of return on assets (if any) are often other contributing factors. The short-term nature of the pressure for reform and the
impetus for emergency action may at times allow more drastic actions
than otherwise would occur. These conditions are, however, not conducive to the design and introduction of reform measures that address
long-term objectives.

Most public schemes were not designed in a way that is financially
sustainable even in the absence of demographic change; that is, they cannot deliver current and future benefits at the established contribution
rate without budgetary transfers or future benefit cuts. In many cases,
the system was designed so that budgetary transfers will compensate for
distributive or noninsurance objectives. The actual budgetary requirements are hardly ever calculated in a comprehensive or transparent manner and in most cases result from the basic lack of actuarial soundness of
the scheme.

This lack of sustainability has two main negative consequences. First,
these transfers often are the main cause of a country's high and rising budgetary deficit, with negative macroeconomic consequences that accentuate
periods of crisis. The most drastic recent example so far is that of Brazil in
1998, where a fiscal deficit of more than 6 percent of gross domestic product (GDP) triggered a crisis in the aftermath of the East Asian and Russian
financial meltdowns. Some two-thirds of this deficit, or 4 percent of GDP,
was due to the cost of pensions. In Lebanon, pension payments for civil
service and military retirees that cover only about 3 percent of the population are the third largest expenditure item in the budget, after interest
payment on the public debt and wages. In poorer countries, the deficit
induced by the pension system may appear less dramatic but, given the
small size of the public sector, can be equally devastating. Second, if the
government wants to minimize the destabilizing effects of high budgetary
transfers, it has to generate more taxes or make cuts elsewhere in the budget. In view of the difficulty of raising taxes, governments in many developing countries choose to cut other social expenditures, typically
expenditures for health and education. In many cases, rapidly rising pension costs are not visible as an increased expenditure. Higher pension
costs for retired teachers simply reduce the number of new teachers that
can be hired under an already constrained budget envelope for education.
In other cases, teachers have to stay on the payroll after retirement age
because there are insufficient resources in the retirement fund to pay their
pension; as a result, no new teachers can be hired. This sort of substitution
occurs in many countries, including the strong procyclical pattern of

expenditures for health and education compared with the more neutral pattern of expenditures for pensions (see Schwarz and Vashakmadze 2002; Snyder and Yackovlev 2000). The longer-term fiscal pressure is clearly linked to the aging of the population, a phenomenon that affects essentially all countries in the world. This was the focus of the Bank's publication *Averting the Old-Age Crisis* some 10 years ago (World Bank 1994). The importance of these forces remains unchanged, although the intervening years brought considerable analysis of their consequences and broader thinking on approaches to the problem and possible solutions. The necessity to act and the broader political and economic implications came into sharper focus during this period. Examples include the "Second World Assembly on Ageing" in Madrid in 2002 and associated follow-up actions (see United Nations 2004) as well as the work performed both by the Center for Strategic and International Studies (see CSIS and Watson Wyatt International 1999) and very recently by the International Monetary Fund (IMF 2004). Three issues are of particular relevance for the Bank's work. First, most of the future aging will take place in the developing world. Second, aging and population stagnation (or even declines) among the wealthier nations of the Northern Hemisphere will create opportunities for arbitrage with the much younger and growing population in the developing nations of the Southern Hemisphere. And third, managing population aging will require more efficient use of both capital and labor in all regions.

Population aging is the result of increasing life expectancy and falling fertility rates. While this process differs in pace and sequencing among regions and countries, it is a worldwide phenomenon (IMF 2004; United Nations 2004). It will result in a steadily rising average age of the population throughout the world, a rising number of elderly (age 65 and above), an even greater increase in the number of very elderly (85 and above), and a rising ratio of elderly (65 and above) to working-age population (15 to 64). This trend is most pronounced in Europe and Japan and least pronounced in Africa and the Middle East, but it is a reality in all regions and nearly all countries, and it is occurring at a much faster pace in the developing than in the developed world. This has two main implications. First, while nearly 60 percent of the elderly live in developing countries, that share is projected to increase to 80 percent by 2050. Second, while the developed economies got rich before they got old, developing countries are getting old before they get rich. This makes it even more important to design and implement effective retirement-income support for the elderly in the developing world and to assess very carefully the tradeoffs as well as synergies between money spent to achieve growth objectives (such as education and health expenditure) and funds directed to alleviate the vulnerability to poverty of groups such as children and the disabled, which may help to safeguard human capital.

Population aging in the North is most pronounced in the European Union, Central and Eastern Europe, and Japan. In these regions, the population is projected to start shrinking within the next decade or so at an annual rate of about 0.5 percent. The cumulative effect of population aging, a deteriorating old-age dependency ratio, and a shrinking labor force make the financing of old-age income support, particularly of the pay-as-you-go type, very difficult and increasingly less attractive. This is significantly due to the fall in the implicit rate of return from an unfunded system that is determined by the rate of growth in the size of the workforce and increases in average real wages (that is, labor productivity). Population aging reduces productivity growth through a variety of channels, including lower innovation and entrepreneurship. Cross-country econometric evidence for 115 countries suggests that the share of the elderly population has a statistically significant impact on growth of real GDP per capita (IMF 2004, table 3.1). Using the coefficient from this research and the demographic forecast for advanced economies suggests that the annual real growth rate of GDP per capita will decline 0.5 percent, on average, by 2050; that is, per capita growth will be 0.5 percent lower than it would have been had the demographic structure remained unchanged. In conjunction with the projected reduction in the size of the labor force of about 0.5 percent a year in much of Europe, this could lead to a fall in the implicit rate of return for pay-as-you-go systems of a full 1 percent. With productivity growth in Europe reaching no higher than 1.5 percent in recent years, this would reduce the internal rate of return to a meager 0.5 percent. If one were to add the effects of rising health costs, the internal rate of return may become zero or negative.

These effects could be reduced or even eliminated through migration. Encouraging migration, however, will not keep the demographic dependency ratio constant, because this would require exponentially rising migration and is unlikely to be the best way of dealing with rising life expectancy. Instead, the objective would be to stabilize the workforce (and, roughly, the share of elderly in the population). The level of migration required to achieve this appears to be manageable and could be recruited from the Middle East and North Africa alone. This is because the economically active population of Europe (EU25 plus Norway and Switzerland) is projected to decrease by almost 50 million from 2000 to 2050, while that of the 20 countries comprising the Middle East and North Africa is projected to increase by more than 150 million. Opportunities for such a demographic (and economic) arbitrage that achieves a solution beneficial to both regions, and the migrants, do exist (Holzmann and Münz 2004). However, such a dramatic approach carries with it profound political, economic, and cultural consequences. The need for fundamental reform of existing pay-as-you-go systems and the attractiveness of funded systems that are less likely to be vulnerable to demographic change because of their capacity for international investment will continue to be accentuated.

Delivering on Promises

Pension systems have four central objectives (Barr 2005). From the individual's perspective, pensions have two purposes: (a) consumption smoothing over the life cycle and (b) insurance against risks, notably the uncertainty of life expectancy after retirement. Consumption smoothing primarily addresses issues of saving and allocation of resources, transferring resources from a period of economic activity and earnings to a period of retirement, while insurance against risks is concerned with managing risks through pooling, in particular, addressing the uncertainty of how long one can expect to live following retirement. Additional public policy objectives are incorporated into pension systems as well, in particular (c) poverty alleviation among the elderly and (d) income redistribution by using the public pension scheme to achieve a more equal distribution of income through transfers from the rich to the poor. These purposes, however, need to be reassessed in the context of a typical developing country with low coverage under a formal scheme, high poverty among the population, and the very distant concept of "retirement" for most, particularly in the rural areas.

For those lucky individuals covered under a formal and earnings-related scheme, mandated systems are expected to deliver adequate and affordable benefits in a sustainable manner and remain a fair system across generations, professions, and cohorts. This should at least exclude perverse redistribution—for example, the often-hidden transfers from the poor to the rich. Most existing pension systems, including some of the recently reformed systems, are unable to deliver on these promises.[3]

The most basic shortcoming of many existing arrangements is that they are inconsistent and unfair across occupations. In countries at all levels of development, retirement-income systems are often created in a sequential manner, with new provisions added to existing ones according to political expediency and short-term financial capacity. In most cases, this occurs without full consideration of their consistency with the more general objectives. As a result, some segments of the population may be overprovided for, while a much larger part remains totally uncovered.

Two examples make this point. First, redundancy or severance pay in many countries constitutes the first step to retirement-income support for formal sector workers, providing for unemployment-type benefits during economically active periods and lump-sum payments on retirement. When earnings-related pension benefits are introduced, the retirement elements of the redundancy payments typically remain unchanged and are not integrated into the policy objectives for retirement income. This lack of integration often leads to overprovision and an excessively high level of total contributions (from both employer and employee). Second, benefit provisions develop mostly along professional lines, starting with civil servants and public enterprises and extending gradually to the private sector—first to employees of larger enterprises, gradually to smaller ones, and in a few cases to farmers and the self-employed. In many cases, the new schemes are established separately from existing ones, with different benefit rules, contribution requirements, and levels of transfers from the government budget. This leads to distributive injustices, difficulties in ensuring portability of benefits, and a lack of mobility between sectors, often most prominently between the public and private sector.

A second main criticism is that existing schemes often promise much but deliver little. Many mandated schemes in developing countries promise a high income-replacement rate (often 60 to 80 percent and more) at retirement ages (commonly at age 60 for men and age 55 for women, but in a number of countries five or more years earlier) that is not sustainable under current conditions and even less so at future levels of life expectancy. They have short participation requirements to qualify for full benefits and provide overly generous early-retirement benefits. Problems on the benefit expenditure side are often exacerbated on the revenue side by poor collection of contributions, poorly managed funded reserves with low or negative rates of return, and high administrative costs (whether funded or unfunded). Consequently, once these systems start to mature, the benefits cannot be delivered at established contribution rates. Benefit levels are rapidly reduced through inflation and only sporadic indexation, ad hoc benefit cuts and freezes are imposed, benefits are cut following a sequence of unannounced reforms, or benefit arrears emerge that can extend to many months and sometimes even years. Cases like these abound in client countries and result from a mixture of inadequate design, implementation, and administration of benefits and contributions as well as governance issues.

A final main criticism of the ability of traditional systems—as well as a number of recently reformed systems for formal sector workers—to deliver on their promises concerns their limited capacity to extend coverage to other groups. Coverage under formal schemes in most developing countries has been at best stagnating and more often decreasing from already low levels. This has been attributed to the reduced role of the public sector as the main engine of employment, a lack of formal job creation in the private sector, and inadequate design of the pension system. The issue of inadequate design has been addressed in a number of reforms by creating a closer link between contributions and benefits and moving partially or completely toward a funded scheme. However, these reforms have achieved only limited, if any, effects on coverage. This result can be rationalized with a number of more or less convincing explanations suggesting that it is rational for many individuals, particularly in low- and middle-income countries, to stay outside even well-structured systems (Holzmann 2000). Whatever the explanation, if consumption smoothing through public policy support is considered important for the whole population, new approaches are required.

The inevitable increase in the number and proportion of elderly in developing countries also raises the issue of whether the informal support delivered by the family and community that is predominant in many settings can alleviate poverty among the elderly. Owing to a variety of both systemic and idiosyncratic factors, the informal support system is crumbling and cannot meet the challenge of poverty among the elderly in many developing countries. Three factors are of greatest significance. First, in some countries the burden on the elderly has risen enormously due to rural-to-urban migration, the rapid dissolution of traditional extended family structures, and mortality among working-age adults resulting from the pandemic of the human immunodeficiency virus/acquired immune deficiency syndrome (HIV/AIDS) and regional conflicts (Kakwani and Subbarao 2005). Second, traditional family support systems, while reasonably reliable during normal times, break down under the kinds of covariate shocks experienced in developing countries, a process that even extends to middle-income countries such as Republic of Korea (Subbarao 1999). Traditional family support is particularly weak if shocks, such as drought, are intertwined with another major systemic trend, such as the HIV/AIDS pandemic (Deininger, García, and Subbarao 2003). Third, the vulnerability of the elderly is often exacerbated by their inability to find paid employment and access credit. Their assets are either used up or depleted in value, and they are often called on to head families and become principal breadwinners as household composition changes (Kakwani and Subbarao 2005). For all these reasons, poverty among the elderly is seemingly widespread in developing countries (see table A.1). Although conclusive documentation is still limited, advocacy for the need to provide some type of social pension is running high (HelpAge International 2004).

While informal family support remains the primary means of keeping the elderly out of poverty, it is becoming increasingly less reliable. Savings, either individual or through past employment, is not a feasible source of old-age income for the lifetime poor. Moreover, even for workers in the formal sector, most jobs do not provide pensions. In low-income countries, reliable instruments for savings may not be available. It is, therefore, not surprising to find the pervasive importance of private (member-based) savings systems, which are essentially informal risk-pooling arrangements such as the funeral societies in East and West Africa. Cash and in-kind gifts and remittances are another important source of support.

The main drawback of such informal arrangements is enforcement, especially during periods of covariate shock, when whole communities are exposed to severe income (consumption) shortfalls. Dercon (2003) cites direct evidence of the extent of risk sharing, which reveals its limitations. Detailed analysis of data on northern Ghana shows that community contracts do not insure many idiosyncratic risks. Evidence for Tanzania indicates that poorer households have fewer such contracts to turn to in times of need. Theoretical and empirical work also shows the limits of informal risk-pooling arrangements, highlighting, in particular, their possible negative consequences on poverty. Inequality and patronage associated with informal risk-pooling arrangements have also been noted by scholars (see, for example, Coate and Ravallion 1993). Other problems with informal arrangements include information asymmetry and long-run sustainability, especially in the face of persistent systemic shocks. The limitations of existing formal and informal systems of retirement-income support in dealing with consumption smoothing and poverty alleviation suggest that virtually all existing systems can benefit from a comprehensive look and are open to substantial improvements. Thinking outside the box is required.

Aligning Systems with Socioeconomic Changes

The public provision of retirement income for workers in the private sector originated in the late nineteenth century as a political response to urbanization and industrialization in today's developed countries. As individuals moved out of the traditional agricultural family structure, there was a need to establish formal risk management arrangements that could substitute for the informal arrangements that were eroding in the face of the transition. The new public arrangements were based largely on the model of a working husband and a housekeeping wife taking care of children. In many cases, they copied the design of benefits for civil servants, which had a much longer tradition and often served as a benchmark.

Social insurance programs for the private sector that provided benefits for old age, disability, and surviving spouses and dependents of workers were established in most industrial countries at the end of the nineteenth century. Retirement age was originally set high (age 70 in Germany), which only a small share of contributors could expect to reach. In the century that followed, in line with individual preferences and because of rising income and political expediency, retirement age and other eligibility conditions were relaxed. The basic structure, however, remained largely unchanged. Developing countries typically inherited or copied this system design from the colonial powers or were encouraged by the International Labour Organization to do so.

By the late twentieth century, three main socioeconomic changes— population aging, rising female labor force participation, and changing family structures—began to pose a major challenge for public pension systems worldwide. Furthermore, rising life expectancy and other changes require a rethinking of the design of disability benefits. While these changes are most pronounced in the industrial countries, they are also being felt in the developing world.

The magnitude of population aging and the role of population structure and labor force growth in the implicit rate of return of an unfunded system have been discussed. In addition, immigration has been used in the more developed countries to compensate for the effects of a fertility rate below the population replacement rate. Using migration policy to manage the effects of rising life expectancy is less feasible because it would require ever-increasing migration flows of a politically unacceptable magnitude. Dealing with rising life expectancy in both developing and developed countries requires a different approach, namely, splitting the increase in life expectancy between an increase in lifetime work and leisure. Such an approach is also in line with rational retirement decisions of individuals (unless they can pass on the effects of increased life expectancy to the next generation) and the financial sustainability of the schemes. The main challenge is to establish systems in which retirement decisions have a benefit-contribution structure that provides incentives for individuals to make a rational choice to distribute their longer lifespan among retirement, leisure, economic participation, and training. Too many pension schemes today are still based on the strict separation of education, work, and retirement leisure. A modern economy and the need for lifelong learning require a pension scheme that encourages rather than impedes the mixing of the three activities—for example, going back to school after years of work, bringing forward (retirement) leisure, or taking up work again after retirement (say, from ages 70 to 72). Most current pension schemes discourage such flexibility. A related challenge is to introduce changes in the labor market so that firms offer the elderly jobs that they have the capacity to perform. The call for lifelong learning also requires changes in wage setting between labor market partners and the addition of in-service training to negotiations concerning wages and working hours.

With rising female labor force participation, the main elements of traditional widow's pensions need to be rethought. Women continue to have less work experience, earn lower wages, and have less pension coverage than men. They also tend to outlive their husbands by several years, which creates a common problem of low incomes for elderly women, poverty among very old women, and falling living standards for widows. Provisions that shelter the needy whether or not they have participated in the formal labor market and survivor benefits that extend beyond the poverty level are obviously needed. The challenge is to structure these in ways that do not create a dependency trap, discourage labor market participation, or become a burden on the public treasury. Traditional arrangements have created inefficiencies and inequities that we can hope to improve on as the traditional role of women changes (James, Cox-Edwards, and Wong 2003a, 2003b). Furthermore, lifelong marriage has become the exception rather than the rule in many countries. In many developed economies, the probability of a marriage ending in divorce is around 50 percent, resulting in large numbers of older individuals living in single households. This has further eroded traditional informal sources of old-age support and made the underlying assumptions for the traditional benefit structure largely obsolete.

Socioeconomic changes also call for a review and redesign of disability benefits, including the delinking of design, delivery, and financing of old-age benefits. At the beginning of the Bismarckian type of pension scheme, disability benefits were much more important for individuals than old-age benefits, as only one in six workers could expect to reach the advanced retirement age of 70. Under these conditions, old-age pensions can be conceptualized as generalized or categorical disability pensions; that is, they insure much the same risk. Today, in most countries, more than five of six workers can expect to reach retirement age, and the old-age pension has evolved to become a life annuity that is paid with accumulated funds or acquired rights and provides insurance against uncertain life expectancy. Conceptually, it is totally delinked from a disability pension that insures against income loss due to a worker's incapacity. However, the original design of disability pensions and the close link to old-age pensions still prevail in many pension systems, and the mixed design has also led to the use of disability pensions as a form of unemployment or early-retirement benefits in many countries. Furthermore, at least in developed economies, sport and car accidents instead of general incapacity have become a major reason for the granting of disability benefits, in particular at younger ages. Disability benefits—insurance based and means tested—need to be reviewed and integrated into the design of an overall work-benefit package for the disabled (OECD 2003).

Challenges and Opportunities of Globalization

Globalization—the increasing integration of markets for goods and services, factors of production, and knowledge—requires changes in the way public programs operate, including pensions. Such reforms are needed not only to reap the benefits of globalization but also to deal with the challenges it creates, including profound shocks resulting from technical innovations and shifts in the demand for and supply of goods and other factors. This calls for more flexibility across labor markets, improved financial markets, and lifelong learning.

A main factor in the fate of nations and their economic performance in a globalized world is their capacity to deal with shocks, in particular those requiring significant adjustments to the existing economic structure. It is claimed that the more flexible and adjustable an economy is in reaction to such shocks, the better it will fare. Such flexibility requires mobility of individuals across professions, not only between the public and private sector but also among states and regions. In some 50 percent of the countries in the world, such mobility is hampered by separate pension schemes for public and private sector workers that create barriers to mobility by imposing large losses on job leavers. In addition, separate schemes render the application of some reform measures difficult or counterproductive. For example, increasing the retirement age for primary schoolteachers to, say, 67 may not be in the best interest of all participants, but it is feasible if a teacher can move easily to a related or different profession.

Mobility across states is also needed with rising economic integration, particularly if integration, as in the European Union, is advanced to the stage of a single currency. In a common currency area, exchange rate and interest rate policies are not set by the individual states, and only a few other policy instruments remain (essentially fiscal policy, wage policy, and migration) to deal with asymmetric shocks that hit some member states and not others. While each of these remaining policies has its own restrictions in a federation that is not fully fledged, the most promising policy may be migration. This requires a pension benefit and financing structure that makes migration possible without high losses for the migrants. A similar question emerges for migrants who return after working many years abroad, perhaps in different countries and pension regimes. A benefit and financing design that provides high flexibility, while securing retirement benefits that are truly transferable, is required to ensure that this sort of migration can occur.

The integration of countries into the world economy is significantly linked with their own financial sector development. A developed domestic financial market is a main ingredient for full capital account convertibility, including the capacity to diversify pension assets internationally (Karacadag, Sundararajan, and Elliot 2003). International diversification is, perhaps, the only free lunch in the world and promises major welfare effects, as national and international rates of return on retirement assets (beyond shares) have low correlation. This requires, however, the existence of some minimum domestic financial market. Forcing individuals to hold most or all of their pension assets in illiquid pay-as-you-go assets is not an optimal strategy for dealing with the diverse risks to which individuals are exposed and clearly does not enhance welfare. Pension reforms that introduce or strengthen a funded pillar allow such a diversification of risk and can contribute to the development of the domestic financial market. Well-developed domestic financial markets are a critical pillar of a market-based economy because they mobilize and intermediate savings, allocate price risk, absorb external financial shocks, and foster good governance through market-based incentives. The level of financial market development is positively linked to the level of output and quite likely also to economic growth (Beck, Levine, and Loayza 2000; Levine 2003). All of this is discussed in more detail in later chapters.

The Contours of Promising Reform Directions

Against this background of diverse reform needs, what type of pension system could promise to deliver on most, if not all, objectives? Quite likely such a system does not exist (yet), but recent experience throughout the world provides some clues about the contours of promising directions for reform. They are part of the conceptualization developed in the remainder of this report. The most important principles are the following:

- *Have well-defined retirement-income objectives and reform criteria.* The international discussion on pension reform over the past 10 and more years was dominated by disputes over structure, such as the number of pillars, a near-religious war about the virtue of funded versus unfunded provisions, and the merits of defined-benefit versus defined-contribution plans. Moving the discussion away from structure and toward objectives and clear criteria, when the latter can be productively introduced in a country, should advance the reform process and enrich the dialogue considerably.
- *Cater to three main groups in society.* Developing countries will have to devise instruments that provide old-age income for three main groups in society: the lifetime poor, informal sector workers who are at risk of becoming poor once they stop working, and formal sector workers who are covered by a formal pension arrangement. Doing so suggests more consideration of noncontributory basic provisions, developing well-regulated and well-supervised voluntary retirement-income instruments, and avoiding mandated systems that are an obstacle to increased formalization of the labor force.
- *Keep the formal and earnings-related system small, simple, and universal.* Small refers to the mandated replacement rate, which should be kept modest for reasons of financing and compliance. Simple refers

to the design of benefits and the need for the closest possible link between contributions and benefits. Universal refers to the application to all sectors of an economy in order to allow mobility across professions. Distributive elements for lower-income groups or other considerations (such as the period for receiving unemployment benefits) can still be introduced, but this needs to be done in a transparent manner. Such a system should help to minimize distortions in the labor market and to deal with population aging in an incentive-oriented manner.

- *Allow for diversification of systems and resources to enhance stability and security of retirement income.* Pension systems are exposed to multiple risks—the most important being economic, demographic, and political risks—and a diversified system should provide more security. A diversified scheme relying in part on funded provisions may increase national savings and provide an important impetus for financial market development. The output and growth effects should foster income security for old age.
- *Pay more attention to process in addition to design issues.* The experience with pension systems suggests that very close attention must be paid to the governance structure, with a focus on rules to deal with conflicting interests, the importance of the political economy of reform, and the myriad implementation challenges.
- *Take account of country circumstances.* A successful pension reform can best be conceptualized as the pursuit of a clearly defined system and reform objectives, while taking account of specific pressures for reform, the inherited system, and the enabling environment.

Chapter 2

Conceptual Foundations of the World Bank's Perspective

THIS CHAPTER OUTLINES THE CONCEPTUAL FOUNDATIONS of the World Bank's thinking on pension systems and reforms. They are important to understand and appreciate because they exert a strong influence over policy analysis, system design, and implementation proposals. Five important areas are highlighted: the social risk management framework, which provides a unifying paradigm for considering risks and risk management instruments in client countries; the rationale for public interventions revisited, appreciated, and applied; the Bank's central arguments for the multipillar approach; the perceived benefits of funding; and the Bank's multipillar approach as a benchmark, not a blueprint.

The Social Risk Management Framework

The World Bank's thinking about pensions and more broadly about old-age income security has moved in parallel with the development of the social risk management framework. This framework provides the conceptual underpinnings for dealing with the diverse risks to which individuals or households are exposed in a world characterized by asymmetric information and malfunctioning or nonexistent markets.[4]

For such an environment, which reflects the real world for our client countries, the framework suggests, among other things, that (a) the sources and characteristics of risks matter for the design and implementation of instruments; (b) there are three main strategies (prevention, mitigation, coping) and three main arrangements (informal, market based, public) for dealing with natural or man-made risks; and (c) different groups that supply and demand risk management instruments can be usefully distinguished. Application of this framework to the risks related

37

to old age advances thinking more broadly about old-age income support and guides the development and design of policy in client countries. Several main considerations are germane to this process.

System design is strongly influenced not only by risks related to general and age-related disability, death, and longevity but also by the many other risks and the enabling environment.

In view of the many risks to which poor individuals are exposed during their life cycle, old-age income provisions are not high on their agenda. Vulnerabilities such as the lack of sufficient resources in old age and uncertain timing of death are likely to be considered less threatening than short-term risks such as war, drought, flooding, unemployment, disability, and sickness. Consequently, mandating the participation of the very poor in a public, earnings-related pension scheme is likely to be welfare decreasing and difficult to enforce. This reasoning is supported by recent advances in the theory of annuity demand. Davidoff, Brown, and Diamond (2003) suggest that full annuitization may not be optimal when markets (for other risks) are incomplete; this incompleteness of markets can lead to zero annuitization and the holding of traditional financial assets only.

For poor people, the most damaging everyday risks are those that prevent them from working to sustain themselves and their families. The loss of work and earnings capacity (a risk that increases with age) is the threat most feared. Informal arrangements help but seem to be much less effective at dealing with the long-term consequences of working incapacity because the family often is much less caring and supporting than many believe. This strongly suggests placing disability and work-injury support before old-age insurance for low-income countries and considering a generalized disability pension (that is, a social or noncontributory pension) beginning at an age when work is not feasible anymore.

Since unemployment risks and old-age-related risks are imperfectly correlated, more-developed countries may gain from pooling these risks over time. In view of the moral hazard problems with unemployment insurance, introducing unemployment savings accounts that become old-age savings accounts on retirement may create efficiency gains. Thinking about risk contributes to rethinking severance payments and their integration with unemployment cum old-age income support (Holzmann and Vodopivec 2005; Vodopivec 2004).

The rate of return under any contributory system is subject to diverse risks, with the most important being economic, demographic, and political risks. These risks affect all types of pension systems—defined contribution or defined benefit, funded or unfunded—but in a differentiated manner. The fact that the rates of return of different schemes or pillars are imperfectly correlated and the robustness of the schemes in relation to covariate risks is different strongly favors a multipillar pension structure in which savings are put into different baskets and a risk floor is provided.

To deal with the diverse risks related to old age, there are three main strategies and many related risk management instruments:

- Informal arrangements, based on family or community support, will remain important for a large share of elderly for the foreseeable future. The main policy question is what governments can do, or should not do, to make them work better (that is, do various forms of subsidies directed to these populations, including tax incentives, help?). With falling birth rates, rising life expectancy, urbanization, and changing family structures, including the effects of HIV/AIDS, the reach and scope of informal arrangements are weakening. This calls for more formal support in the form of government provisions or market-based arrangements to complement or substitute for informal arrangements.
- Public arrangements are largely market-substituting approaches. Hence, the question for countries moving from predominantly informal old-age arrangements is the extent to which they should move to full-scale public and unfunded arrangements before relying (partially) on funded arrangements or whether they can and should develop market-based, funded arrangements from the beginning. This is an issue for the path of reform rather than the need for diversification and the design of effective systems to manage the differing type of risks. The potential risk of failing to move to the second stage of such a transition is a key strategic consideration.
- The better output and factor markets work, the more reliance can be placed on market-based arrangements and individual choice. The extent to which this is feasible depends on the degree to which markets are able to provide the appropriate instruments and whether government can provide effective and reliable regulation and supervision.

As introduced in chapter 1, three main groups demand old-age income support: the lifetime poor, nonpoor informal sector workers, and formal sector workers. These groups demand different risk management instruments, which calls for a differentiated supply of instruments and a multipillar system design that caters to the needs of these large and differentiated groups (presented in part 2 of this report).

Rationale for Public Intervention

The textbook rationale for public intervention also applies to the provision of retirement income: market failure and income redistribution—that is, the lack or suboptimal supply of market-based retirement products and the wish to redistribute from the rich to the poor or at least to alleviate poverty. As these interventions occur in an imperfect world, they are bound to have economic distortions: hence the need to balance potential distortions against risk-pooling and redistribution objectives (Diamond 2003). But the redistributive effects must be seen in a life-cycle context in which incomplete markets and measured income provide an insufficient yardstick with which to gauge the redistributive effects of public intervention (Holzmann 1990).

Public intervention due to perceived market failure may arise because of demand- and supply-side deficiencies. If there is no demand due to myopia, supply will not emerge, and even if there is demand, supply by the private sector may not be assured if left unregulated. This section discusses the following justifications for public intervention: myopia, absence of financial products, the need for regulation and supervision, the need for government protection, the desire to distribute income more equitably, and solidarity.

Individuals may have a short planning horizon and, hence, when left on their own, may undertake insufficient, if any, retirement saving. Myopia may be the result of an insufficient planning horizon or a high personal discount rate. Empirically, it is difficult to distinguish between both causes, but there are strong indications for the latter. A perceived high discount rate can be the result of restricted credit markets, the existence of other, more urgent, lifetime risks (such as sickness, disability, and family dissolution) or natural and political risks (such as flooding and drought, civil war, and inflation), and the incompleteness of markets for these other risks. Hence, improving the provision of appropriate risk management instruments for the broader set of risks to which individuals are exposed may be crucial to reducing the high personal discount rate and thus the need for public intervention in retirement income.

Even if individuals want to provide for their old age, they need adequate financial products with characteristics consistent with the requirements of long-term retirement savings: savings products (for example, bank deposits, stocks, bonds) for transferring funds to the future and annuity products (which guarantee a monthly income until death against the payment of an initial lump-sum amount) for insuring against an uncertain date of death. Without such annuities and the capacity to pool and manage mortality risks efficiently, individuals would either consume too little in old age and hence leave involuntary bequests or consume too much and end up in poverty. Even when such products exist, they often require public intervention in the form of education and guarantee funds to address behavioral impediments to their use. Without such products, governments need to intervene and provide the required products in a market-substituting manner.

Creating a functioning and stable financial market requires government regulation and supervision. Financial markets left to their own may not develop at all, only some segments may develop, or, if they develop, they might not deliver the long-term savings and annuity products that individuals need. To ensure that the private sector delivers on the policy objectives related to the "outsourcing" of retirement income requires additional care and consumer protections, in particular, if participation in market-based systems is mandated.

Even if the private sector can provide market-based retirement products and ordinary workers demand them, the government may want to intervene in order to alleviate poverty and achieve a more equitable distribution of income. The first public intervention for the benefit of the poor may lead to a second one, namely, mandating participation in a retirement-income scheme. The government wish for more equitable income distribution needs to be seen in perspective.

All societies have an interest in reducing the poverty of individuals at all ages. Direct government intervention can achieve this through means-tested real and monetary transfers. Society is inclined to support the elderly poor, who are assumed to have limited capacity to work, but this very provision may induce individuals not to undertake voluntary retirement saving, creating a moral hazard issue. Government may protect itself against such opportunistic behavior by mandating the participation of workers in a pension scheme, whether publicly or privately managed. But mandating is likely to involve welfare costs, especially for the lowest-income groups, which may have strong incentives to evade, and enforcement of participation is difficult and costly.

More equitable (lifetime) income distribution requires redistributing income from the lifetime rich to the lifetime poor. This redistribution can be achieved by a combination of benefit design and revenue measures, including special budget transfers to low-income contributors or the unemployed in market-based systems. But the redistributive effects of these interpersonal transfers is likely to be small compared with the effects created by the access of lower-income groups to retirement products and their capacity to redistribute income over the life cycle in a welfare-enhancing manner (Holzmann 1990). Simulations indicate that redistributive effects of these intrapersonal transfers have a much stronger impact on an appropriately measured lifetime income than any interpersonal transfers.

A major aspect of the discussion about the public provision of a pension scheme is the concept of solidarity, at least when viewed from a typical European welfare economics perspective. Although the notion of solidarity is fairly vague, solidarity can be defined as the redistribution of actual earnings from the rich to poor, the pooling of risks among the insured, and the provision of (some) insurance, even if the risks are not fully specified. These three aspects of solidarity, which typically are linked with unfunded provisions, can be emulated in multipillar provisions but require public intervention, such as the provision of a basic pension, budgetary transfers to low-income contributors, central pooling, or some public guarantees in decentralized funded pillars.

The Multipillar Approach: Diversification and Efficiency

Pension systems are fundamentally methods of addressing and managing the risks of aging.[5] This is approached by creating the capacity for individuals and society as a whole to maintain consumption for older populations when they are either unable or unwilling to remain economically productive. As risk management devices, their design should be based on an assessment of their capacity to manage the relevant risks efficiently on both an individual and a collective basis.

Pension systems comprise elements that are essentially consumption-allocation mechanisms that either in form or in function can be viewed as assets (and liabilities) of the affected individuals and society. The principle of efficiency in the management of risks—the optimization of expected returns in relation to risks through diversification of the elements (or assets) of the system as a whole—is as important an element in the design of the overall system as it is in the management of any portfolio. In pension systems, this manifests itself in the potential advantages of a multipillar system that comprises several elements with varying characteristics that, in conjunction with each other, achieve the desired individual and societal benefits, while minimizing the relevant risks.

The suggested multipillar pension system is composed of some combination of five basic elements: (a) a noncontributory or "zero pillar" (in the form of a demogrant or social pension) that provides a minimal level of protection;[6] (b) a "first-pillar" contributory system that is linked to varying degrees to earnings and seeks to replace some portion of income; (c) a mandatory "second pillar" that is essentially an individual savings account; (d) voluntary "third-pillar" arrangements that can take many forms (individual, employer sponsored, defined benefit, defined contribution) but are essentially flexible and discretionary in nature; and (e) informal intrafamily or intergenerational sources of both financial and nonfinancial support to the elderly, including access to health care and housing.

Each of these potential elements both addresses and is characterized by its own particular type of risks. Zero pillars address the risk of lifetime poverty and liquidity constraints. These may preclude, or be strongly associated with, minimal participation in the formal or wage economy and the related capacity to accumulate meaningful individual savings. First pillars address, among others, the risks of individual myopia, low earnings even within the formal economy, and inappropriate planning horizons due to the uncertainty of life expectancies and financial market risks, but they typically are financed on a pay-as-you-go basis and thus are subject to demographic and political risks. Mandatory second pillars address myopia and, if effectively designed and operated, can better insulate individuals from political risks. They subject participants to financial market volatility, the risk of high transaction costs, and demographic risks if they require some mandatory annuitization. Third pillars compensate for rigidities in the design of other systems but entail financial and agency risks as a result of the private management of assets.

For a variety of reasons, a system that incorporates as many of these elements as possible, depending on the capacity and preferences of individual countries, can, through risk diversification, deliver retirement income more effectively and efficiently. At the most basic level, the rationale behind this statement is that the factors affecting each pillar are not perfectly correlated and, in some cases, have minimal or even negative association. This means that almost any given level of expected retirement income, or "return," can be achieved at a lower "risk" by diversifying to a multipillar system. Perhaps the simplest example of this is the relationship between a traditional public defined benefit (first pillar) that is linked to lifetime or final earnings and funded individual accounts (second or third pillar, depending on their construction). The earnings-based, defined-benefit system provides benefits that are a function of wage growth and thus are subject to the risks of variation in individual or average wages, depending on their design. Individual accounts that are invested in financial assets are subject to the risks associated with the return on these assets. Because wage growth and financial returns are not perfectly correlated, the efficiency gains from diversification across the two "asset categories" can be readily demonstrated (Holzmann 2000; Lindbeck and Persson 2003; Nataraj and Shoven 2003; Shiller 2003).

There is a variety of similar examples of the diversification gains that result from multipillar designs. Pure capitalized individual savings systems, which seek to translate stock savings into a flow of retirement income at the point of withdrawal from the labor market, expose participants to substantial risks due to interest rate volatility or limited capacity to manage mortality risk through inefficiencies in private annuity markets.[7] These risks are substantially truncated through staggered purchases of annuities instead of conversion at a given point in time, participation in public defined-benefit schemes that pool mortality risk across cohorts or generations, and the presence of a zero-pillar safety net. The risks of earnings volatility and employment dislocation that underlie voluntary employment-based third pillars are significantly offset by first- and second-pillar arrangements. The political risk of default on benefit promises due to macro shocks or long-term demographic change can be mitigated through second- and third-pillar systems. These and a wide range of other factors make compelling arguments for the need to diversify the instruments of retirement savings and income.

In addition, a multipillar structure allows for tactical sequencing, strategic bundling, packaging, and compensation and thus is useful for overcoming resistance to reform (Müller 2003a, 2003b). The proposed paradigm change has been credited with enabling successful reforms throughout the world (Holzmann, Orenstein, and Rutkowski 2003).

The (Net) Benefits of Funding

The advantages of (pre)funding or capitalization to the degree appropriate for the overall system design and applicable conditions remain a basic element of the World Bank's perspective on pension reform.[8] The prevailing view of most Bank staff on the benefits and costs of funding has benefited from intensive discussion within and outside the Bank. New theoretical and empirical insights have changed some positions, while strengthening others. Overall we hold the view that—where appropriate—some funding creates net benefits that can be found at a social, economic, and political level. While such prefunding can, in principle, take place in any of the pillars, for a typical client country the net benefits are quite likely the highest in the mandated or voluntary (second or third) pillar.

While we claim that funding provides some (gross) benefits in many circumstances, we are also very much aware that it introduces new or additional costs, most importantly through additional risks (such as investment risks), higher transaction costs (such as fees), and fiscal transition costs (when replacing an unfunded scheme). For most reforming countries, the transition costs of moving toward more funded provisions play a crucial role in assessing the net benefits and are discussed here. The other costs and limits are dealt with in part 2.

The overall benefits of funding are best developed at some length under three scenarios:

- *Scenario I* describes countries with a mature pension system operating a fully funded pillar and outlines the benefits of such an approach. If a multipillar scheme promises only very limited benefits under such steady-state conditions, the transition toward such a design is unlikely to produce net benefits.
- *Scenario II* describes the transition toward a multipillar system starting from a fully developed and dominant unfunded pillar with broad coverage. This is the situation not only in many developed economies, such as France, Germany, and Italy, but also in transition economies in Europe and Central Asia and a number of middle-income countries in Latin America and the Caribbean and in the Middle East and North Africa.
- *Scenario III* describes the condition of a typical client country in the starting position—namely, low or modest coverage under an unfunded or centrally funded system—and the envisaged move toward a multipillar structure with a pronounced funded second (or third) pillar. In all cases, it is assumed that the conditions

required to operate a funded pillar (financial products and markets, legal and institutional framework) are met; otherwise, it should not be considered an option.

Scenario I

Scenario I describes countries with a mature pension system in terms of coverage and benefit levels that is operating a fully funded and sizable second or third pillar. Two sets of countries fall into this category: countries such as Australia, the Netherlands, and Singapore that have large mandated funded (second) pillars and countries such as Denmark, Brazil (to some extent), New Zealand, and the United States that have large funded and voluntary (third) pillars. Would any of these countries be better off if it were to replace its established funded system by enlarging the size of the unfunded system? The answer would likely be an almost unanimous no from politicians or economists, regardless of their political perspectives. As concerns the affirmed or assumed benefits of such a diversified multipillar approach, the answers may differ between individuals and are likely to cover the whole range of political and economic opinion. Yet one may conjecture that there is more consensus on the political than on the economic or social benefits of the multipillar approach.

Most Bank staff see the potential economic benefits of a multipillar pension scheme with a major second (mandated) or voluntary (third) funded pillar in three main areas: enhancing output, handling population aging, and improving individual welfare.

Enhancing Output

Pensions, like wages, constitute a claim on output, and hence the discussion about the form of financing—unfunded or funded—seems to be moot. Yet the centrality of output to the capacity to pay current and future pension benefits (Barr 2000, 2001) renders the form of financing important if it is not neutral with regard to output level and growth path. There are various conjectures and empirical indications that funding may, in fact, have positive effects on output even within these more developed environments. The suggested mechanisms that determine the effects of funding on output are essentially threefold: through higher aggregate saving, through lower labor market distortions, and through more efficient financial markets. There are also empirical indications that these effects may not occur automatically but are related to institutional structures.

The discussion of the effects of pension systems on aggregate savings began with the introduction of the Bismarckian social insurance system. It has been substantially advanced in recent years by access to data and computers to test the hypotheses econometrically. Most of the investigations and debate have centered on whether the creation of a public pay-as-you-go system reduces national saving, followed by investigations of whether the move from unfunded to partially or fully funded systems has a positive impact on aggregate saving.[9] Although the empirical support for these questions through econometric studies conducted largely at the country level is tentative at best, the dispute has sharpened the analytical concept and heightened recognition of the importance of the institutional setting to outcomes. At the conceptual level, the distinction of narrow versus broad funding has developed. Narrow funding refers to the backing of individual pension claims with financial assets (and property rights) as individual collateral. Broad funding refers to the translation of future pension commitments into increased aggregate saving (and higher output) as macroeconomic collateral. There are many good economic reasons, largely related to institutional arrangements, why an increase in individual saving does not translate into an increase in aggregate saving.

A recent World Bank study (López-Murphy and Musalem 2004) confirms the findings of other cross-country studies that funding matters for the aggregate saving rate and that the institutional setup is important (Bailliu and Reisen 1997; Edwards 1995). The study of 50 (developing and developed) countries suggests that the accumulation of pension fund assets increases national saving when these funds are the result of a mandatory pension program. In contrast, national saving may be unaffected under voluntary programs. The difference may be explained by credit constraints and restricted savings substitution in mandated compared to voluntary schemes.

The impact of the institutional setup on aggregate saving is also suggested by recent studies of the pension systems operated for the employees of state-level governments in the United States and OECD countries (Bosworth and Burtless 2003; Smetters 2004). The analysis of state employee plans in the United States suggests positive effects from a high degree of separation between the accumulation of assets in pension funds and the operation of the nonpension operating budgets of the states. States that accumulate large reserves within their pension funds do not act as though the funds were available to finance nonpension government operations. This behavior contrasts with the experience in national-level governments that have attempted to prefund a portion of their public pension liability. A large proportion (60–100 percent) of the pension fund accumulation in national social insurance systems is found to be offset by larger deficits in other budgetary accounts. Smetters (2004) claims that the offset for the United States exceeds 100 percent. The difference between these two examples can be attributed to differences in the governance of the pension system and the extent to which pension funding is separated from other budget activities.

In summary, while the establishment of funded pillars does not guarantee an increase in aggregate saving and output, the empirical evidence suggests that mandating a funded scheme with decentralized administration or central funding with an appropriate governance structure can, if properly structured, have a positive effect on national saving.

Pension schemes may also influence the level and growth of output through labor market performance. Pension systems that distort the labor market through contribution and benefit formulas that effectively impose a major tax on wages or impair labor mobility will lead to a lower level of output. The negative effects of such tax elements on labor force participation by the elderly are internationally well documented (Gruber and Wise 1999; Hofer and Koman 2001) and are also claimed to explain the difference in labor supply between Europe and the United States (Prescott 2004). Furthermore, if the tax element leads to a higher level of informality that uses a lower level of technology, the growth rate may also be negatively affected (Corsetti and Schmidt-Hebbel 1997). To the extent that a funded system (or a funded pillar within a mixed system) links contributions more directly to benefits and thus leads to lower labor market distortions (including those emerging from financing the transition), positive output and even growth effects should emerge. An unfunded system may also create a closer link between contributions and benefits, but the implicit tax element remains potentially larger. Macroeconomic evidence consistent with the claim of positive labor market effects has been found in studies examining the experience of Chile (Corbo and Schmidt-Hebbel 2003).

While the effect of funding on aggregate savings is still open to discussion and is quite likely dependent on institutions and regulations, the positive effect of funding on the composition of national saving and financial market development is well established, with World Bank research making important contributions to this literature. Funded schemes clearly seem to promote the development of securities markets (Impavido, Musalem, and Tressel 2003), making them more liquid and deeper as well as more sophisticated and innovative (Walker and Lefort 2001). Either the development of contractual savings (pension and life insurance) in shallow financial markets leads to the development of stock markets or causality operates in both directions (Catalán, Impavido, and Musalem 2001); it also increases competition in financial markets by reducing bank spreads (Impavido, Musalem, and Tressel 2002a); and last, but not least, the lengthening maturity of debt is likely to imply shifting resources from low-return, short-term to higher-return, long-term projects, thus fostering growth (Musalem and Tressel 2003).[10]

Developed financial markets, in turn, are crucial for sustainable and high economic growth (Beck, Levine, and Loayza 2000; Levine 1997, 1999, 2003). Such effects on growth have been documented for Chile (Corbo and Schmidt-Hebbel 2003; Holzmann 1997b), and recent empirical evidence claims growth effects in both OECD and emerging-market economies (Davis and Hu 2004).

The development of contractual savings also reduces the volatility of output because it increases the resilience of banks and enterprises to interest rates and demand shocks. This occurs because contractual savings improve the financial structure of banks and firms. It also reduces refinancing risks by lengthening the maturity of debts and improves resilience to shocks by favoring equity finance over debt finance. In bank-based financial systems, although contractual savings development increases the debt-to-equity ratio of firms, it also increases the maturity of their debt; in market-based financial systems, it reduces the debt-to-equity ratio of firms (Impavido, Musalem, and Tressel 2002b). Finally, contractual savings development is associated with greater resilience to credit and liquidity risks of the banking system (Impavido, Musalem, and Tressel 2002a). The difference in recent growth experience of the United Kingdom and United States compared to France and Germany can be related to differences in the stage of financial market development and in the importance of funded pensions.

Addressing Population Aging

As a prima vista, there should be no main advantage of funded provisions with regard to population aging. Both unfunded and funded pillars (and schemes) need the next generation, either to pay contributions or to purchase the accumulated assets. Stated differently, (pre)funding of pension liabilities is no panacea for population aging. Funded pillars in addition to, or instead of, an unfunded (first) pillar are likely, however, to be essential to coping with population aging for three main reasons. First, funding makes it technically and politically easier to make the current working generation cofinance their increase in life expectancy by constraining their ability to pass the bill on to the next generation. Second, while the rate of return for both forms of financing is negatively influenced by population aging, the capacity of the funded pillar to invest internationally allows it to cushion some of the demographic effect, as aging is not symmetric among regions. Finally, the most appropriate approach to handling population aging is to split the increase in life expectancy between retirement leisure and additional work. Yet individuals have different career paths and preferences and wish to retire at different ages and with different retirement assets (annuitized and not annuitized). Access to well-established funded pillars can provide the flexibility for individuals to implement their varying retirement paths and strategies.

Improving Individual Welfare

Multipillar schemes with substantial funded pillars may also have effects at the level of individual welfare, with five main outcomes possible in mature systems: diversification, political isolation, choice, rate of return, and lower excess taxation. The advantages of diversification have been discussed and comprise the diversification of risk at economic, demographic, and political levels, both nationally and internationally. The claim that funded pillar(s) do a better job of isolating benefits against political risk goes beyond risk diversification. In a decentralized and market-based structure with well-defined property rights and functioning courts, the capacity of governments to reduce benefits is considerably less than under unfunded and centralized structures. Although this isolation is likely to exist in many countries, funding is not a panacea for political risks, as recently demonstrated by the events in Argentina.

Enhanced individual choice of retirement provisions and instruments under a scheme with funded pillar(s) is another potential benefit of funding that is important for at least a subset of the population. Funding creates more flexible retirement arrangements that are considered crucial to facilitating labor mobility across professions and countries. In view of the documented high financial illiteracy of individuals in the developed and developing world, the value of this benefit is often doubted and, if achieved, may come at a price. There are strong indications of a tradeoff between individual choice and costs (for example, James, Smalhout, and Vittas 2001). Undoubtedly, many individuals benefit from access to at least the voluntary funded provisions in their retirement portfolio.

A (partially) funded scheme should also provide a higher rate of return than an unfunded system (especially where there is no tax burden to fund transition costs, as in this scenario). This should allow lower contributions for a given replacement rate (or a higher replacement rate for a given contribution rate). On a conceptual level, some claim that the higher return only reflects higher risks and, hence, that the higher return may not matter for welfare overall (Sinn 2000). Others claim that, in a dynamically efficient economy, returns on capital must outpace growth in output, independent of risk (Valdés-Prieto 2002). On an empirical level, evidence supports the hypothesis that the real rate of return on a balanced portfolio of stock and bonds available in the financial market exceeds the growth rate of covered wage bill in most economies most of the time (Abel and others 1989). Long-run data for major industrial countries support the perception that the rate of return of stocks, and to some extent bonds, is above the growth rate of wages (Thompson 1998). Whatever the difference, if the gross rate of return is offset by the high transaction costs of funded provisions, it will not matter.

Funding per se does not reduce labor market distortions. Funded defined-benefit plans can create major obstacles to mobility and distortions in individual labor supply decisions. Funded final-salary arrangements are likely to be more distortionary than an unfunded defined-benefit scheme based on lifetime earnings. There are strong indications that the link between benefits and contributions matters for the incidence of contributions and, hence, the degree to which they are considered as taxes and thus distort markets

(Ooghe, Schokkaert, and Flechet 2003). Funded defined-contribution plans are the closest to an actuarially fair system, so the labor market distortions should be low. This theoretical view is consistent with estimated coverage for Latin America and the positive influence that the share of contributions in funded schemes has on participation in the formal sector (Packard 2001).

Scenario II

Scenario II describes the transition toward a partially funded multipillar system starting from a fully developed and dominant unfunded pillar with comprehensive coverage. This is the situation for many developed economies in Europe (such as France, Germany, and Italy) but is also valid for Japan, for the transition economies in Central and Eastern Europe and in Central Asia, and for a few Latin American countries (such as Uruguay). While the potential benefits of partial funding in a multipillar scheme are still valid, substantial fiscal costs result from the move to funding. The optimal degree of funding in these circumstances is derived largely through cost-benefit analysis that needs to weigh the benefits, and their probability, against the anticipated fiscal costs, keeping in mind that not all costs are economic.

The critical cost value for the move toward funding is the implicit pension debt (IPD) resulting from the current pension obligations to retirees and workers. The relevant definition of implicit debt (accrued-to-date liability) in mature pension systems amounts to 20–30 times the annual public pension expenditure (Holzmann 1997a). These expenditures are in the range of 5–15 percent of GDP in these countries, equivalent to an implicit debt of 100–450 percent of GDP. Moving from an unfunded to a funded system makes the implicit pension debt explicit. To achieve the economic benefits requires the repayment of this debt (and hence a reversion of the initial income transfer toward the start-up generation). Debt repayments of this size create a major cost for current (and future) generations, and, despite the potential advantages, the net benefits of a major move toward funding may not be positive.

Such an assessment has to be seen in perspective. Some move to funding is already occurring as governments across the developed world begin to reduce unfunded pension benefits and to tighten eligibility conditions. This leads to individuals offsetting these reductions by increasing their savings in financial and nonfinancial retirement products (such as housing). Hence, governments in many parts of the world have implicitly decided that allowing individual savings in the third (or fourth) pillar is preferable to expanding or keeping unfunded benefits.

This implicit debt and its economic costs may be smaller than the figures suggest. Moving toward funding does not move a pension system back to a sustainable basis. Reforms such as an increase in retirement age and a reduction in benefit levels typically are required. Such reforms amount to a default on debt, and the magnitude of recent reforms in OECD countries and certain others has amounted to cuts in IDP of 25 percent or more. Another mechanism to reduce the economic burden of the fiscal transition is through lower economic distortion (such as on the labor market; see Smetters 2005 for an interesting suggestion) and positive externalities of the funded pillar(s), such as a higher growth path through a higher national saving rate and financial market developments (Holzmann 1997a, 1997b, 1999; Lindbeck and Persson 2003). Such effects are important not only for developing but also for developed economies.

In addition to the benefits of funding outlined in scenario I, the move from an unfunded single to a multipillar scheme is also likely to improve the capacity to undertake reform through effects on the political economy of the reform process. Two avenues for this effect are particularly relevant: enhanced credibility of a new (multipillar) paradigm and an improved policy process. The argument of enhanced credibility essentially states that reforms of unfunded schemes are not credible because they never become sustainable. The sequence of small parametric reforms with no clear direction raises the resistance to reform as individuals react rationally to oppose a small reform that will be followed by an unknown reform in the future (Holzmann 2000). The multipillar structure that incorporates some funding can facilitate the reform process because it permits tactical sequencing, and strategic bundling, packaging, and compensation and thus is useful for overcoming resistance to reform (Müller 2003a, 2003b).

The assessment of future economic and current political benefits of reform in contrast to the economic burden of transition has led many middle- and high-income countries to move toward a (more or less) pronounced multipillar structure: the reform approach in the transition countries of Central and Eastern Europe (as in Latin America) is largely paradigmatic. It implies a systemic reform and a conscious reduction of the unfunded first pillar to the benefit of a new and funded second pillar. In contrast, Japan and most countries in the European Union (EU), with exceptions such as Sweden, follow a parametric approach to scale down the obligations of the first pillar. The different approaches reflect different levels of IPD as well as different expected economic and political benefits of programmatic compared to parametric reforms. In all cases, however, the reforms signal a positive assessment of the benefits of some funding.

Scenario III

Scenario III describes the typical client-country conditions, low to modest coverage under an unfunded or centrally funded system, and the envisaged move toward a multipillar structure with a pronounced funded second (or third) pillar. For these countries, the net benefits of funding are potentially much higher, although many of them may not be ready to operate such a system at an acceptable level of risk and therefore should not do so.

The benefits of a multipillar system with substantive funded pillars in these countries are potentially very high and may exceed those of countries in the other scenarios, at least as far as the effects on output are concerned. These countries are in dire need of national savings for investment and capital accumulation, as domestic savings are often insufficient and access to foreign savings is limited and loaded with problems of its own. Labor markets in these countries are largely informal, and a well-designed multipillar scheme should be conducive to increased formalization, at least over the medium term. Perhaps most important, the financial markets in these countries are largely underdeveloped and do not support a path of sustained growth. Hence, if the appropriate conditions are fulfilled, a funded pillar can contribute significantly to financial market development and output growth.

In addition, the argument regarding transition costs is less relevant for these countries. For many, the starting point is an unfunded scheme that covers between none and some 20–30 percent of the labor force with the benefit level often still in maturation. The implicit debt is consequently much smaller. In a selection of 35 low-middle- to middle-income countries in which the Bank has been involved, the estimated IPD for 15 of the countries is below 100 percent of GDP, roughly the magnitude in Chile at the time of reform (Holzmann, Palacios, and Zviniene 2004). Most client countries in Africa and Asia also have this level of implicit pension debt. Although this is still a sizable amount of debt to be repaid, it may be manageable if the debt is reduced with the reform or if only a partial move toward funding takes place. Furthermore, the welfare gains for the other 70 and more percent of the labor force that is potentially covered under the new (partly or fully funded) scheme are large. If history is a predictor, the alternative is quite likely an unbounded expansion of the unfunded scheme and an increase in implicit debt to a scope of 300, 400, or even 500 percent of GDP before a painful adjustment takes place. This was the experience in Brazil.

In summary, the World Bank recognizes that there are limitations to the beneficial effects of funding but concludes that, in consideration of both the economic and the political economy of pension reform, some degree of funding promises the best combination of potential benefits and risk management. This perspective acknowledges the uncertainty of funding by itself to have all of the positive benefits for growth but also recognizes the capacity of pension reform through funding to "frame" the problem of diminishing the wedge between capital returns and market interest rates (which may lead to suboptimal levels of capital stocks) in a manner that is politically feasible when lowering taxes in other ways is not possible (Lindbeck and Persson 2003). In addition, research at the Bank and elsewhere shows that the contractual commitment of savings for the long term enables them to be used in ways that enhance growth. This perspective essentially concludes that the many positive results of funding over the long run, when it can be implemented at a reasonable level of transaction cost, ultimately outweigh the relatively small costs of its implementation.

A Benchmark, Not a Blueprint

Acceptance of the multipillar approach and the advantages of funding could lead to a simplistic policy prescription that mimics what is perceived to be a model of successful implementation: the substitution of a mandatory system of individual savings accounts for a substantial proportion of a public pay-as-you-go defined-benefit system, as has been put in place in Latin America.

The World Bank recognizes the value of this particular multipillar model as a frame of reference for which there is real-world experience and measurable outcomes against which other approaches to reform may be usefully evaluated. More important, however, the extensive experience with pension reform across widely varied circumstances during the past decade has demonstrated that initial conditions, existing pension systems, and the economic and political environment of a country will determine the feasible path of reform. The approach embodied in this policy note therefore seeks to use the experience of mandated individual retirement-savings systems as a baseline or starting point for analysis of the outcomes of a proposed reform rather than as any type of prescriptive model that would define or limit possible alternatives.

During the critical process of defining and evaluating the design of a reform, a mandated fully funded individual account system can effectively serve as a reference point against which to evaluate the crucial decisions and alternatives. It can establish an effective means to frame the policy discussions, contributing a common vocabulary and serving as a point of departure for the measurement of basic issues such as distributional outcomes, fiscal consequences, and welfare gains. Without such a reference point, the evaluation of these critical considerations may become too abstract to be meaningful or conclusive in any relevant time frame.

The concept of a benchmark must be clearly distinguished from a default option or policy prescription. The World Bank explicitly recognizes that the primary determinants of an appropriate pension reform are the unique conditions and circumstances of the environment in which it occurs and has supported a diverse range of approaches and outcomes. As a practical matter, however, the process of reform and, in particular, the consideration of alternative designs require some grounding in experience and a common metric for the measurement of expected results in order to proceed in an expeditious manner.

Chapter 3

Goals and Criteria That Define the World Bank's Perspective

EVALUATING THE VALUE AND FEASIBILITY OF PENSION REFORMS on the basis of the expected outcomes and viability of the process requires the articulation of goals toward which reform should be directed and the formulation of criteria against which these and the process of reform will be judged. These goals and criteria define the standards that a reform must achieve in order for the World Bank to provide financial and other support for it.

Primary Goals:
Adequate, Affordable, Sustainable, and Robust Pensions

What are the primary goals that mandated schemes should achieve? The World Bank holds that pension systems should provide adequate, affordable, sustainable, and robust benefits.

Adequate refers to both the absolute level (preventing old-age poverty) as well as the relative level (replacing sufficient lifetime earnings) of retirement income that the pension system will provide. The goal of any pension reform should be to ensure that all people regardless of their level or form of economic activity have access to the capacity to remain out of extreme poverty in old age and that the system as a whole provides assurances that those individuals who live beyond the expected norms will be protected from the "risk" of extreme longevity.

How much lifetime earnings should be replaced on a mandatory basis will depend on a number of factors that are specific to the conditions in which the reform is undertaken. These include access to housing, health care, and other basic services, average propensity to save, level of economic development, and level of income in the country. World Bank experience generally indicates that, for a typical, full-career worker, an initial target of net-of-tax income replacement from mandatory systems is likely to be about 40 percent of real earnings to maintain subsistence levels of income in retirement.[11] Lower-income workers require somewhat higher rates, while higher-income workers require lower rates. The age at retirement will also affect the measure of adequacy, with older workers requiring higher replacement rates because they have little potential to supplement their pension benefits. Targeting average replacement rates above 60 percent is not likely to be viable over the long term because the required contribution rates would impose an untenable burden.

Whether and how a zero-pillar pension is provided will depend very much on the circumstances in a given country. While providing income support to the most vulnerable elderly should be a clear objective of system design and reform, in many client countries the sparse budget resources will have to be evaluated against alternative uses, such as support for the most vulnerable children and youth. While targeted approaches will, in principle, ease the issue of choice and selection, many client countries may be lacking administrative capacity, and community-driven approaches may not yet be available.

Affordable refers to the financing capacity of individuals and society. Although higher replacement rates seem desirable, they come at a cost. The direct cost is through higher contribution payments for individuals, which interfere with more pressing needs (such as child raising) or investment needs (such as housing). The indirect cost is through higher incentives for evading contributions by engaging in informal sector activities, with negative consequences for individual lifetime opportunities and macroeconomic consequences for budget sustainability and economic growth. World Bank experience indicates that mandated contribution rates in excess of 20 percent are likely to be quite detrimental for middle- and high-income countries with a well-developed structure of collection; for low-income countries, the threshold may be as low as 10 percent.

Sustainable refers to the financial soundness of the scheme, now and in the future. The pension program should be structured so that the financial situation does not require unannounced future hikes in contributions, unannounced future cuts in benefits, or major and unforeseen transfers from the budget. Put differently, all the adjustments needed to keep the scheme financially sound (through changes in contributions, benefits, or age of retirement) should be decided, announced, and factored into the design of the program. These may include mechanisms to adjust the program to address economic shocks in a manner that keeps financing within the established macroeconomic envelope. Since the whole population (active and retired) lives off current output (actually gross national product), the amount of available resources is highly significant to the extent that countries cannot borrow from abroad indefinitely to sustain high consumption. Sustainability, therefore, ultimately refers to the primacy of output in determining overall constraints and the capacity of any reform to provide the promised benefits without unduly displacing other claims on future resources.

Robust refers to the capacity of the system to withstand major shocks and to remain viable in the face of unforeseen conditions and circumstances. The key outcome in this regard is the capacity of the system to sustain income-replacement targets in a predictable manner over the long term. Main shocks to the system may come in the form of economic, demographic, or political risks. Any pension system must be designed to withstand the range of stresses from these and other sources, explicitly taking into account the anticipated stability of the environment in which it is implemented.[12] A central element in meeting this goal is a credible analysis of the financing of reform across the full range of likely scenarios and over the full term required for a reform to mature and reach long-term stability. To fulfill this goal, countries are likely to need to develop or adapt one of the sophisticated modeling tools to their own conditions and to present analyses that incorporate a significant range of variation in basic assumptions to demonstrate the viability of a reform over the long term.

Secondary Goal: Contribution to Economic Development

The secondary goal of mandated pension provisions (and their reform) is to create developmental effects, either by minimizing negative impacts, such as the effects on labor markets or macroeconomic (in)stability created by imbalanced systems, or by leveraging positive impacts, especially by increasing national saving and by promoting financial market development. Pension schemes have an important impact on the level and growth of output and distributable resources. Hence, the goal of creating economic effects is important since all retirement income—whether funded or unfunded—is essentially financed out of a country's output.

The centrality of output for a pension system's ability to deliver on its primary goals makes it imperative that the design and implementation of a pension system be evaluated in terms of the developmental effects (Barr 2000, 2001). There is rising empirical evidence that the system's characteristics—most important being the design, financing mechanisms, and administrative implementation of benefits—have an important bearing on developmental effects and hence on level of output. But there is not yet enough empirical evidence to unequivocally guide the design and implementation in detail, making reform assessments and knowledge sharing even more important.

Reform Criteria

Because the World Bank is willing to support a broad range of reform attempts, sound and transparent criteria are needed to define those approaches to which the World Bank will lend its support (Holzmann 2000). While the World Bank reacts flexibly to country preferences and circumstances, it does not support all reforms proposed by a country. Too much is at stake for the current and future retirees, and the country as a whole, to engage in a pension reform that is unlikely to attain the country's social and economic objectives. The suggested criteria address both the content of the reform and the process through which it is to be undertaken. Four primary content criteria are currently applied.

First, *does the reform make sufficient progress toward the goals of a pension system?* Will the reform provide reasonable protections against the risks of poverty in old age by efficiently allocating resources to the elderly? Does it provide the capacity to sustain consumption levels and provide social stability across the full range of socioeconomic conditions that are prevalent in the country? Does the reform meet distributive concerns? Will it offer access to retirement savings and poverty protection on an equivalent basis to all persons with significant economic participation? Does the reform offer savings mechanisms and basic poverty protection to informal sector workers and those performing mainly noneconomic work (for example, through a basic pillar and joint annuity requirements)? Does it provide different groups of workers (for example, men, women, high-income workers, low-income workers) equal incentives in principle (that is, no special rules) to participate in the labor market? Gender equity must be explicitly considered within these criteria.

Second, *is the macro and fiscal environment capable of supporting the reform?* Have financial projections been thoroughly evaluated over the long time periods appropriate to pension systems and rigorously tested across the range of likely variation in economic conditions over these time periods? This includes detailed projections of the scheme's long-term fiscal sustainability; an assessment of the proposed measures to finance the transition toward a funded pension (the level of transitory debt financing and budgetary financing); and the proposed reforms of revenue and expenditure programs. Is the proposed financing within the limits reasonably imposed on both public and private sources? Quantitative assessments of the long-run fiscal and distributive implications of the current pension scheme and of alternative schemes under consideration are basic ingredients of any reform process. Because most client countries with an ailing pension scheme do not possess the required model, the World Bank has developed a generic pension model, PROST (Pension Reform Options Simulation Toolkit), which, when filled with country-specific data and system information, provides long-term projections of the current scheme and main alternatives, including the reform of an unfunded scheme and the introduction of a (partially or fully) funded scheme.

Third, *can the administrative structure operate the new (multipillar) pension scheme efficiently?* Does the government have the institutional infrastructure and capacity to implement and operate publicly managed elements of the reform? Can the private sector be reasonably expected to develop and operate the institutions required for any privately managed elements? This includes an assessment of the capacity to levy contributions, to channel them to the different pillars, and to pay benefits in a timely fashion; the level of computerization; the availability of personal identification numbers (important for individualized accounts both on a notional and funded basis); and the level of competence and training needed for administrative staff.

Fourth, *have steps been prepared to establish the regulatory and supervisory arrangements and institutions to operate the funded pillar(s) with acceptable risks?* Is the government able to put in place sustainable and effective regulatory and supervisory systems to oversee and control the governance, accountability, and investment practices of publicly and privately managed components? This includes an assessment of the regulatory agencies and their strength of supervision and the powers of intervention for pension funds and insurance companies; the criteria for entry and exit of funded pension institutions; the availability of sound custodian banks; and an assessment of the proposed internal versus external management of assets, fee structure, and a variety of other aspects of operating a pension system.

The experience of the World Bank also indicates that the process and political environment under which a reform is undertaken are significant determinants of the likelihood of success. Consequently, three criteria are considered relevant to process; they are centered around the issues of commitment building, consensus building, and implementation (see also part 2 on the political economy of reform).

First, *is there a long-term, credible commitment by the government?* Is the reform effectively aligned with the political economy of the country and supported by a clear political mandate? Are the political conditions under which the reform will be implemented sufficiently stable to provide a high likelihood for a full implementation and maturation of the reform? This is, perhaps, the most difficult reform criteria because it is subjective. Political indicators include broad consensus among the central ministers and ministries about the need for and direction of reform, the existence of a champion of reform and empowerment of a technical group to develop the supporting analysis, the willingness to undertake broad-range parallel reforms (such as taxation and financial sector and budget reforms), and a high probability that a new government will not undo the reform. Other related indicators are the development of sound analysis and effective communication of the objectives, costs, and outcomes of the reform to the public and the inclusiveness of the reform process, including the involvement of trade unions or other worker representatives.

Second, *is there consensus building through local buy-in and leadership?* Even the best technically prepared pension reform is bound to fail if it does not reflect the preferences of a country and is not credible to the population at-large. To achieve this, the preparation of a pension reform has to be undertaken primarily by the country itself, by its politicians and technicians, and be effectively communicated to and accepted by the population. Outsiders, such as the World Bank, can assist with advice and technical support, but ownership and public support must come from the client country.

A major challenge for any comprehensive pension reform is to create an awareness of the issues among politicians and the population at-large. Once the seeds for pension reform are sown, the challenge is to train technicians in the new skills required in administration, regulation, and supervision. The activities of the World Bank, headed by the World Bank Institute, include (a) an annual workshop together with reputable academic institutions (originally with the Harvard Institute for International Development, then with the Harvard Kennedy School of Government, and as of summer 2004 with Oxford University); (b) a core course on pensions targeting technical staff from our client countries and World Bank staff, which was launched in December 1999 and is now offered on a regional basis; (c) an annual conference on public pension fund management; (d) an annual conference on contractual savings; and (d) regional workshops and conferences to discuss broad policy issues in the area of pensions or to draw lessons from regional experiences with reform (including the October 2003 Stockholm conference to review critically the concept and implementation of notional defined-contribution schemes; see Holzmann and Palmer 2005).

Third, *does it include sufficient capacity building and implementation?* Pension reform is not simply a change of laws but a change in how retirement income is provided. Accomplishing this typically requires major reforms in governance, collection of contributions, record keeping, client information, asset management, regulation and supervision, and benefit disbursement. With passage of a legal framework, only a small part of the task has been achieved. A major emphasis on and investment in local capacity building and implementation and continued work with the client and other international and bilateral institutions beyond reform projects or adjustment loans are still required.

The World Bank is increasingly involved in pension reform in all regions of the world. On the one hand, this exposure requires that cutting-edge knowledge be available within the World Bank to provide the best advice, to address the specific needs of a country, and to issue innovative proposals for solutions. In short, this requires knowledge to empower the country to find its own specific solution. On the other hand, the lessons learned in each country provide a unique set of information that can be productively applied in other reforms. This requires the analysis and sharing of information within the World Bank, with the outside world, and with the countries implementing reform. The World Bank has created a Primer on Pension Reform series that provides comprehensive information on design and implementation issues, including case studies of country experiences for the benefit of World Bank task managers as well as politicians and technicians in client countries. For the dissemination and sharing of reform-related information, emphasis is being placed on the development of a Web site, including the publication of conference and workshop proceedings, basic pension data, and links to other reform-related Web sites from academic, financial sector, and partner institutions (http://www.worldbank.org/pensions).

The World Bank also supports outreach to old and new international partners in order to strengthen the message and impact of reform. In the past, countries too often received sharply conflicting advice from different international institutions and bilateral donors. The World Bank is seeking to engage partner institutions in a constructive dialogue in order to determine areas of agreement and difference and to examine the reasons behind them (such as differences in objectives, values, assumptions, views on the functioning of the world, or constituencies). This approach will not dissipate all disagreements and perhaps should not do so. The outcome of such a dialogue, however, should help client countries to assess the differences and arrive at their own judgments.

To this end, dialogue has been strengthened with the International Labour Organization, which traditionally has been opposed to enhancing funded provisions to the detriment of unfunded provisions but has recently adopted a more open stance (see, for example, Beattie and McGillivray 1995; Gillion 2000; Gillion and others 2000; ILO 2002a). One forum for such an exchange of views has been created by the International Social Security Association (ISSA) through its Stockholm Initiative, a worthwhile attempt to create a new consensus on social security (ISSA 1998; Thompson 1998). The World Bank has also established partnerships with nongovernmental organizations such as HelpAge to deal with income support for the vulnerable elderly. Intensive contacts with regard to the design and implementation of reform exist with the World Bank's sister institution, the International Monetary Fund. In the past, the fiscal stance of the IMF and its defense of government deficits have hampered the move toward funded pensions. A note by the Fiscal Affairs Department to the IMF board in 1998, however, recognized that reform-induced deficits do not reflect an expansionary fiscal policy if they are caused by a reduction in the implicit pension debt. The application in a country context occurs on a case-by-case approach. More recently, cooperation in the pension area has been established with the regional development banks such as African Development Bank, Asian Development Bank, and Inter-American Development Bank. Last, but not least, the World Bank cooperates with the OECD's Working Party on Private Pensions and the recently established International Organization of Pension Supervisors (IOPS) on the regulation and supervision of private schemes.

Chapter 4

World Bank Lending to Support Pension Reform

THE DISCUSSION IN CHAPTER 3 ARTICULATES the concepts and principles that constitute the World Bank's perspective on pension reform among its client countries. These are the result of an ongoing process of development, research, and evaluation over more than a decade of work in this field. Although there has been considerable evolution and refinement of this perspective, the essential foundations of World Bank policy have been relatively constant throughout the period. These embody two essential principles: (1) a focus on enhancing the stability and sustainability of pension systems by diversifying the risks and establishing some degree of prefunding and (2) the need to accommodate the conditions and circumstances of a given country in developing a path to reform.

The most readily accessible evidence of the application of any policy framework, however, is in its implementation. For the World Bank, this takes the form of direct financial support for pension reforms through its lending activities. This chapter reviews the record of the Bank's lending related to pension reforms during the period of fiscal 1984 through fiscal 2004. This record indicates that the World Bank has made a substantial commitment to pension reforms within a broad range of settings over an extended period. It also demonstrates that, while there is strong adherence to the policy of supporting the multipillar framework, the financial support is also characterized by a highly diverse range of reform designs, with only a relatively small proportion of loans directed toward a dominant, mandatory second pillar. This evidence describing the World Bank's pension reform activities demonstrates its commitment to the diversity, flexibility, and application of the World Bank's framework as a benchmark rather than as a blueprint for pension reform.

As part of the regular process of internal review of World Bank operations, the Operations Evaluation Department (OED) has compiled data on all of the loans made since 1984 with a meaningful pension component. Information on these loans was obtained from original documentation in the World Bank's archives and includes the classification of loans by amounts, the nature of the loan (investment, technical assistance, or structural adjustment), and the characteristics of the pension reform involved (first, second, third, or multipillar). These data provide a comprehensive look at World Bank financial support for pension reforms and the capacity to evaluate the level and characteristics of World Bank activities in this area.

Scope of the World Bank's Pension Lending

The World Bank made 204 loans involving 68 countries with some pension reform component over the 21 years from fiscal 1984 through fiscal 2004.[13] Pension lending activities were both in the form of direct support for specific reforms through technical assistance and investment loans and in the form of indirect support through program and structural adjustment lending (a type of lending that currently is included in the category of Bank operations termed development policy lending). A rough estimate of the full scope of pension-related lending in this second category can be developed by assigning the share of "adjustment" loans in proportion to the share of pension-related conditions associated with the loans.

Over this 21-year period, loans that had some pension element represented more than $34 billion of World Bank lending, a substantial portion of the Bank's operations.[14] Using the rough measure for assessing the share of adjustment lending in combination with lending in which the pension component is explicit indicates that about $5.5 billion, or 16 percent of the aggregate dollar value of these loans, was related directly to pension issues. As shown in table 4.1, there was significant lending activity for pension reforms in every year during the period, although the total amounts varied considerably. The highest levels of pension lending were from 1997 to 1999, during which pension lending averaged more than $1 billion a year. The average pension component of loans was $26.8 million, indicating that pension issues were a major share of the lending activity when present in a loan. This figure may understate the significance of Bank financial support for pension reform because pension lending tends to be associated with larger loans. Among all of the loans (weighing each equally rather than in proportion to total dollars), nearly 20 percent of the loan, on average, was associated with pensions.

When a narrower measure of Bank financial support, which includes only technical assistance and investment lending, was used, the significance of pension components of loans was found to be similar. Within this

Table 4.1. World Bank Lending with Pension Components,
Fiscal 1984–2004

Fiscal year	Total Bank lending with pension component (US$ million)	Value of the pension component (US$ million)	Pension component as a percentage of total
1984	5.0	0.4	8.0
1987	80.0	11.4	14.3
1989	181.1	16.3	9.0
1990	295.2	14.2	4.8
1991	654.3	12.3	1.9
1992	1,777.2	163.0	9.2
1993	1,003.1	159.3	15.9
1994	929.0	39.5	4.3
1995	2,237.0	161.9	7.2
1996	947.4	46.7	4.9
1997	2,591.2	985.6	38.0
1998	8,500.8	1,286.5	15.1
1999	7,013.0	1,309.3	18.7
2000	2,342.5	788.7	33.7
2001	1,184.5	50.0	4.2
2002	2,687.7	197.5	7.3
2003	1,147.2	149.0	13.0
2004	603.6	76.3	12.6
Total	34,179.8	5,468.0	16.0

Source: OED forthcoming.

narrower category of loans, the total dollars associated with pension elements accounted for 13.6 percent of the lending operations, and the average among loans (weighing each loan equally) was 26.5 percent.

The World Bank's lending activities were broadly distributed geographically during the past decade, covering countries in all regions of the world. Table 4.2 shows the regional distribution of Bank loans. The Latin America and Caribbean region received 56 percent of the dollar value of pension lending, with a pension component of $3.1 billion. The largest number of loans (93) was in the Europe and Central Asia region.

Diversity of Pension Reforms

The World Bank supported a wide range of pension reforms over the relevant period. In reviewing the underlying loan documents, a simple descriptor that classifies lending as related to a first, second, or third pillar—or

Table 4.2. Regional Distribution of World Bank Lending Activities, 1984–2004

Region	Number of countries	Value of the pension component (US$ million)	Number of loans
Sub-Saharan Africa	14	122.2	26
East Asia and Pacific	4	518.4	7
Europe and Central Asia	25	1,626.2	93
Latin America and Caribbean	15	3,067.5	57
Middle East and North Africa	6	76.0	9
South Asia	4	59.0	12
Total	68	5,468.0	204

Source: OED forthcoming.

some combination—was assigned to each loan. This classification provides the basis for some simple measures to evaluate whether and to what extent the Bank did, in practice, implement the policy of flexibility and adaptation to local conditions or whether it pursued an agenda focusing on one particular reform design or, as some observers have suggested, placed a pronounced emphasis on reforms that involved the implementation of a funded and privately managed second pillar.

This is essentially a simple test of whether there is any indication of the imposition of a pension "blueprint." To this end, a classification among the Bank's pension experts and the Bank's independent evaluation department (OED) assessed the extent to which financial support was distributed among the various types of pension systems and reforms. In addition, for loans focusing on more than one pillar but with a second-pillar-dominated reform, a judgment was made to determine whether the lending occurred before or after enactment of the reform to assess whether there is evidence that lending exerted a significant degree of policy influence on these types of reforms.

Single and Multipillar Reforms

The distribution of pension lending between the different kinds of reforms (combination of pillars) demonstrates that World Bank lending supported a wide range of pension system design and reforms. Table 4.3 indicates that Bank lending supported all types of basic reform designs and was broadly distributed across the full range of pillars and potential combinations. The table indicates that lending was distributed approximately equally between single and multipillar reform efforts, with 120 loans and $2.4 billion associated with single pillars and 80 loans and $3.1

Table 4.3. World Bank Pension-Related Lending Classified by Pillar Support, 1984–2004

Type of pension project	Number of loans	Total Bank lending with a pension component (US$ million)	Value of the pension component (US$ million)	Pension-related lending as a percentage of total lending
Loans associated with a single pillar	120	18,694.8	2,373.9	43.4
First pillar	92	13,356.4	2,078.2	38.0
Second pillar	10	322.6	125.5	2.3
Third pillar	18	5,015.8	170.2	3.1
Loans associated with more than one pillar	80	13,824.8	3,094.0	56.6
First and second	24	4,105.8	1,432.1	26.2
First and third	22	5,634.9	1,170.3	21.4
Second and third	2	167.0	12.1	0.2
All three	32	3,917.1	479.4	8.8
Loans not associated with any pillar	4	1,660.0	0.0	0.0
Total	204	34,179.8	5,468.0	100.0

Source: OED forthcoming.

billion associated with multipillar efforts. The vast majority of the lending ($5.2 billion or more than 90 percent) was associated with reforms of first-pillar arrangements, either alone or in combination with other components. Well over half of the dollar value of the lending (57 percent) was associated with reforms involving multiple pillars of the pension system. Only 10 of the loans and $125 million (less than 5 percent by either measure) were associated with the second pillar alone, and less than 40 percent of the lending related to pensions ($2 billion involving 68 of the loans) was attributable to second-pillar reforms, either alone or in combination with other pillars (usually the first pillar).

Lending for Second-Pillar Reforms

It has been suggested that, even within this broad range of reform structures, the World Bank has focused primarily on lending to support the implementation of mandatory privately managed funded second pillars.

Table 4.4. Proportion of Pension-Related Lending for Second-Pillar Implementation, 1984–2004

Type of lending	Loans		Value		Countries	
	Number	Percent	Amount (US$ million)	Percent	Number	Percent
Second-pillar implementation	43	21	1,648.3	30	24	35
All lending	204	100	5,468.0	100	68	100

Source: OED forthcoming.

Table 4.4 indicates the proportion of lending throughout this period in which some portion of the loan was associated with either "actual reform measures" or "institutional capacity building" for a second pillar. (It does not include loans with "general analytical support," which may or may not have resulted in the implementation of a second pillar). Because it is not possible to distinguish the proportion of any individual loan associated with each pillar (many of these are multipillar reforms), this represents an upper bound of the proportion of Bank operations that supported second-pillar implementation during this period. This shows that just slightly more than one-fifth (21 percent) of pension-related loan operations had some element of second-pillar implementation, representing 30 percent of the value of lending and involving a similar proportion (24 of 68) of the countries in which the Bank engaged in some pension-related operations.

Similarly, some observers have suggested that the World Bank's lending for second-pillar pension reforms have been oriented exclusively toward reforms associated with a dominant second pillar. Only a handful of the pension reforms over this period met these criteria: Bolivia, Chile, Kazakhstan, Mexico, and Peru. Table 4.5 shows the lending related to these reforms in proportion to the total value of pension lending over the period. The pension component of these loans was $943.1 million out of the total pension component of $5.4 billion, indicating that 17.2 percent of all pension-related lending was associated with reforms with a dominant second pillar. This represents less than half of the approximately $2 billion in lending (including general analytical support) for loans that had any association with second-pillar reforms.

Supporting Implementation

The manner in which the World Bank has engaged in pension reform activities with its clients can also be viewed in relation to the extent to which its loans were made in advance of the enactment of a reform (and

Table 4.5. World Bank Lending for Reforms with a Dominant Second Pillar, 1984–2004

Type of lending	Value (US$ million)	Percent of all loans with a pension component
All loans with a pension component	5,400	100
Loans for reforms with a dominant second pillar	943.1	17

Source: OED forthcoming.

thus may have influenced the design of the reform) compared with the extent to which loans were approved and disbursed after enactment of the reform (and thus responded to a policy framework that the country had already put in place). Figure 4.1 indicates that most of the pension-related loans were made in the years immediately following enactment of the reform rather than prior to enactment.

The World Bank's role in multipillar reforms emerges even more clearly when the value of World Bank lending before and after reform is considered. Figure 4.2 shows that most of the World Bank's pension lending went to postreform implementation loans. About half of total pension lending was made in the two years following reform. Preform lending

Figure 4.1. Timing of World Bank Loans to Multipillar Schemes, by Number of Loans

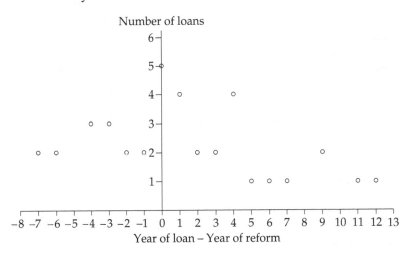

Source: OED forthcoming.

Figure 4.2. Timing of World Bank Loans to Multipillar Schemes, by Amount of Loans

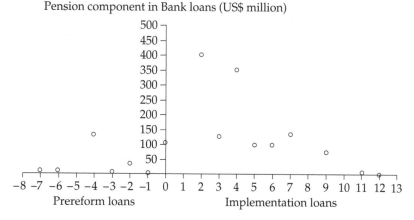

Source: OED forthcoming.

was relatively small, and, within this subset, lending in the two years prior to reform was negligible.

As this analysis indicates, the pension-related lending operations of the World Bank were a very significant part of the overall activities of the Bank. These loans were widely dispersed over time and among regions, reflecting an approach that strongly emphasizes multipillar system designs. The majority of the lending involved some reform of existing publicly managed first-pillar systems, and there was an important, but certainly not dominant, focus on the development of funded second pillars. A large part of the lending took place after enactment of the reform, indicating a significant orientation to the implementation of client-enacted reforms rather than the use of lending to impose a policy "blueprint."

PART 2

DESIGN AND
IMPLEMENTATION ISSUES

The second part of this presentation of the World Bank's perspective on pension systems and reform elaborates in some detail relevant issues of design and implementation. Chapter 5 reviews the generic options for reform and presents a stylized policy choice framework; while the goals of reform are universal, the policy choices of each country are substantially determined by the inherited system, the impetus for reform, and the (enabling or disenabling) policy environment. Chapter 6 provides a quite extensive but still incomplete review of key reform issues. While Bank staff have developed fairly firm positions in some areas, we are still in search of good solutions in others. Chapter 7 presents a summary review of reform experience from the two regions in which the greatest activity has occurred—Latin America and Europe and Central Asia—and a less extensive overview of reform developments in other regions. Chapter 8 offers a few concluding remarks summarizing the discussion.

Chapter 5

General and Country-Specific Options for the Reform of Pension Systems

THE POLICY FRAMEWORK ARTICULATED IN CHAPTER 4 is oriented toward both process and outcome and looks to goals and criteria based on functional rather than structural concepts.[15] This is bound to produce a broad range of approaches to pension reform and system design. Despite the individual character of pension reform efforts, the scope of feasible outcomes remains sufficiently constrained by common realities that make certain principles and patterns discernable. A review of these is useful in defining the range of reasonable results in a generic manner. Considering the nature of the options and their strengths and weaknesses provides a useful starting point for considering how various types of reforms may be able to fulfill the requirements articulated in chapter 4. The actual reform options for a country have to consider very specifically the inherited system(s), the specific reform needs, and the (enabling or disenabling) policy environment.

General Options for Reform

There are essentially five main options for reforming a typical publicly managed, unfunded defined-benefit scheme. These are a subset of a potentially larger set of options resulting from different combinations of benefit type (defined benefit or defined contribution), administration (public or private), and funding (unfunded, fully funded, or prefunded). The relevant subset comprises (a) parametric reforms that keep the benefit structure, public administration, and unfunded nature of the scheme and merely change the system's parameters; (b) a notional defined-contribution reform that changes the structure of benefits but keeps public administration and the unfunded nature; (c) a market-based approach

73

that provides fully funded defined-contribution or defined-benefit arrangements under primarily private management (especially the investment of assets); (d) public prefunding that provides defined benefits or defined contributions that are publicly administered; and (e) multipillar reforms that diversify the structure of benefits, administration, and funding of the pension system. Each of these main options is discussed in turn. While these reform options are particularly relevant for unfunded systems, a subset is also relevant for centrally funded systems.

Parametric Reform

Parametric reforms leave the existing structure unchanged but adjust the parameters of the scheme to improve the delivery of social and economic objectives. Such parametric reforms include lengthening the assessment period for calculating initial benefits (for example, from the past three years of earnings to lifetime earnings), introducing actuarial increments (decrements) for earlier (later) retirement (typically from 0 or 2 percent to some 6 percent a year), reducing the annual accrual rate (for example, from 2 to 1.25 percent a year), increasing the retirement age, changing from wage to price indexation of benefits, and reviewing the minimum pension guarantee provisions but also increasing the contribution rate to make the scheme fiscally sound.

Such reforms can, in principle, deliver the social and economic objectives, but they have three main shortfalls. First, and most important, for largely political reasons, they are never fully implemented. No single country has undertaken a parametric reform that, by itself, delivers adequate, affordable, and sustainable pensions. Such parametric reforms simply are not politically attractive because many of the gains would be achieved after the politicians responsible have retired. For this reason, they engage in partial parametric reforms to keep the system afloat; that is, they react but do not act. Since individuals know that more is to come but the full game plan is not known, the reform is not credible, and many individuals have an incentive to oppose even minor changes.

Second, and as a result of the typically incomplete parametric reforms, while some distortions in the labor market may be eliminated, many distortions are likely to remain. For example, the obstacles to mobility between public and private sector employees persist because parametric reforms are rarely able to lead a common and harmonized general pension scheme. While a reduction in mandated benefits is likely to increase the demand for voluntary and funded arrangements, the impact on financial market development can be expected to be small. Third, any effort to deal with aging would require long-term, announced, or discretionary changes in the retirement age and other system parameters in line with changing life expectancy—again, not politically attractive and almost never done. In nearly all cases, it is simply not politically feasible to reform a traditional defined-benefit structure to provide the flexibility needed for individuals to make adjustments among learning, work, and retirement leisure.

Nevertheless, parametric reforms are important and constitute the majority of actual pension reforms in recent decades (see, for example, Fox and Palmer 2001; Gillion and others 2000; OECD 1988; Schwarz and Demirgüç-Kunt 1999; World Bank 1994). Although in most instances they will not by themselves lead to reformed, modern pension systems, these parametric reforms can be a crucial precursor to more far-reaching paradigmatic reform, as they change the liabilities under the old system and may thus allow for a smoother transition toward a new system and benefit structure.

Notional Defined-Contribution Reform

In a nonfinancial or notional defined-contribution system, an individual account is established to which contributions by the individual (and his or her employer) are earmarked and on which a notional interest rate is paid (Palmer 2005b). The notional interest rate is consistent with the interest rate that an unfunded scheme can pay—that is, the "natural" growth rate (essentially the growth rate of covered wages in a mature system). At retirement, an annuitization factor that reflects the remaining life expectancy of the cohort at retirement and the relevant interest rate is applied to the accumulated notional individual account to determine the benefit payout. The benefits are typically price indexed—or at least are not fully wage indexed—to allow for the buildup of a reserve for dealing with economic or demographic shocks.

This type of reform changes the benefit structure from defined benefit to defined contribution but retains the unfunded nature of the system. The move from an unfunded defined-benefit scheme to a nonfinancial defined-contribution scheme essentially makes the underlying financial relationship more explicit and transparent. Formally, an unfunded defined-benefit system can be adjusted parametrically to mimic a notional defined-contribution system, and a full-fledged defined-benefit system (such as the German or French point system) may come close to that (Disney 1999; Góra and Palmer 2004; Legros 2005). Full equivalence, however, would also require the defined-benefit formula to exhibit variable and actuarially adjusted decrements (increments) for earlier (later) retirement and to build increasing (remaining) life expectancy into the benefit formula. The reform experience in Brazil, Ecuador, France, or Germany suggests that such adjustments in the defined-benefit system are politically difficult to implement; hence, a notional defined-contribution reform is not simply a subset of a parametric reform.

This nonfinancial defined-contribution structure is appealing for its simplicity and transparency, its incentive effects on labor supply and retirement decisions, its adjustment to changing professional and family structures (including divorce), and automatic adjustment to increasing life expectancy. Specifically, as in funded individual schemes, workers have an interest in, and can easily verify, the amount of contribution paid on their behalf. Contributions are much less likely to be perceived as taxes, and the labor market distortions are reduced (but not eliminated, as long as the notional risk-adjusted interest rate remains below the risk-adjusted market interest rate or personal discount rate). Distortions on retirement decisions are reduced as well. Increments (decrements) for earlier (later) retirement are part of the benefit design and do not require extra political decisions.

The approach also allows for an easy and quick harmonization between different schemes (such as for public and private sector workers) because higher benefits for public sector workers are essentially conserved for those close to retirement (if accrued rights are transformed into the appropriate notional amounts), while new entrants are subject to the same rights as private sector workers. In its pure form, the notional defined contribution is intentionally nonredistributive within a cohort (that is, each worker gets back his or her contributions plus a notional interest rate), but redistributive elements can be introduced (such as matching contributions to low-income workers or during periods of sickness and unemployment). However, these redistributions should be accomplished through an explicit and transparent transfer of money, to avoid idiosyncratic or excessive giveaways of unfunded promises. The individual account structure allows an easy buildup of individual rights for women and splitting of the accrued value of benefits after divorce and death; it does not, however, provide survivor insurance for widows unless some of the notional capital is put aside for this purpose. When the estimated life expectancy of a cohort increases, individuals receive, through a reduced annuitization factor, a lower pension and can adjust by retiring later or saving more.

Some of these arguments have convinced policy makers in Italy, Latvia, Poland, and Sweden—and also in Brazil, the Kyrgyz Republic, and Mongolia—to undertake reforms that transform their defined-benefit systems into nonfinancial defined-contribution schemes (some doubt that Brazil's reform can be called a notional defined-contribution reform). These reforms highlight alternative approaches to reform, such as an immediate change toward notional defined contribution as opposed to a gradual phasing in, and different methods of transforming accrued rights into notional amounts (see Palmer 2005a). In addition, the experience in these countries also brings to light some basic weaknesses, with Sweden generally considered the benchmark country (see Palmer 2000).

The experience demonstrates that the notional defined-contribution concept can be hijacked by politicians and lead to less-than-optimal system designs. For example, financial unsustainability may persist if the "wrong" notional interest rate is chosen, such as per capita GDP or wage growth instead of growth of the total wage base (adjusted for changes in the contribution-benefit profile and demographics; see Settergren and Mikula 2005). The remaining cohort life expectancy needs to be projected and implemented; it should not be used as a fixed factor, as in China (James 2002). As the system remains unfunded, a financial balancing mechanism, such as a buffer fund, is needed to deal with demographic and economic shocks. Such a buffer fund may have the same fate as other reserve funds of unfunded systems in the past; that is, they get emptied. Contributions to the individual account should not be granted if they have not been paid, as in Italy. The substantial administrative requirements to run such a scheme should not be underestimated, as in the Kyrgyz Republic or in Mongolia. Despite these challenges, reforming along notional defined-contribution lines, if done well, is likely the best way to restructure a typical unfunded defined-benefit scheme within a multipillar structure (that is, securing redistribution through the zero pillar or explicit transfers through the notional defined-contribution pillar and having funded provisions in place to allow individuals to compensate for the likely lower replacement rate with individual saving efforts).[16]

A Full Market-Based Reform

This type of reform changes, most importantly, the manner of funding (from unfunded to prefunded) and can also involve a move from public to private administration. Market-based reforms can involve both defined-benefit and defined-contribution systems and may be linked with the conversion of a defined-benefit system to a defined-contribution arrangement. These reforms may involve comprehensive changes—from the collection of contributions to the disbursement of investments and benefits—or focus on the establishment of market-based investments only. Typically, the movement to market-driven investments is what really matters. Under this kind of a reform, publicly administered, unfunded arrangements are restricted to the zero or basic pillar dealing with pure poverty alleviation objectives. This would be accomplished through a noncontributory or social assistance scheme in addition to, perhaps, some form of redistribution to low-earning contributors through the first pillar, such as a minimum pension, and minimum rate-of-return guarantees in the new funded pillar. The Chilean pension reform of 1981, which provides a means-tested pension to poor noncontributors and a minimum pension guarantee to low-earning contributors (and similar reforms in the 1990s in Bolivia, El Salvador, Mexico, and Peru), or the reforms in Australia and Hong Kong (China) are examples of such an approach.

Ideally, market-based reforms offer many advantages. In particular, providing market interest rates on individual and funded accounts that exceed long-term wage growth affords the potential to produce higher replacement rates for a given contribution rate or demands a lower contribution rate for a given target replacement rate. But this potential gain also carries risks with regard to the rate of return and replacement rate. At the same time, the distortions on labor supply and retirement decisions should be reduced. Pension payouts adjust automatically to an increase in life expectancy, making the system less subject to demographic risk. By definition, the scheme is financially sound and sustainable, and the funding should increase national saving and contribute to financial market development and economic growth. Of course, various advantages of the notional defined-contribution structure—introducing distributive elements, granting individual rights for women, and adjusting to an increase in life expectancy—apply as well.

In reality, various obstacles have to be overcome to attain all or even some of these advantages. As discussed in part 1 of this report, the transition from pay-as-you-go toward full funding makes the implicit debt explicit. The repayment of the now-explicit debt requires an extra tax to pay the interest in order to prevent government debt as a percentage of GDP from becoming excessive. As a labor tax (for a given replacement rate), it exactly consumes the difference between the prior higher contribution rate and the lower premium in the funded scheme (Sinn 2000). Repaying the implicit debt requires a tighter fiscal stance (a higher tax burden or a lower expenditure on other budget items) to undo the original windfall profit that unfunded schemes confer on the start-up generation. Only if the reform lowers the excess tax burden (by changing the tax structure) or creates positive externalities (by encouraging a higher growth path as a result of increasing savings and stimulating financial market development) can a potentially double burden on the transition generation be mitigated (Holzmann 1997a, 1999). Most important for the Bank's client countries, such a reform prevents an increase in the unfunded debt and the implicit burden on future generations as coverage increases.

Mandating that a pension scheme be delivered through the private sector does not eliminate conjectural liabilities for the government. For social and political reasons, many governments will not be able to leave all retirement-income risks with the individual. Providing a minimum pension or minimum rate guarantee is equivalent to writing an option that may reduce the implicit debt very little (Smetters 2002). Finally, to deliver the higher rates of return in a funded scheme at reasonable risks requires a sound, well-regulated, and well-supervised financial sector. Although such a sector need not be fully established at the inception of the scheme, it must be there well before maturation. International diversification may provide major support to this end, but it also creates requirements and issues of its own (Chan-Lau

2004; Holzmann 2002). Full privatization, therefore, may be a reform option for countries with low implicit debt in the existing system (due to a relatively immature system for both benefit levels and coverage), with the potential to create a strong financial sector in a relatively short period (while allowing international diversification of assets), and with the ability to use budgetary means to compensate for major income shocks from adverse rate developments. Indeed, a full market-based reform has been found to be more likely among countries with low pension debt (James and Brooks 2001).

Public Prefunding

Public or centralized prefunding of defined-benefit or defined-contribution systems has been proposed (among others, by Orszag and Stiglitz 2001) and is being implemented in some developed economies in order to cope with the problem of an aging population. Canada, Ireland, New Zealand, and the United States all have some degree of partial prefunding. Additionally, provident funds that, in principle, provide retirement savings through a defined-contribution system have a long tradition in former British colonies in Africa and Asia, and a centrally managed defined-contribution system was recently established in Kosovo and is proposed for civil servants in Eritrea, in both cases as a first step toward greater choice. The common characteristic of these arrangements is that prefunding is centralized in one government-administered fund, although investment management may be outsourced to private asset managers.

To deliver on the primary and secondary goals of a pension system, prefunding requires the same changes in the benefit formula as the other reform options. Central prefunding is intended to achieve two objectives: (a) to reduce the fiscal burden on future generations by improving the intertemporal budget position of government (in much the same way as a reduction in explicit public debt but, perhaps, in a politically more palatable manner) and (b) to use one central public fund (compared with multiple privately managed funds) in order to improve risk pooling and keep administrative costs low.

To deliver on the potential benefits of central prefunding, the key requirement is to create a governance structure that keeps politics out of investment decisions and does not produce a looser fiscal stance because government has easy access to funds (Hess and Impavido 2004; Impavido 2002). The degree of government control of the capital stock in these types of arrangements imposes significant challenges. Although some of the recent changes and approaches in highly developed countries may provide some optimism (Palacios 2002), the track record on central funds worldwide is poor, including the well-known examples of Malaysia and Singapore (Asher 2002; Palacios and Iglesias 2001). Furthermore, the approach raises major questions with regard to corporate governance of private sector enterprises in possession of the central fund. The experience of Kosovo and Russia during the next few years will indicate whether such an approach can be used as a transitional device toward decentralized fund management (see Musalem and Palacios 2004).

Multipillar Pension System

A multipillar approach simultaneously diversifies the structure, funding, and administration of benefits. The World Bank (1994) has proposed a specific definition of a multipillar pension scheme: (a) a (mandated) unfunded system of defined flat or means-tested benefits that is publicly managed and seeks to alleviate poverty; (b) a mandated funded (usually defined-contribution during the accumulation phase) system in which the assets are privately managed and that seeks to replace income; and (c) voluntary funded retirement provisions that compensate for any perceived retirement-income gap for individuals, in particular those with higher lifetime incomes.

Within this definition, some 20 countries now have a multipillar system, including, Argentina, Australia, Bolivia, Chile, Costa Rica, Kazakhstan, Switzerland, Uruguay, and other countries in Latin America. However, if we were to adopt a loose definition, almost all countries could be said to have a multipillar scheme because most have some kind of social assistance scheme for the general public (and the elderly poor), most have some form of occupational scheme that, in principle, is funded and covers some part of the formal labor force, and all countries offer access to voluntary retirement savings (via savings accounts or housing). Other considerations, however, render a straightforward definition of a multipillar pension scheme difficult:

- Tension between what an "ideal" system should look like (and this will depend on the eyes of the beholder) and what definition best characterizes the schemes existing in the world today.
- Differences in the use of the terms "second" and "third" pillar in the world (see OECD 2001b). In Europe and elsewhere, the second pillar refers to occupational pension plans, and the third refers to personal pension plans (whether mandated or voluntary); in the Americas and elsewhere, the second pillar refers to mandated plans, and the third pillar refers to voluntary plans (whether occupational or personal).
- Differences in the use of mandating or type of funding to define the pillars. A few public schemes are partially prefunded (Canada, Ireland), whereas some occupational schemes are unfunded (a few quasi-mandated schemes, as in France, and voluntary schemes through book reserves, as in Germany).
- Differences in the focus on the main groups of society to be covered. The traditional definition of a multipillar scheme focuses largely on formal sector workers only. Given the low coverage and the existence of two other main groups in society with different needs and

capacity—the lifetime poor and informal sector workers—the availability of different pillars has real-life significance.

As a result, the Bank proposes the following categorization of pillars targeted to the three main groups in society. Table 5.1 sets out the pillars, target groups, and main characteristics, which are detailed below.

The target groups constitute a rough characterization of the three main groups in the Bank's client countries:

- *The lifetime poor,* who do not participate in formal sector activities in a sustained manner, if at all. Labor is their main asset, and they are too poor to save for an extended retirement. When they become very old and are unable to work in a full-time capacity, they become very vulnerable, in particular those living alone or widowed.
- *Informal sector workers,* many of whom could participate in a formal scheme but do not for various reasons. While working, they are not in deep poverty but may become so if financial instruments are not available to transfer resources into the future.
- *Formal sector workers,* who, almost by definition, are mandated to participate in formal pension schemes. Some of them may have an insufficient work record, which makes them ineligible for even a minimum pension.

The suggested pillars go beyond the Bank's original three-pillar terminology. The zero or basic pillar is intended to deal more effectively with the lifetime poor as well as with informal or formal sector workers who reach old age with insufficient resources or are not eligible for a formal pension. The importance of the basic pillar is expected to decrease as income levels rise and the economy becomes more formal.

The first pillar is the typical public pension scheme, funded from social security contributions, with perhaps some reserves, with defined benefits or nonfinancial defined contributions, under public management, and possibly with an additional redistributive goal. Initially, this category comprises different plans for various occupations (such as civil servants, private sector employees, independent workers, or farmers), with a trend toward harmonization between the schemes as development occurs and labor mobility becomes increasingly important. Its essential feature is to provide a minimum level of longevity insurance to retirees, financed through intergenerational transfers.

For the second pillar—mandating—full funding and private asset management are the primary characteristics (whether for occupational or personal plans). Second pillars are typically defined contribution during the accumulation phase but, when mature, incorporate a means for individuals to convert account balances into a lifetime annuity. They may, however, be constructed with defined-benefit elements and should be designed with specific income-replacement targets.

Table 5.1. Multipillar Pension Taxonomy

	Target groups			Main criteria		
Pillar	Lifetime poor	Informal sector	Formal sector	Characteristics	Participation	Funding or collateral
0	X	X	x	"Basic" or "social pension," at least social assistance (universal or means tested)	Universal or residual	Budget or general revenues
1			X	Public pension plan, publicly managed (defined benefit or notional defined contribution)	Mandated	Contributions, perhaps with some financial reserves
2			X	Occupational or personal pension plans (fully funded defined benefit or fully funded defined contribution)	Mandated	Financial assets
3	x	X	X	Occupational or personal pension plans (partially or fully funded defined benefit or funded defined contribution)	Voluntary	Financial assets
4	X	X	X	Access to informal support (family), other formal social programs (health care), and other individual financial and nonfinancial assets (homeownership)	Voluntary	Financial and nonfinancial assets

Note: The size and appearance of x reflect the importance of each pillar for each target group in the following increasing order of importance: x, X, **X**.

The third pillar comprises voluntary and prefunded pension plans (whether occupational or personal plans) established and regulated to ensure a clear retirement objective. Depending on the form of benefits, the third pillar can also provide longevity insurance, but its provision would rely on private sector institutions. The fourth pillar is added because a large part of retirement consumption may be derived from sources that are not formally defined as pensions, such as homeownership, interfamily transfers, and personal savings accounts.

The *type of funding* refers to the form of collateral of the pension liability, with economic development, strength of the legal framework, and political economy determining the quality of the collateral. Since the quality of collateral is linked to GDP and the underlying demographic structure, the traditional distinction between unfunded and funded is blurred. Furthermore, a funded defined-contribution scheme that is invested in an expanded supply of government paper or a corporate and personal pension scheme that lends to the government and allows an increase in the fiscal deficit and explicit public debt may be as unfunded as a nonfinancial defined-contribution scheme.[17] One may think of unfunded versus funded in terms of how the creation of the pension liability contributes to implicit or explicit public debt. If no public debt, including contingent liabilities, is created, then the scheme may be called funded; if public debt is created, then it may be called unfunded. An alternative definition is presented in part 1, distinguishing between narrow and broad funding. Narrow funding refers to the backing of individual pension claims with financial assets (and property rights) as individual collateral. Broad funding refers to the translation of future pension commitments into increased aggregate saving (and higher output) as macroeconomic collateral. However, the latter definition makes the notion of funding dependent on behavior that is well outside any control.

The *type of benefits*—defined benefit or defined contribution—can, in principle, be distinguished by who carries the (investment and mortality) risk. In a (funded or unfunded) defined-benefit system, the sponsor of the pension plan typically carries the risk—that is, the enterprise or the government. In a (funded or unfunded) defined-contribution system, the individual carries the risk. The reality, however, is more complex. In an unsustainable, unfunded defined-benefit system, the economic or demographic risk is passed on to the next generation through higher contributions or higher government transfers. In an unsustainable company plan, the risk is passed on to pensioners and workers who are still alive when the plan becomes insolvent. The individuals also carry a risk that the benefit formula or indexation practice may change. In a defined-contribution system, the demographic and investment risk can either be borne by insurance companies if annuitization is common or be passed on to future generations if benefits are ultimately provided through nationwide public pooling.

Country-Specific Options for Reform:
Policy Progression and Path Dependency

The pension systems and reforms will be guided by the main reform options discussed above. However, the actual choices will depend on a number of country-specific considerations, most important being the existing pension scheme (and other related public programs); the special reform need(s) of schemes; and the (enabling or disabling) environment. All these considerations are broadly linked with the development status and income level of a country. This has led to suggestions that the Bank offer a policy framework or progression that presents the breadth of reform options in relation to the enabling environment, addressing linkages to such factors as development status and fiscal and institutional capacity. This section attempts to address this suggestion, although, in order to condense the many potential combinations and variations, the result is more stylized than prescriptive.

While it is generally true that poorer countries with lower fiscal and administrative capacity have fewer options and that richer countries with a more supportive environment have more options, the progression of options is not linear. This is due to the shadow or absence of the existing system(s). Most critically, while a rich OECD country with full fiscal and administrative capacity could, from an enabling environment point of view, move toward any system, the actual (best) choice will have to consider the inherited system, including the implicit pension debt and institutional setup. As a result, the introduction of a second pillar may be a potential option, but not the best or even a feasible policy choice. In contrast, in a reform-minded middle-income country with moderate implicit debt and sufficient fiscal and administrative capacity, such a choice may be viable and desirable.

Table 5.2 highlights the central reform options and suggested choices by broad country groupings. It is a stylized representation of the choices because it limits constraints to three broad areas—existing system, need for reform, and reform environment—and, within each set, to a few central features with limited properties. Going through a larger set of features and properties would create a decision or choice tree of a few thousand entries, but not necessarily produce a better understanding of the operative principles. The choice of constraints, features, and properties is clearly influenced by actual experience with reform. For the inherited system, the crucial features are the existence or absence of pension systems, their heterogeneity, the level of coverage (and implicit debt), and the type of benefit and funding. For reform needs, the suggested crucial features are fiscal issues, low rate of return, multiplicity of systems, and coverage. With regard to the enabling environment, the suggested key features are macro and fiscal room, administrative capacity, minimum financial sector, and government commitment to reform (as suggested in the reform support criteria in part 1).

Table 5.2. Stylized Reform Choices for Countries: Matching Reform Needs with Constraints and Opportunities

Type of country	Existing system	Reform needs	Reform environment	Central reform options
Low income				
Postconflict	No system and coverage	Protect the most vulnerable	All capabilities essentially absent	Provide basic support and services via social funds, nongovernmental organizations, and international aid and avoid the introduction of costly civil servant schemes and the compensation of freedom fighters via pensions
Low-level equilibrium	Notional defined benefit for public sector with limited coverage	Deal with fiscal costs; extend coverage	No macro and fiscal room, limited administrative capacity, no financial sector, some government willingness to reform	Undertake a parametric adjustment of the unfunded system and provide community-based support for the vulnerable elderly

Continued on next page

Table 5.2. (continued)

Type of country	Existing system	Reform needs	Reform environment	Central reform options
Emerging and reform oriented	Notional defined benefit for public sector with limited coverage	Deal with fiscal costs; extend coverage	Limited macro and fiscal room, administrative capacity, and financial sector, but willingness to reform	Undertake parametric reform of the unfunded system (perhaps with a view to notional defined contribution); introduce, regulate, and supervise the voluntary system; introduce and test noncontributory pensions
	Funded defined contribution or defined benefit for public sector with limited coverage	Improve rate of return; extend coverage	Limited macro and fiscal room, administrative capacity, and financial sector, but willingness to reform	Improve governance of the central or provident fund; introduce, regulate, and supervise a voluntary system; introduce and test non contributory pensions

Table 5.2. (*continued*)

Type of country	Existing system	Reform needs	Reform environment	Central reform options
Middle income				
Under stress	Multiple notional defined benefit (and funded defined contribution) with moderate coverage	Deal with fiscal costs, low rate of return, multiplicity of systems, and labor market issues; extend coverage	Limited fiscal room, administrative capacity, financial sector, as well as willingness to reform	Undertake parametric adjustment or reforms of the unfunded systems; improve governance of central and provident fund; regulate and supervise a voluntary system
Emerging and reform oriented	Multiple notional defined benefit with moderate coverage (and implicit pension debt)	Deal with fiscal costs, multiplicity of systems, and labor market issues; extend coverage	Some fiscal room, administrative capacity, and financial sector and strong willingness to reform	Introduce a single unfunded system (such as notional defined contribution), move toward a fully funded system, or adopt a mixture of both; introduce, regulate, and supervise a voluntary system; introduce noncontributory pensions (social pension)

Continued on next page

Table 5.2. (*continued*)

Type of country	Existing system	Reform needs	Reform environment	Central reform options
	Multiple funded defined contribution with moderate coverage	Deal with low rate of return (and captive public bond market); extend coverage	Some fiscal room, administrative capacity, and financial sector and strong willingness to reform	Introduce a single funded system (funded defined contribution); introduce, regulate, and supervise voluntary system; introduce noncontributory pensions (social pensions)
High income				
Under stress	Multiple notional defined benefit with high coverage (and implicit pension debt)	Deal with fiscal costs, multiplicity of systems, and labor market issues; keep or extend coverage	Some administrative capacity and financial sector, but limited macro and fiscal room and political willingness to reform	Undertake coordinated parametric reforms of the unfunded systems; improve regulation and supervision of the voluntary system; improve the existing non-contributory pension systems

Table 5.2. (*continued*)

Type of country	Existing system	Reform needs	Reform environment	Central reform options
Maturing tiger	Basic income support but not mandated earnings-related scheme	Deal with current and future fiscal costs (aging); improve consumption smoothing for population	Strong administrative capacity, macro and fiscal position, financial sector, and willingness to reform	Introduce a (limited) mandated and fully funded scheme; improve regulation and supervision of the voluntary system
	Centralized funded defined contribution (provident fund) with limited basic income support	Deal with low rate of return; keep or extend coverage	Strong administrative capacity, macro and fiscal position, financial sector, and willingness to reform	Improve governance of the centralized scheme, including opting out after minimum balance; improve regulation and supervision of the voluntary system; improve the existing and introduce noncontributory pension systems

Continued on next page

Table 5.2. *(continued)*

Type of country	Existing system	Reform needs	Reform environment	Central reform options
With continuous reforms	Multiple notional defined benefit with high coverage (and implicit pension debt)	Deal with fiscal costs, multiplicity of systems, and labor market issues; keep or extend coverage	Strong administrative capacity, macro and fiscal position, financial sector, and willingness to reform	Move toward a single unfunded system (such as notional defined contribution); strengthen regulation and supervision of the voluntary system; introduce and strengthen noncontributory pensions

Note: Level of income loosely refers to the classification used by the World Bank, with low income referring to International Development Association countries and high income referring to OECD-type economies.

The suggested progression of policy choice for *low-income countries* is relatively straightforward, but perhaps less simple than expected. In postconflict countries without a prior scheme, the emphasis for the elderly should clearly be on poverty relief and the most vulnerable. However, the elderly may not be the most vulnerable, and the most vulnerable may include persons of all ages who are disabled by civil strife, including many children. In these circumstances, war veterans expect compensation for their efforts, preferably in the form of a pension, which risks becoming mixed with the perceived need to provide some pension to civil servants, in part to reduce the vulnerability to corruption. If obligations toward public sector employees under a preconflict scheme need to be honored, in what form and how should they be linked to a new system, and what should it look like? Countries currently facing such choices are, for example, Afghanistan and Eritrea.

Most low-income countries have a pension system for at least a subset of their population—public sector employees (that is, civil servants and workers in parastatals). These systems are typically in dire financial condition and urgently require reform. The reform direction will be very much determined by the reform environment. With low capacity and political willingness for reform, little more than minimum adjustments of the existing scheme(s) and stronger community support for the vulnerable elderly can be expected. However, in a reform-oriented environment with some, albeit limited, capacity, the reform options are much more comprehensive: a comprehensive parametric or even a notional defined-contribution-oriented reform of the unfunded scheme; improved governance of funded schemes; the introduction or at least the testing of a noncontributory pension scheme; and the introduction and improved regulation of emerging voluntary schemes are appropriate to these conditions. Countries in this set include Kenya, Senegal, and Uganda.

For *middle-income countries*, the set of feasible policy choices is already more enhanced. The limitations for this quite heterogeneous group of countries are derived more from the capacity constraints than from inherited systems. As a result, for countries with limited capacity and political willingness to reform, the basic reform choices boil down to damage control and basic adjustments. Strongly reform-oriented countries with sufficient capacity at the fiscal and administrative levels have the full array of options open to reform an unfunded or funded (mandated) public scheme. As the coverage—and hence implicit debt—of the inherited system is typically small, the move toward a full second pillar can be envisaged. If the inherited unfunded scheme is large (as in most transition economies), the set of options is restricted, and the move toward a funded, mandated pillar may be partial.

For *high-income countries*, the set of feasible policy choices may appear to be even more enhanced, but this may not be the case. For these countries, which are also quite heterogeneous in their composition, the limitations are quite likely to derive from the inherited system rather than from capacity issues, although the latter can be significant. As in middle-income (and low-income) countries, a rich country under (macro and fiscal) stress, with a government not fully committed to reform, will be restricted to damage control and incremental parametric reforms. A reform-oriented country, with all of the needed capacity but with an inherited Bismarckian system with high implicit debt, is likely to exclude a move toward a funded (second) pillar among its choices, even if it is only partial. Presumably, many countries in continental Europe fall into this category. Those few economies with full capacity but only basic income provisions will move toward mandated funded provisions (as more recently was done by Australia and Hong Kong, China).

Conclusions

While there is, indeed, a link between capacity and reform space, the link is not linear. The feasible options and actual choices will be (co)determined by the inherited system. This suggested path dependence of reform space implies that reform-oriented, middle-income countries need to assess their choices carefully and work diligently on their capacity for reform if they do not want to be constrained in the future. By extension, the same applies to low-income countries and their need to find the appropriate moment to introduce and better regulate and supervise voluntary systems.

Chapter 6

Key Reform Issues: Firm Positions and Open Questions

THIS CHAPTER PRESENTS SOME OF THE KEY ISSUES REGARDING THE DESIGN of pension systems and the implementation of reform, highlighting areas where the World Bank holds a solid position and areas where it is still searching for good answers. Specifically, it presents the Bank staff's views on pillar design, poverty relief, and redistribution; financial sustainability; administrative and implementation issues; regulatory and supervisory issues; the options for countries with small financial markets; and issues of political economy. The chapter ends by acknowledging some major reform dilemmas—that is, areas where there is substantial disagreement or simply an absence of well-developed knowledge of the optimal design of reform.

Pillar Design, Poverty Relief, and Redistribution

Ideally, every elderly person should have access to old-age income, at a minimum in the form of poverty relief or, even better, an income-replacing pension. In reality, access to one or the other is scarce in a typical client country because the income level and coverage rate are closely related. Coverage for the typical low- to middle-income country ranges from a single-digit percentage of the labor force and elderly population to almost 50 percent, with an average of about 20 percent. Exceptions are the former transition economies in Eastern Europe and Central Asia, where coverage is still very high among the elderly (and partially among the workforce), and a few countries in Southern Africa (Botswana, Mauritius, Namibia, South Africa) and some Latin American countries (Brazil, Costa Rica) that have basic pension provisions. Traditional wisdom is that coverage under an earnings-related scheme is simply a question of per capita income level, with almost full coverage in rich OECD countries a benchmark that will be reached over time. This wisdom, however, is increasingly challenged, as coverage in OECD countries is decreasing and coverage in developing countries has not increased as envisaged (Gill, Packard, and Yermo 2004; Holzmann 2003; Holzmann, Packard, and Cuesta 2001). This creates special challenges for the priorities and design of pillars, the level of benefits, and the role of redistribution. In addition, the design of disability and survivor pensions needs to be reviewed—in its own right and as part of the design of a multipillar pension scheme.

Role of Pillars

The role of pillars is largely dependent on the country context and stage of development. While in more developed countries all pillars may be assigned a function in pursuit of the primary and secondary goals of a pension system, the inherited system typically creates a constraint on the choices. In contrast, less-developed countries are often essentially unconstrained by an inherited pension system. However, lacking both financial markets as well as the capacity to implement and administer new systems limits the choices among the various pillars for these countries.

In countries where coverage and administrative capacity are high, the zero or basic pillar can serve as a safety net and should be means tested. Even in countries with high coverage, some individuals, particularly those working primarily in the informal sector, do not have sufficient years of service or did not participate in the labor force and therefore are at risk of becoming poor in old age. The contributory system can be covered under pillar one (a public pay-as-you-go, or partially funded, defined-benefit system—perhaps revamped as a notional defined contribution), pillar two (a market-based and fully funded defined-contribution system), or a combination of pillar one and pillar two. These pillars may be complemented by a (usually tax) subsidized voluntary system organized at either the occupational or the personal level (pillar three).

In countries where coverage is low, the zero pillar ideally is the dominant tool to protect against old-age risk, offered either to all individuals above a certain age or to a large percentage of individuals rationed by a means test or other mechanism. There could be a pillar one, a pillar two, or a combination of the two. But in many low-income countries, neither the public nor the private sector can deliver coverage, which creates a dilemma. Under such circumstances, pillar three (voluntary pensions) should be envisaged and promoted, with the basic pillar only covering the most basic needs of the most vulnerable. Voluntary savings instruments are of particular importance for covering the retirement needs of the large informal sector in low-income countries and for addressing the high incentives for micro-entrepreneurs and workers to avoid formal earnings-related schemes. There are usually pressures from civil servants or other special groups to offer special pension plans, which then are extended to other groups, as well as pressures to comply with international labor standards (see ILO 2002b). As a result, despite the low coverage and difficulty of administering such systems in the lowest-income countries, the tendency is to embrace a mandatory pillar one or pillar two for at least some segments of the population, with nothing for the remainder.

Design Issues for a Basic Pillar

The first step in structuring the basic pillar is to consider the pros and cons of the available design options.[18] Four options are worth considering: (a) expanding the contributory system, (b) integrating programs to address elderly poverty with the general social safety net (that is, general poverty-targeted social assistance for households regardless of age), (c) a universal basic pension, and (d) a means-tested basic pension.

EXPANSION OF THE CONTRIBUTORY SYSTEM

The main problem with a contributory system is that it cannot cover everyone, especially the lifetime poor, those with incomplete employment history, and workers in the informal sector who may stay outside the formal sector. Even if it were possible to cover all of the categories of vulnerable individuals, an enormous data collection and record-keeping effort would be required, which is nearly impossible, especially in rural areas where information constraints preclude such programs in nearly every country. Similarly, simply mandating increased coverage will not be effective in most settings because of the practical problems of identifying the relevant population and establishing cost-effective enforcement.

INTEGRATION WITH THE GENERAL SOCIAL SAFETY NET

In principle, integration with the general social safety net—poverty-targeted social assistance for all households, including households with elderly—is possible, but it does not empower the elderly or provide them with some choices to look after themselves. It also may create adverse incentive effects on the labor market if it targets households where both the able-bodied and the elderly are living together. The potential stigma associated with enrollment of the elderly in these types of programs is also a significant impediment. Given these considerations, most countries do not adopt the social assistance route to protect the elderly.

UNIVERSAL (NONCONTRIBUTORY) BASIC PENSIONS

A number of countries, both developed and developing, are implementing a noncontributory pension program. Table A.2 provides a list of countries and the basic features of the universal pension program. This is probably the best way to provide poverty relief to the elderly. Considering the difficulty of identifying who among the elderly is poor, the principal merit of the program is that its universality avoids the targeting issue.

However, its principal merit is also the principal problem: fiscal afford-ability, especially in low-income countries. Consequently, many countries where a universal pension program is currently in operation are consider-ing ways to target the program or reduce the benefit levels (by letting inflation erode the real value of benefits).

Fiscal affordability of universal pensions leads one to consider several central questions prior to considering this policy option, especially in low-income countries, where the value of a marginal dollar of public money may have valuable alternative uses aimed at national poverty reduction (as opposed to poverty reduction solely among the elderly). Addressing these questions requires evaluation of the poverty status and living condi-tions of the elderly, their vulnerability compared to other groups (such as children), the impact of targeting the poor elderly on the national poverty rate, as well as the alternative use of resources for poverty reduction (such as investment in physical and human capital).

Initial empirical investigations in this direction are currently being undertaken by the World Bank for 15 African countries (Kakwani and Subbarao 2005) and select countries in other parts of the world (such as Nepal). While the preliminary results do not undermine the request to investigate the contribution of social pensions to social and economic development in a country context, neither do they support this policy option in all developing countries. The study points, in particular, to the heterogeneity among African countries with respect to the proportion of the population that is elderly and their living conditions and arrange-ments. Most elderly live in extended families, and in some countries, the elderly living with children (usually grandchildren) appear to be the most vulnerable. The budgetary resources required to fill the poverty gap among the single elderly and the elderly living with children are not high, but a much larger envelope is needed to move from the single elderly to all elderly-headed households (table A.3).

Targeting a social pension program only to the poor among the elderly is undoubtedly a less costly option and has greater impact on group and national poverty rates. But such a benefit assessment abstracts from the (administrative) costs of targeting. Providing a fixed benefit level (0.70 percent of the poverty threshold) to all of the elderly is a very expensive option, even when the benefit is limited to the poor among the elderly (table A.4). In the case of an eligibility age of 60, it ranges from 1 percent to more than 3 percent of GDP if given to all elderly and is more than half of this level if provided only to the poor elderly. In many low-income coun-tries, 2 percent of GDP represents 15 percent of tax resources: about 5 to 10 times the amount of total social assistance resources for all other vulnera-ble groups and more than half of the amount typically spent on education. Furthermore, even if these benefits could be financed, we still know very little about how to disburse small amounts of money to people in thinly populated rural areas, where the age of many potential recipients is difficult to establish.

Nevertheless, the rationale for investigating the vulnerability of the elderly in general, and in developing countries in particular, remains strong. Careful consideration needs to be given to three design parameters: (a) the level of the benefit, (b) the age of eligibility, and (c) other eligibility requirements. In this context, Nepal's experience is of particular interest. Nepal kept the level of the benefit low (under $2 per month per person) and set the age cutoff point at 75, maintaining the universality feature. The result has been excellent coverage (87 percent of all eligible participants are covered by the program, with minimal errors of exclusion) at a low budgetary cost so that the country not only can afford the pension but also can sustain the fiscal cost of the program over time. India is also implementing old-age pensions with age cutoffs and benefit levels that differ across states, costing no more than 0.1 percent of GDP.

It is not surprising that many countries where universal pension programs are currently in place are attempting either to target the program or to allow the benefit level to erode over time, largely driven by fiscal considerations. If the features of program design are well constructed from the outset, this policy option still merits serious consideration in many countries. However, any decision regarding the best instruments and the tradeoffs between a universal pension and reduced programs for other groups (such as children and widows) needs to be placed in the context of the specific country.

MEANS-TESTED BASIC PENSION

A basic pension for the elderly is provided based on a means test (which may take the form of an affluence test), persons living in particular geographic locations, or other categories determined to indicate vulnerability (such as families with AIDS patients). The main impediment to implementing this type of program is the cost of service delivery, especially in countries where means testing involves significant administrative costs. Countries differ a great deal with respect to their ability to administer a means test, and implementation modalities need to recognize that the degree of decentralization has a major influence on costs and effectiveness. For example, in Thailand village social workers are able to identify the elderly poor relatively easily and cost-effectively. This may not be the case in other countries. Yet cross-country evidence suggests that targeting in developing countries does work (Coady, Grosh, and Hoddinott 2004).

SUMMARY AND IMPLICATIONS FOR POLICY

For most developing countries, an optimal strategy would be to begin with a basic pension at an advanced age, keeping the level of benefit small. This would ensure self-selection with a low budgetary cost. It is important to consider explicitly the size of the benefit and intended coverage in low-income countries because of competing fiscal needs: widows and women with many children may be worse off than the elderly. In a fiscally strapped economy, more for the elderly means less for other programs (such as health and education). Also, a risk and vulnerability assessment is needed to determine whether the elderly as a group faces risks significantly more onerous than other groups. Based on such an assessment, benefit levels could be revised upward or downward. Regardless of the current level of benefits, the fiscal cost is bound to increase as the number of elderly increases, which, given the current demographic patterns, will occur in virtually all settings. When that happens, other policy options to consider are keeping the benefit level constant at a low level so that it continues to be unattractive to the nonpoor, raising the age of initial eligibility for benefits as life expectancies improve, and gradually introducing means testing as the information base becomes more robust and reliable.

Design Issues for a Contributory System, Pillars One and Two

The actual shape of a country's contributory system is strongly influenced by historical precedent and the country's preferences. However, several principles should be applied regardless of the distribution of pillars. Contributory systems should be self-financing and fiscally sustainable. The labor market implications of the level of overall contribution rates and the benefits provided need to be considered, recognizing that high contribution rates often lead to evasion and a decline in revenue and that generous benefits simply encourage skilled labor to withdraw from the covered labor force. Moreover, it is important to avoid fragmenting the labor market by offering different pension systems to different occupational groups. Finally, to minimize welfare costs, relatively modest replacement rates under a mandatory system are preferred over higher replacement rates. Any obligatory system entails welfare costs for many. Pension systems are obligatory to counteract myopia during one's working years, which might lead to old-age poverty, and to prevent the elderly poor from becoming a burden on the state. A fairly modest pension is required to fulfill these objectives.

High-coverage countries might want to include some income redistribution within the contributory pension system. This can be done through a progressive benefit formula in defined-benefit systems or explicit transfers to match contributions for low-income workers in nonfinancial as well as funded defined-contribution systems. While the financing of this redistribution in an unfunded scheme can, and perhaps should, be done fully internally, for funded defined-contribution schemes, this would require explicit government transfers. Special periods of noncontribution (sickness, maternity, military service, and unemployment during which benefits are received, but not education) should be financed explicitly out of the corresponding social insurance funds in a highly transparent and individualized manner (not as unspecified transfers). Another approach would be to redistribute earnings with pillar one and to replace income with pillar two. A third approach would be to recognize the risks involved with both pillar one and pillar two. To diversify risks, pillar one could be used for both redistribution and income replacement, while pillar two could add further income replacement.

In low-coverage countries, the situation is different. The need for redistribution within the contributory system—at least in the short run—is less compelling because redistribution only occurs within the covered population. As a result, the country could adopt pillar one, pillar two, or a combination of the two. It is absolutely imperative, regardless of the shape of the contributory system, that the system be self-financing. Since pillar two is more efficient at income replacement and is self-financed more easily, pillar two may be preferable. However, financial sector conditions, historical precedents, and the country's own preferences would determine the choice of pillars.

Design Choices for Pillars One to Three

Pillar one could be designed in a variety of ways. It could be a flat benefit (or a means-tested flat benefit with regard to a minimum pension), a proportional or progressive earnings-related defined benefit, or a defined benefit in the form of a nonfinancial defined-contribution system. A tight link between contributions and benefits helps to combat evasion and makes the system fairer, but this has to be balanced against the objective of redistribution, the provision of insurance, and the way it is provided. The benefits should also be based on lifetime average earnings rather than final earnings. This would make the system fairer and less open to gaming, in which individuals declare too few earnings during their working years and then declare huge wage increases right before retirement in order to maximize their pension. The benefits should also be explicitly indexed for inflation after retirement to avoid having the oldest and most vulnerable fall into poverty.

Pillar two would be defined contribution regarding the manner in which benefit levels accrue, and the management and investment of the accumulated assets should be market based. Second pillars should, however, on reaching the benefit payout phase, provide a means for participants to convert account balances to a lifetime annuity. Consequently, they cannot be perceived as purely defined contribution in nature. The international experience with centralized public management has been dismal, and the encouraging recent experience in some OECD countries is still too untested and may not be transferable to a typical low-income client country. Introducing competition among private providers by auctioning the fund management or using multiple fund managers is, in principle, encouraged. Key design issues include the means of keeping administrative costs reasonable, the scope of choice (as there are strong indications of a tradeoff between choice and costs), the structure of private providers and the savings instruments offered, and the design, implementation, and regulation of payouts. The basis for these often-difficult choices is discussed below.

If the role of pillars one and two is to provide modest pensions, the role of *pillar three* is to enable and encourage individuals and businesses to save for more generous benefits or earlier retirement, if desired. Since long-term savings generate positive externalities for the economy as a whole, tax advantages usually are provided to encourage pillar-three savings. However, discretionary savings are more likely for high-income individuals than for low-income individuals. Tax advantages also are less likely to induce the poor to save, since poor individuals often pay few taxes to begin with. The high-income individuals who take advantage of these programs often have savings, which they move from one investment vehicle to another to take advantage of tax preferences, reducing the potential gain to the economy. Since scarce tax revenue is being given up, the redistributive impact of tax preferences is usually regressive. Targeted subsidies are, in theory, preferable but impose major administrative challenges that may make tax preferences the only practical alternative. Finally, pillar three cannot be a full substitute for pillars zero, one, and two, since one of the primary reasons for public involvement in pension provision is to counter myopia and prevent old-age poverty.

Disability Benefits

How best to provide disability benefits is an open question in both traditional single-pillar schemes as well as newly established multipillar schemes. Traditional disability programs tend to be more open to abuse than the basic old-age pensions and are often used by countries as a substitute for unemployment benefits (Andrews 1999). This has led to proposals to delink the design and financing of disability from (earnings-related) old-age benefits and to establish them as distinct benefits. Conceptually, the separation can be seen as a reaction to rising life expectancy and the increasing distinctions between the two. At the start of the Bismarckian-type pension scheme, disability benefits were much more important for individuals than old-age benefits, as only one in six workers could expect to reach the advanced retirement age of 70. Old-age pensions then could be conceptualized as generalized or categorical disability pensions—that is, as insurance for much the same risk. Nowadays an old-age pension is a life annuity paid with accumulated funds or acquired rights that insures against the uncertainty of death; conceptually it is totally delinked from a disability pension, which insures against income loss due to incapacity to work.

The countries that have adopted multipillar schemes have devised an array of solutions to disability pensions, including keeping them in the public system, outsourcing them to insurers, and adopting solutions in between, such as outsourcing with a public top-up. The systems to date have not existed for that long and have not been studied sufficiently to provide sound advice. The challenge in most countries is to design a program that shows compassion for those falling under unfortunate circumstances, which is what social insurance is intended to do, but is not subject to rampant abuse. Much more work and experience in this area are needed. A recent review of 10 Latin American countries that have undertaken pension reform suggests that an important degree of freedom exists for defining the structure of the disability subsystem under a multipillar system (Grushka and Demarco 2003). A review of OECD country approaches to disability benefits provides another (but not necessarily replicable) information set (OECD 2003).

The design, provision, and reform of disability benefits in the Bank's client countries will receive much more emphasis in the Bank's conceptual and operational work in the years to come. This reflects the increased recognition of the importance of this benefit for those in both formal and informal employment (and the neglect so far). Furthermore, in 2002 the Bank created a Disability and Development Unit, which looks at the broader development issues of disability and disability benefits and their importance for the poverty mission of the World Bank.

Survivor Pensions

Traditional survivor benefits are based on the concept of a working husband and a housekeeping wife taking care of children and a low incidence of divorce. In some cases the resulting benefits have been overly generous and redistributions have been perverse, placing a burden on the public purse to finance large benefits to women from high-income families. In other cases, they have been meager or have discouraged work because women have had to give up their own benefit in order to qualify for the widow's benefit. A redesign of spousal survivor benefits is needed as a result of increasing (formal) labor force participation of women in both developing and developed countries and also because of changing family structures due to rising divorces. In many developed countries, the divorce rate is more than 50 percent of the marriage rate, and many developing countries are catching up quickly. How this redesign is best implemented in client countries is still open for discussion.

The conceptual, administrative, and budgetary issues of designing and running survivor pensions in the face of changing family structures and the existence of own and derived pensions have reinforced the need to establish individual pension rights for women. These rights may be derived from their own claims and contributions, from the work history or contributions of the prior partner for the period of a joint household (for example, determined by splitting pension rights or accumulated amounts), and, perhaps, from transfers by the insurance pool or government budget. Nonfinancial and funded defined-contribution schemes enable the implementation of such an approach (Holzmann and Palmer 2005).

An alternative view states that survivor benefits will remain essential for the well-being of older women. It is less clear how they should be provided and what the relative public and private roles are. Two simple principles have been suggested for this approach: access to widow's benefits should not drive out the woman's own benefit and thereby discourage her own work, and women from low-income families should have first claim on public subsidies. Some countries with multipillar systems require the husband, when he retires, to purchase joint annuities or other joint pensions that cover his spouse. For example, in Chile and Mexico, husbands must finance a survivor benefit that is 60 percent of their own benefit; in Argentina the mandated level is 70 percent. When the husband dies, the widow gets the survivor benefit in addition to her own pension. The combination of the two brings her income to two-thirds of the prior combined household income (on average), which is just enough to maintain her prior standard of living without putting a burden on the public treasury. In effect, these joint pension requirements compensate for household economies and scale and formalize the informal family contract that led women to work and earn less in the first place (James, Cox-Edwards, and Wong 2003a, 2003b).

Civil Service Pensions

In most countries, pensions for civil servants were the first to be developed, and in about half of the countries they remain distinct from pensions for private sector workers, often without explicit contributions from employees or employers (government; see figure 6.1). The promised benefits, often still calculated on the last salary paid, are typically very high relative to the real value of lifetime earnings and often are considered compensation for the low remuneration during active life (this is not necessarily true for many developing countries, where civil servants often profit both from higher active wages and pensions and from more job security).

Such pension schemes have major implications. They virtually eliminate labor mobility between the public and private sector, especially at older ages, since the civil servant would lose a major share of his or her lifetime income. They limit the ability to raise the retirement age as a cost-saving tool, since the government still would have to pay wages, instead of pensions, often based on the seniority principle. And, in many cases, continued services for the government beyond a certain age may not be feasible (military) or useful (teachers). They also create major problems for reform since the lower active wages and higher pensions constitute a

Figure 6.1. Parallel and Integrated Civil Service Pensions, by Region

Number of countries

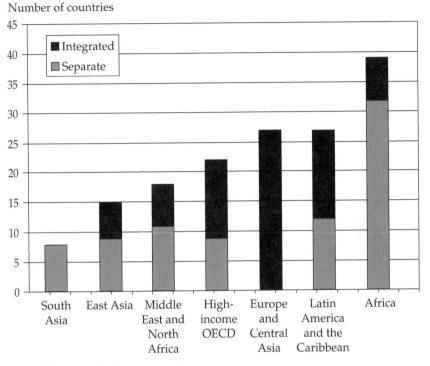

Source: Palacios and Whitehouse 2004.

loan by the civil servants to the government (implicit debt), which needs, in principle, to be repaid if the system is changed.

Nevertheless, various countries have started to reform their civil service pensions (Palacios and Whitehouse 2004). While the design of reform differs, these efforts have similar goals: to align the civil servants' scheme with that of the private sector to allow full mobility; to see such a reform as part of an overall review of civil servants' remuneration and as an alignment with private sector pay as the benchmark; and to fund supplementary pensions for civil servants, if provided, in a way similar to occupational pensions in the private sector. India, for example, has eliminated the defined-benefit scheme for all civil servants of the central government hired after January 1, 2004, and replaced it with a funded defined-contribution system in which 20 percent of pay is contributed, designed to be a rough approximation of the replacement value of its predecessor without the associated fiscal and labor mobility implications. Many civil service systems will require parametric reforms to reduce benefit accrual rates, change overly generous commutation formulas, or raise minimum retirement ages to make them fiscally sustainable and bring them in line with pensions provided to other formal sector workers. Another strategy, not yet implemented, is to move all sector schemes, including for civil servants, to nonfinancial defined contributions in which the accrued rights under the old scheme are immediately transformed into a notional amount. Over time this would lower the replacement rate for civil servants to sustainable levels, while creating a smooth transition between new entrants to the labor market and workers close to retirement (Holzmann 2005).

Financial Sustainability Issues

One of the main goals of pension reform is to achieve financial sustainability—the payment of current and future benefits according to an announced path of contribution rates—without unanticipated hikes in contribution rates, cuts in benefits, or deficits that need to be covered by budgetary resources. To be credible, a pension reform must make progress in this direction; this requires, above all, credible financial projections, a view of both short-term and long-term flows, and an assessment of both the stocks and flows involved. In the case of funded pillars, it also requires assessment of the rates of return achieved, including the role of foreign investment in diversification and management of returns.

Pension reforms are often driven by short-term financial disequilibria to which politicians react by making ad hoc adjustments (cutting benefits or hiking contribution rates) and by submitting reform proposals in an effort to put the scheme on a sustainable basis. However, unless it is fully costed and compared with a current scheme, such a reform should not be undertaken (and will not be supported by the Bank). Credible projections are based on detailed modeling of the pension system(s); the demographic, labor market, and economic structure; and conservative assumptions about key parameters such as future growth rates of wages, labor market participation, and investment returns. Countries can use their own models, commission projections from actuarial bodies, or use the Bank-developed PROST model to undertake these projections. The use of multiple models is helpful, because different models may project different outcomes, and these differences need to be explained.

To prevent ad hoc adjustments and reforms, the Bank encourages countries to undertake periodic assessments of the financial sustainability of the pension scheme (this is best done every year but should be done at least every three years). Such assessments should be conducted by independent bodies with an agreed set of assumptions about demographic and economic development, and the results should be published and discussed in open public forums.

To assess financial sustainability (in particular of unfunded schemes) requires taking a long-term view and considering flows as well as stocks. A short- and medium-term view of newly established, unfunded schemes provides no assessment of financial sustainability. After its creation, the scheme pays few or no benefits for many years, while levying contributions from an increasingly covered labor force. This resulting cash surplus is no indicator of financial sustainability, since the inflow and contributions create a liability that needs to be honored in the future as a pension payment, often 40 years away and then for a period of 20, 30, and more years. For this reason, flows (expenditure, revenue, and balance) need to be projected for 75 years or more.

In the same vein, an evaluation of flows should be enhanced by a calculation and assessment of the stock of commitments and assets (as suggested for other and future fiscal challenges as well; see Heller 2003). The first is done through the implicit pension debt, operationally best defined as the accrued-to-date liability (Holzmann, Palacios, and Zviniene 2004)—that is, the present value of accrued pension rights to retirees and contributors. The second is done through a mark-to-market evaluation of accumulated reserves, if any. A large and rising implicit pension debt needs to be covered by future contributions and, together with low and stagnant assets, provides an early warning of financial lack of sustainability.

The calculation of implicit debt is also important to assess the progress in pension reform. In a parametric reform of an unfunded scheme, the effects on the flows are felt only gradually through lower expenditure (for example, after a change from wage to price indexation). In an evaluation of stocks, the effects are capitalized immediately, and the fall in implicit pension debt from changes in benefit indexation can amount to 20 percent (and more) of the original value (Holzmann 1999).[19]

The evaluation of reform through stocks becomes even more important when moving away from unfunded and toward fully or partially funded schemes. In such a reform, the implicit pension debt is gradually reduced because part of the contribution is now paid to the funded scheme, which diminishes the liability of the unfunded scheme. But old commitments need to be honored (and pension benefits paid); therefore, some contributions are lost, and the deficit of the scheme grows. Unless covered by higher taxes or lower public expenditure on other items, the fiscal deficit and debt increase. Partial debt financing can be justified for reasons of tax and consumption smoothing. As a result, and in order to assess the overall progress of the reform, the total pension debt—the implicit debt plus the reform-related explicit debt (including capitalized interest rates)—needs to be calculated and evaluated annually. Knowledge about the scope and development of this total pension debt is important not only for tracking progress in reform but also for signaling the financial markets, which otherwise may react negatively to a temporary rise in explicit financial debt (and deficit).

In defined-benefit schemes (both partially and fully funded) as well as in funded, defined-contribution schemes (both centrally and privately managed), the rate of return on financial assets is critical for financial sustainability. In defined-benefit systems (such as a typical first-pillar scheme with reserves), a sustained higher real rate of return on assets requires a lower contribution rate or fewer transfers by sponsors or from government than otherwise and thus directly enhances financial sustainability. In the case of funded defined-contribution systems—which, by definition, are financially sustainable—issues of unsustainability through low or even negative real rates of return enter through contingent liabilities (Smetters 2002): a guaranteed minimum rate of return or a minimum pension, a substitution for social pensions, or simply a political obligation to pay if the amount is too low.

Management of Public Pension Funds

In various regions of the world, mandated pension systems with sizable publicly managed funds are the dominant retirement scheme, at least for a main subset of the covered population (see figure 6.2). These sizable funds and the defined-contribution nature of the systems reflect the legacy of the British Empire and its strong preference for provident funds for both the public and private sector. Many defined-benefit-type systems with substantial reserve funds are a legacy of the "phased-premium systems" promoted by the ILO after World War II, in which a large surplus of revenues over expenditures was intended to allow substantially lower future contribution rates if the invested funds delivered sufficiently positive rates of return (Cichon and others 2004).

Many of these partially or fully funded systems are in dire need of reform, and most of the pressures for reform are similar to those of unfunded schemes: the inability to deliver on social objectives, the need to harmonize public and private sector schemes, and financial (un)sustainability due to low and in many cases negative rates of return. Publicly managed pension funds have a poor record on rates of return (Iglesias and Palacios 2001). In most cases, the rates are negative in real terms (for a period of 20 and more years), but even if they are positive, they are seldom above wage growth and compare unfavorably with privately managed funds.

Main Reform Options

Given this consistent record of failing fund management in many countries, what are the alternatives for reform of such systems? There are essentially three: (a) abandoning the illusion of funding and moving to a pure unfunded—pay-as-you-go—system; (b) keeping the funding but reforming the system toward market-based and decentralized manage-

Figure 6.2. Distribution and Importance of Public Pension Funds, by Region

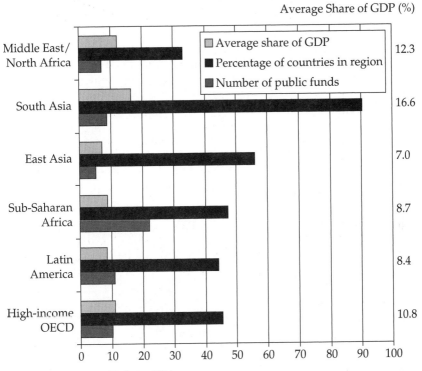

Average Share of GDP (%)

Region	Average Share of GDP (%)
Middle East/North Africa	12.3
South Asia	16.6
East Asia	7.0
Sub-Saharan Africa	8.7
Latin America	8.4
High-income OECD	10.8

Legend:
- Average share of GDP
- Percentage of countries in region
- Number of public funds

Source: Carmichael and Palacios 2004.

ment of pension funds (as in Chile or Switzerland); and (c) keeping the funding structure of the system as is, but improving the governance structure of the fund by applying best practice from private and public pension funds.

MOVING TOWARD AN UNFUNDED, PAY-AS-YOU-GO SYSTEM

Such an approach may be desirable if the country does not have the capacity to operate a public fund due to the lack of appropriate financial instruments or the incapacity to defend the fund against the political pressure for inappropriate use. Such situations clearly occurred in the aftermath of decolonization, when large provident funds were present. Provident funds were an ideal retirement-income system for expatriates in an empire with a dominant currency and the presence of currency boards in the colonies. During the accumulation stage, the provident fund had access to domestic as well as international assets with essentially no currency risk. At retirement, the individual would repatriate the funds, mostly to Great Britain, and purchase an annuity in what were then the most sophisticated annuity markets. With independence, these funds typically lost their access to international markets, potential investments in the new currency became very limited, and the capacity to withstand political pressure to use the funds for other purposes disappeared. Many were simply forced to buy government securities in captive markets. Various countries in Sub-Saharan Africa have experienced similar conditions, leading to the erosion of such public funds until the formal move to a pay-as-you-go system has become unavoidable. In others, such a move may need to be seriously considered.

MOVING TOWARD A MARKET-BASED AND DECENTRALIZED SYSTEM

Such an approach may be beneficial if the financial market conditions with regard to instruments as well as regulation and supervision are fulfilled, but serious doubt exists that the capacity to withstand political pressure for suboptimal use of funds can be expected soon. A main challenge for such a reform is the need to replace the predominant investment in government bonds with a more diversified portfolio and to address the fiscal consequences of such a change. When the fund holds a large share of outstanding government debt, such a change in portfolio requires shifting the fiscal stance and repaying the debt, as required by a move from an unfunded to a funded scheme. From the pension or provident fund's point of view, a move toward a more diversified portfolio may not increase the rate of return (even less the risk-adjusted rate of return). In some countries (such as India) the rates paid on government bonds issued to the provident funds are quite high for political reasons but are not sustainable in view of the government's high deficit and public debt.

In a partial approach to a more decentralized investment regime, a few countries have allowed individuals with accumulated assets above a minimum amount to invest the surplus in the private market (for example, Malaysia and Singapore). The attractiveness of this reform has diminished in these countries because it was implemented during the onset of the Asian financial crisis of the late 1990s. This has led private sector asset managers to claim that a level playing field has not been achieved.

IMPROVING THE GOVERNANCE STRUCTURE OF THE EXISTING PENSION FUND

Using centralized public funds has advantages if the problem of investment performance and the use of ownership rights in the "private" enterprises can be solved. The two main advantages are (a) the capacity to pool risks across individuals, as every participant receives the same rate of return, and (b) efficiencies attained from the centralized collection of contributions, administration of records, management of consumer information, disbursement of benefits, and management of investments. A more individualized risk-return approach could be envisaged if the fund offered a limited set of portfolios from which the individual could choose. Except for gains from the consolidation of investment management, all of these advantages may, however, also be achieved with a clearinghouse approach. To address the issue of ownership rights in private sector enterprises held by the centralized fund requires the use of proxy rights and other instruments to avoid a nationalization of enterprises. To address the issue of investment performance requires major changes in the governance structure of funds.

Central public funds appear to have become more feasible with recent developments in Canada, Ireland, New Zealand, and Norway (see Musalem and Palacios 2004; Palacios 2002), which have created some optimism among economists about the usefulness and feasibility of central funding (Orszag and Stiglitz 2001). National and international experience with the governance of private and public pension funds provides important lessons and suggests principles of good investment process design that may also be introduced in advanced client countries.[20]

Suggested Principles of Good Investment Process Design

As it became clear that governance matters for performance, countries as well as international organizations started to develop guidelines for governance. For example, the Association of Canadian Pension Management, the Office of the Superintendent for Financial Institutions, and the Pension Investment Association of Canada have all developed independent sets of governance guidelines. As these guidelines contain many common principles, these organizations have formed a Joint Task Force on Pension Plan Governance in order to develop a common set of governance principles as well as a guide for plan administrators to conduct an assessment of their governance practices.

Very recently the International Social Security Administration also began to develop guidelines for public pension fund management. The ISSA fund management guidelines focus on governance structure, governance prerequisites, and the investment function (ISSA 2004). They clearly highlight the problem of the politicization of public fund management and the need to improve investment performance while managing risk. ISSA (2004) contains very similar prescriptions to what is detailed below. Despite appearing less stringent than desirable on the exclusion of social mandates, they clearly indicate that "where investment in a particular venture of economic and social utility is considered desirable by the government and/or by the governing body of the social security scheme but the returns likely to be achieved are below market norms, the investment should be structured so that the subsidy is made from other government resources, in order to avoid compromising the fiduciary responsibilities of the social security scheme" (ISSA 2004, 7).

These and other guidelines provide the central contours of principles for good investment processes. These contours are strengthened by international experience and the research and field experience of Bank staff with financial sector and pension fund reforms. While there is clearly a need to develop further understanding of how governance mechanisms that work in more advanced countries can be translated and implemented in the reality of our client countries, we believe that the following general principles should apply to the design of the investment process of public pension plans.[21]

The public pension plan should be free from inappropriate interference from the government in pursuing its objectives and meeting its responsibilities. Ideally, the government should remain at arm's-length from the investment decisions of the fund manager. To this end, countries have introduced different approaches. New Zealand has chosen the disclosure route. The legislation sets restrictions on when, and at what rate, the government can draw on the Fund—and the use needs to be published. Ireland directly restricts one possible avenue toward misuse of the public pension fund for the government's own purposes by explicitly prohibiting investment by the fund in Irish government securities. Canada has established the CPP Investment Board as a separate crown corporation for the management of CPP assets. Japan has established a separate Government Pension Investment Fund to manage public pension funds.

Public pension plans should have to clearly disclose their overall commercial mandates. Multiple (and unclear) mandates induce a strong bias in the control structure of the plan, compound the problem associated with the multiple-constituency structure of plan stakeholders, and should be avoided. Ideally, public pension plans should have a unique and unequivocal commercial mandate.

The optimal control structure of a public pension plan should be linked to the structure of residual claimants. The control structure of public plans should be aligned with the structure of residual claimants of the plan. As residual claimants of public pension plans, active members and, more generally, taxpayers should be granted more control in the deliberations of governing bodies. This can only be achieved if clear commercial mandates are provided for in the law or in the plan documents.

Since granting direct control to taxpayers is problematic in practice, several mechanisms (mostly behavioral) should be established to correct the de facto bias in favor of passive members, such as the government.

The number of independent, professional governors should be maximized. Even if active members are granted more responsibility in public pension plans, this does not ensure that effective monitoring of management takes place. Active members are a dispersed group of stakeholders, and a governance structure that reduces the collective action problem of public plan stakeholders is still necessary. Furthermore, since many governance mechanisms traditionally used by corporations are not available for public pension plans, a strong governing body is required to monitor the performance of management. The role of independent directors appears to be more necessary in pension plans than in corporations.

The regulatory framework of the plan should detail unequivocally the conditions, such as the use of fit-and-proper and professional qualification tests, under which governors can be appointed and removed. For example, in Canada, the appointment process involves a nominating committee that recommends qualified candidates to the federal and provincial governments. The appointment process is subjected to close public scrutiny, and candidates, in addition to having suitable qualifications, are required to meet demanding skill and character requirements.

Governors should be subject to fiduciary duties, and failure to comply with those duties should result in legal liability. In the United States, private pension plans are subject to the strict fiduciary requirements of the Employee Retirement Income Security Act (ERISA) statute. ERISA's "exclusive purpose" (duty of loyalty), "prudent person" (duty of care, diligence, and skill), and diversification rules require the responsible individuals to have the relevant expertise and to exercise due diligence while making decisions in administering the plan, including the choice of investments. They also require that all decisions be made solely for the purpose of increasing the economic value of the assets of the plans and providing benefits to plan participants. Although these particular standards apply to private employer-sponsored arrangements, they represent a useful framework that should be applied to public plans as well.

All staff, but critically senior management and governors, should abide by a publicly disclosed code of conduct and conflict-of-interest rules. Another tool to control the behavior of governing bodies is a code of ethics (or conduct). For governors, the code covers such issues as conflicts of interest and the acceptance of gratuities. Through such provisions, the code should guide governors toward decisions based on prudence rather than personal gain, and this, in turn, should lead to better overall performance of the pension fund. Similar to the prudent-person standard, a code of ethics should help to control agency problems.

The governing body should establish a governance committee. A governance committee would recommend governance policy, guidelines, and procedures, make recommendations on the board's effectiveness, monitor the application of the code of conduct and the conflict-of-interest guidelines, and conduct periodic governance assessments.

There should be full and open disclosure about the governance structure of the scheme and the managing agency, including rules for selecting members of the governing body and managers. Accountability requires that details about the governance structure be made public. In particular, there should be adequate disclosure of the arrangements put in place to detect and prevent fraud. As part of its disclosure of governance arrangements, the managing agency should be required to publish its formal delegations of powers and responsibilities. Once the agency has formalized its structure of delegations, it should make these available to all stakeholders (for example, through its Web site).

The governing body should establish an internal audit committee. An internal audit committee should be formed with the responsibility for overseeing financial reporting, the external and internal audit, information systems, and internal control policies and practices.

Internal and external financial, accounting, actuarial, and governance audits, as well as their public disclosure, are essential to increase transparency in the operations of the fund and, therefore, improve accountability. The likelihood of mismanagement or undue influence can be drastically reduced if the public is regularly informed about issues such as the governance structure, the financial situation, and the performance of the governance framework as well as the financial performance of the fund. Internal audits should be supported by external audits carried out by independent auditors.

The governing body should establish an investment committee. The role of the investment committee should be to establish the investment policy of the plan. Sound statements of investment policies should be produced, and at the same time there should be a transparent process for disclosing to the public how the investment policy is implemented and adhered to. The investment policy document should clearly express the desired asset mix needed to match assets and liabilities. It could also describe the role and composition of the investment committee, if this is not defined in the governance manual; how investments are recorded; both short- and long-term performance measures; the universe of vehicles that can be used to meet these measures; risk tolerance guidelines either in terms of quantitative limits or outcome of asset-liability models; and, finally, the reporting, compliance structure, and performance reviews. The investment policy should also establish due diligence criteria for investment transactions, valuation of the underlying assets, accounting treatment of the assets, and procedures to be used for approving investments by the investment committee and should require that each investment be recorded with double signatures by an officer of the plan and the chairman of the committee authorizing it. Above all, measures of long-term target performance should be consistent with the long-term target funding ratio of the plan.

The policy statement should outline the fund's approach to corporate governance as a shareholder and potentially dominant force in the domestic market. A final aspect of investment policy that should be addressed by the governing board is its attitude to exercising its voting rights as a shareholder. Since the fund could potentially be a major shareholder, it has a responsibility to exercise its governance rights wisely. The exercise of voice is important, but to avoid a situation in which the government de facto directs private business, it is usually better to delegate this power to the fund managers. One way of minimizing the conflicts of interest that may arise from such situations is for the fund to publish, with a time lag, a summary of the way in which it voted in its various shareholder capacities. In response to the fear that government-controlled investing would mean partial nationalization of major businesses, which, in turn, would allow politicians direct involvement in the economy, some countries have imposed concentration limits or have delegated voting rights to fund managers. Other countries, such as Sweden, have put a cap on the effective voting power of the fund. In all cases, a policy for stakeholder voice should be explicit, documented, and publicly disclosed.

Periodic reporting to active-member representative bodies should be required. Full disclosure of performance in both absolute and relative terms is fundamental to protecting the interests of plan members. Both Canada and Ireland use publicly disclosed benchmarks for performance comparisons. In Canada, the benchmark is private sector fund performance, while Ireland uses a predetermined set of benchmark indexes. In addition, the Canadian fund managers are required to hold public meetings at least every two years in each province to discuss performance. It is worth noting that since instituting public reporting of this type, the Canadian administrative costs have fallen more than 60 percent. If practical reasons preclude taxpayers' representation on the board, clear disclosure procedures (like periodic reporting to Parliament and other representative associations) should be in place to inform taxpayers' representatives about the performance of plans.

Funding shortfalls should be identified and disclosed, along with the government's proposed remedial actions. The process for assessing and dealing with a funding shortfall should be transparent and preferably contained in law. Where the government has an explicit policy of partial funding, the extent of the underfunding with respect to clearly disclosed minimum funding ratios should be assessed and reported in the government's accounts.

To the greatest extent possible, rewards for performance should be linked to delegated responsibilities and should be risk based. Those who make delegated decisions should be rewarded or sanctioned according to the way in which they exercise their delegations. Managers should be required to review periodically the exercise of delegations they have made. Compliance should be rewarded, and breaches of guidelines, regarding either governance or investment, should be penalized, even where the returns are higher than expected.

The government should require that the management agency be regulated and supervised by an authority with sufficient powers and independence to conduct effective oversight. In most cases, this can be accomplished by the same agency that is responsible for regulating private pension funds, and, where feasible, it should meet the same standards imposed on private funds. Canada has not placed its public fund under the jurisdiction of any of its private sector financial regulators, but it has imposed a similar set of standards for governance and investments as those required of the private sector. In contrast, regulatory reforms proposed in Indonesia would see the Indonesian public pension fund come under the same regulator as private pension funds. This is already the case in Costa Rica, Fiji, Honduras, Kenya, Morocco, Namibia, and, to a certain extent, all the countries belonging to the Conférence International de Prévoyance Sociale region in West Africa. Direct supervision of public pension fund management could be enhanced by the establishment of an independent ombudsman with adequate resources to investigate allegations of fraud, waste, and abuse.

Administrative and Implementation Issues

Many administrative and implementation issues are linked with pension reform and the introduction of a multipillar scheme. Some issues are well understood (for example, tax treatment of mandatory schemes), and some recent innovations create optimism (for example, clearinghouses for the collection of contributions and fund management, record keeping, and benefit disbursement in decentralized schemes). Other issues are still awaiting good or best practices (for example, the provision of annuities through the private sector). Although administrative and implementation issues have typically been underestimated and undervalued in the discussion of pension reform, this section highlights the main areas and main topics therein. Even a slightly more comprehensive treatment is well beyond the objective of this report and the space available.

Administrative Preparedness and Institution Building

The key issues in administrative preparedness of the new pension system, especially a defined-contribution one, are the introduction of personal accounts, the unified collection of social contributions, and the issuance of social cards. The introduction of personified reporting is key for tracking individual contributions. It is also difficult, as all employers must submit personified reports, indicating gross wages and pension contributions for each employee. Those individual reports then have to be entered electronically or manually, and data have to be transferred to the central level. The unified collection of social contributions requires a central database that supports the future unification of data collection for pensions and other social contributions, preferably on a frequent schedule (quarterly or even monthly). The purpose of social cards is to ensure direct access to individual records in a way that allows identification of the social status of an individual and prevents abuse of the system. Changes in all three areas take time and effort.

Our experience shows that most difficulties arise in the process of deciding how to integrate the flow of money and the flow of data at the national level. From the point of view of social security institutions, the flow of money could remain decentralized, while the flow of data could be partially or fully centralized. Leaving both flows decentralized would seriously undermine the effort to improve compliance and the efficient collection of pension contributions—and, ultimately, the collection of all social contributions. Centralizing the flow of both data and money at the national level (for example, in a form of clearinghouse) would improve control over the system but could entail new transaction costs in the money-handling process, but the economies of scale should prevail.

One of the most important findings of reforms so far is that ample time is needed for implementation. The reforms in Latvia and Mexico were postponed to allow time for administrative systems to be developed. The Polish reform ran into problems because inadequate time was allotted to implementation. In particular, the obligation to send monthly individual information to the social security institution and to submit new reports should not be introduced without a sufficient waiting period and time for preparation. If not enough time is allowed to test the new procedures, the quality of data in the social insurance system will be poor.

Monthly reporting reduces the time it takes money to get to the individual accounts, compared with annual reporting, but it generates a large and continuing flow of data, making it extremely difficult to check the accuracy of data closely. It may often be appropriate to consider intermediate options, such as quarterly or biannual reporting. This not only would decrease the amount of time that money is held in a central holding fund (earning a government bond rate) but also would minimize the burdens on both employers and administrators that result from monthly reporting.

The quality of the data depends on how information is sent to the social security institution. Usually, there are three ways to communicate information: (a) manually filed forms, (b) printouts from special software, and (c) electronic data transfer. Papers filed manually have the most errors, while data transferred electronically have the fewest. Setting up a system of electronic transfer is a big investment and takes time to design and test. It is usually better to wait until electronic transfer is possible than to initiate a system of manually filed forms, as the change later on may be difficult and time-consuming.

One important decision is the choice of an identification number for contributors. Administrative aspects of any reform should start with a careful assessment of the quality of current systems of account numbering and information transfer. Above all, a clear national strategy is needed concerning the enumeration of workers and their dependents (effectively all citizens) as well as employers. As part of this strategy, governments at the highest level will have to understand the purposes and ownership of the numbering system or systems (and linkages). It is important to pick the best existing number, if a good one already exists, rather than to create a special social security number. In the United States, the social security number serves many purposes, largely because it was the first number ready to use in the 1930s.

Public-Private Partnerships in Contribution Collections: A Clearinghouse Approach

The recommended centralization of the flow of data calls for the creation of a clearinghouse to consolidate some aspects of second-pillar operations with operation of the state's first-pillar agency or tax authority. The word "clearinghouse" has come to encompass a variety of options on a spectrum that includes using a state agency to collect second-pillar contributions and allocate them among second-pillar funds, being an alternative record keeper, and being an exclusive record keeper and information agent for fund participants. The arguments for consolidation include the following:

- *Economies of scale.* Economies of scale would be gained as a result of the operation of a single transfer agent (Demarco and Rofman 1999). This can happen at the level of first pillar (such as in Poland) or second pillar (in Mexico).
- *Smaller burden on employers.* Employers would only have to deal with one collection entity.
- *Information barriers between employers and pension funds.* Because contributions are funneled through the first-pillar agency (as in Costa Rica, Poland, and Uruguay) or the tax authority (as in Argentina), employers would typically not know to which funds their workers are subscribing. This would minimize the fund's ability to use employers as a means to pressure workers to sign up with a particular fund.
- *Greater investment flexibility for second-pillar participants.* Under a centralized registry participants would have the ability to divide their fund accumulations among qualified funds without administrative difficulty.
- *Information barrier between fund managers and fund participants.* Reducing the information barrier would reduce marketing cost and pressure. With a centralized registry, fund managers would not have to know the identity of their individual clients, as they would deal with the aggregate amount of assets lodged with the fund by the collector or registry (blind accounts). The fund would report to this entity the performance of the account and would prepare statements and other reports for participants, indicating the amount of units purchased and owned and the value of each unit.

Figure 6.3. Combined Collection and Clearinghouse

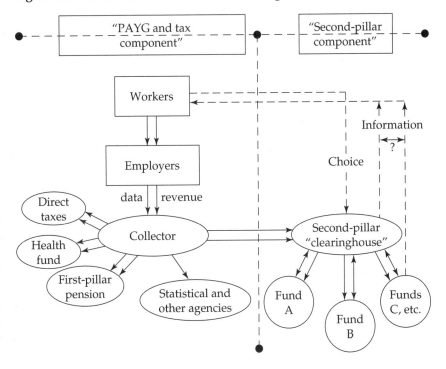

In theory, this second "information barrier" between funds and their clients within a central registry system would greatly reduce the emphasis on direct marketing to increase market share. These direct marketing costs have led to very high costs of acquisition, with a resultant decline in the value of funds accumulated on behalf of clients. This kind of information clearinghouse is part of the Latvian and Swedish second pillars now being implemented. Any information clearinghouse would have to be included in a country's original second-pillar design if it were to be introduced successfully. Once an industry of commissioned agents develops, it becomes a powerful lobby group opposed to its own extinction.

Figure 6.3 illustrates a unified revenue and data collection system, combined with an integrated second-pillar clearinghouse. The much-debated issue of an information barrier between funds and clients is shown as an open question by having dual reporting lines back to workers and a question mark between those lines. A combined collection scheme can be created without a second-pillar clearinghouse (left-hand side of the diagram) in countries that do not have a second pillar. In addition, the function of social insurance collection may *not* be combined with

Figure 6.4. Decentralized Funded Pillar in Chile and Hungary

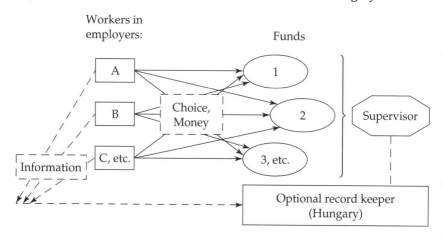

the national tax authority; instead, it may operate as a full or partial clearinghouse for the second-pillar funds. It is conceivable that a second-pillar clearinghouse could operate independently of an otherwise unified collection system or even as a third independent collector, but such institutional arrangements would consume more real resources, placing a greater burden on employers and requiring more state resources.

Some countries will pursue a decentralized model, with direct flows of information between participants and funds (see figure 6.4). Such a model (Chile, Hungary) is quicker to implement, but it imposes a greater transaction burden on employers. Instead of having to deal with one or two potential collectors (tax and social insurance agencies), employers each must sort out second-pillar contributions among a larger number of second-pillar companies. Accordingly, the higher transaction costs to employers probably lead to a higher level of noncompliance, especially regarding the intrayear transmittal of contributions and data. Along with these additional burdens come opportunities for employers to try to influence workers' choice of funds.

A related but separate issue concerns the coexistence of tax collection and social insurance collection units. While there are many good arguments for having only one collection unit in the long run (which is suggested to be the national tax authority), experience in some regions (in particular, the transition economies) indicates that the speed and preparedness to undertake such a merger need to be considered. For example, as social insurance contributions are earmarked revenues, compared with general taxes, the link between revenue and expenditure and the incentives to the involved institutions need to be taken into account. Meanwhile, the existing tax authority may not have enough intimate knowledge of enterprises or technical capacity to levy contributions in a sustained manner. The Bank is working with the Fiscal Affairs Department of the IMF to identify the conditions under which joint collection can take place.

Taxation of Pension Benefits

The tax treatment of pension schemes raises many issues (Dilnot and Johnson 1993; Whitehouse 1999), but three stand out: (1) What taxation concept should be applied: comprehensive income tax or consumption-type taxation? (2) If the latter, should the taxation be front loaded or back loaded? (3) What is the role of preferential tax treatment for voluntary retirement savings?

Most countries tax income under a comprehensive income tax regime. Under such an approach, income is taxed irrespective of the source. Hence, saving is undertaken out of taxed income, and interest income on these savings is taxed again. For mandated retirement income, however, most countries provide an exception. In unfunded systems, contributions typically are tax exempt, while benefits are fully taxed. The same approach is used for funded schemes, where the interest earned is mostly not taxed. For retirement income, a consumption-type tax is applied, which eliminates distortions on intertemporal consumption and savings decisions. We believe that this is the appropriate treatment of retirement income. However, the double taxation on savings should be avoided, as should the lack of taxation. In some countries, retirement savings remain totally untaxed, leading to distortions in the other direction and questionable distributive outcomes, since the higher-income groups profit disproportionately from this treatment.

An expenditure-tax regime maintains tax neutrality of consumption over time and treats savings as deferred consumption, therefore exempting it. Such a regime can, in principle, be achieved either by front loading or back loading taxation, while remaining neutral for the intertemporal budget constraint of government. Under the latter, contributions as well as interest earned remain untaxed, while benefits are taxed (hence an exempt-exempt-tax [EET] treatment). Under the former, contributions are taxed, while interest rates earned and benefits remain untaxed (hence a tax exempt-exempt [TEE] treatment). In a model-type setting (including constant marginal tax rate), both treatments are equivalent. In a real-world setting, differences do emerge. For political purposes, EET treatment may be preferred, since a TEE approach may not be credible (as further taxation can be introduced in the future). For budgetary reasons, however, TEE treatment may be preferred because the extended tax credit to individuals under the EET approach may not be feasibly financed. When the tax system is progressive, TEE is likely to provide more tax revenues, while EET is likely to provide more incentives for individuals to participate. Also, if one stands by the notion that public investments have a lower marginal product than private investments, then EET treatment has the advantage of freeing resources earlier to be invested by the private sector and resulting in a more favorable composition of investments. Hence, in a dynamic sense, EET treatment may provide, at least in theory and ceteris paribus, higher overall tax revenues than TEE treatment. We believe that either EET or TEE treatment is acceptable. The option a country chooses will depend on its politics and the outlook of its fiscal accounts. Any difference in the economic impacts of either option would be of a second order of magnitude.

While there is strong consensus about the tax treatment of mandated schemes (unfunded or funded) in the pension community, there is no consensus about the tax treatment of voluntary schemes—of individual retirement account or employer-sponsored savings arrangements such as 401(k)-type plans in the United States. For some economists inside and outside the Bank, preferential tax treatment (that is, consumption-type taxation) should also be applied—within limits—to voluntary schemes in order to encourage the take-up of these schemes and to allow governments to play a more active role in regulation and supervision. For other economists, such tax treatment does little to increase overall individual saving, and an increase in take-up reflects largely a substitution for other forms of saving. Even worse, the income effect of the preferential tax treatment may even reduce individual and government saving. And recent estimates for OECD countries suggest that the fiscal costs of tax-favored schemes may be sizable, while the effects on saving are still unclear (Antolin, de Serres, and de la Maisonneuve 2004; Yoo and de Serres 2004). Although we do not exclude the reduction in savings, we consider some preferential tax treatment of standardized retirement-income products as useful. Even though it may not increase savings and may not deepen financial markets, it changes the composition of financial intermediation favoring long-term funds. This, in turn, reduces the refinancing risks of governments, banks, and enterprises and reduces the leverage of enterprises, making them more resilient to shocks.

Fee Structure and Levels

The amount of fees or charges levied on financial retirement products is an area of considerable debate and research. For critics of a funded pillar, these fees are much too high, in particular compared with the (best) unfunded and public benchmark; they reduce the net rate of return to sometimes unacceptably low levels and thus eliminate the potential return advantage of a funded pillar; and the structure of fees is often nontransparent and antipoor, which prevents a broader pension coverage of lower-income groups. Also, supporters of a funded pillar (including the Bank) recognize the need to bring fee levels down and to rework fee structures.

But they see the problem as much more manageable, with fee levels in client countries much more in line with those of popular financial services in developed countries and falling after start-up costs have been covered. Still various areas require closer investigation in and across countries and regions (first stock-taking exercises include those by James, Smalhout, and Vittas 2001; OECD 2001a; Whitehouse 2000; World Bank 2003a; Yermo 2002). This subsection concentrates on three issues dealing with the measurement of fee levels and the approaches for their reduction or limitation.

MEASURING AND COMPARING FEE LEVELS

Across countries, charges or fees (administrative charges and management fees) on long-term financial products, such as pensions, are levied in many different ways. Some are one-off fees, usually a fixed sum payable either up-front or at maturity. Others are ongoing and can take the form of a fixed fee per period, a percentage of contributions or premiums, or a percentage of assets. One main problem with international comparisons is that products offer different services and pension systems have different structures. For example, some plans have guaranteed minimum returns or guaranteed minimum pensions, while others do not. Obviously, everything else being equal, guaranteed products should have higher fees. Also, some plans provide better services, such as higher rates of return and immediate benefits to plan members, and could justify being more expensive. Finally, funded pillars that rely on the public pillar to collect contributions (for example, Argentina) should have lower administrative costs than those that are independent of government.

A national and international comparison of fee levels requires a comprehensive and life-cycle-type approach in which all types of charges for, say, a full working life are considered and, for example, the gross amount and the net accumulated amount are compared at retirement (Whitehouse 2000). Time-specific comparison of fees on flows (contributions) and stocks (assets) alone are of little value.

FEE-LEVEL LIMITATION VIA REGULATION OF STRUCTURE

Countries have taken different approaches to regulating the fee structure of pension funds. For example, Australia, Hong Kong (China), the United Kingdom, and the United States have few, if any, explicit restrictions on charges and instead regulate charges under the broader "prudence" or "reasonableness" standards. This is partly explained by the fact that private pensions in the United States remain voluntary, while in other countries they are built on preexisting voluntary systems. Most World Bank client countries limit the structure of charges, and quite a few have restrictive regimes in that companies are limited to two charges (an asset-based and a contribution-based charge), one of which is subject to a ceiling (asset-based charge), while the other can take any value.

It is still unclear to what extent these limitations on the structure lead to effective lower fee levels or what they imply for the longer supply structure (number of funds) or demand structure (scope of coverage). It appears that these limitations may be of lesser relevance than other elements of the second-pillar design and implementation (for a first assessment of four European and Central Asian countries, see World Bank 2003a). We suggest that a simple and transparent fee structure with well-thought-through price caps is a useful approach when such a new pillar is introduced. But these limitations need to be reviewed regularly and adjusted with other pillar characteristics if deemed necessary; it is quite likely that they will be relaxed as time progresses and individuals become more familiar with the system.

FEE-LEVEL LIMITATION VIA SPECIAL ORGANIZATION OF PROVIDERS

Several models of pension fund management are aimed at reducing fees by reducing costs. The basic idea is that, in competitive markets, costs are the major determinant of fees and, moreover, we should be concerned with the real cost of producing the services. International experience indicates that close-end funds (those limiting membership to employees of a firm, industry, or profession) have lower fees than open-end funds, perhaps because they incur lower marketing costs. Some countries use a centralized competitive-bidding process to outsource fund management (Bolivia, Kosovo, and Latvia, but not Sweden). These systems have resulted in lower fees, although it is not clear whether the related reduction in worker choice is sustainable. In this regard, the experience of the Federal Thrift Savings Plan in the United States (covering only federal government workers) is encouraging. Its gross expense ratio has declined steadily as the fund assets have grown, from an average of 0.67 percent of funds in 1988 to 0.07 percent in 1999 (Hustead and Hustead 2001; James, Smalhout, and Vittas 2001). It is by far the lowest fee structure in the industry.[22] Another important case for reducing fees while providing almost unlimited investment choices to plan members is the Swedish scheme. The majority of Latin American and some Eastern European countries adopted a model of open-end and specialized fund managers, with either centralized or decentralized collection and record-keeping systems. These models have produced relatively high management fees, especially in their early years. Although their fees are not higher, and in some cases are lower, than those of personal and stakeholder plans in the United Kingdom, there is still room for reducing them by addressing the issue of industry concentration.

Deregulation of fees and market contestability (for example, providing options to plan members) promote competition but require stronger disclosure of information. Fund managers have to provide affiliates with statements of their accounts. In addition, at least once a year they need to provide affiliates with basic information about the pension fund management company (ownership, managers, directors, and audited financial statements, including the auditor's report) as well as information on the fee structure and rate of return relative to the respective system's average, taking into account the long-term view. The greater the choice and contestability, the greater the incentive of fund managers to spend money on public relations and marketing—costs that eventually are passed on to worker-affiliates.

Again, it is too early to make strong recommendations, but the experience, so far, suggests three promising approaches. First, limit costs by saving on the administrative costs of contribution collection, account administration, and so forth (that is, adopt the clearinghouse approach). Second, limit the incentives for marketing expenditures by pension funds through blind accounts or constraints on the ability of individuals to change funds as a result of laws or exit fees. Last, but not least, limit asset management fees by restricting the choice of individuals, including the use of passive investment options, employers' choice of financial provider, or competitive bidding for a restricted number of service suppliers.

Can the Private Annuity Market Deliver?

A privately managed, funded pillar (mandated or voluntary) requires the provision of annuities that transform at retirement an accumulated amount into a lifelong income stream (that is, until death). This raises a number of issues for which good answers are not always available. For example, how much annuitization is required, in what form, and at what age (or ages if plan members are given the option of purchasing annuities through time) in order to improve risk management? What type of providers should offer what products? To what extent can and should unisex life tables be applied? What prudential and business regulations should be applied? What risk-sharing arrangements can or need to be put in place between providers and annuitants? What is the appropriate allocation of the risk of future changes in mortality among public and private sources? What role is there for governments in ensuring that appropriate financial products are available to back indexed annuity contracts?[23] This subsection concentrates on five issues: (a) What type of providers should be allowed to offer annuities? (b) What kinds of products should be allowed? (c) When must a private annuity market be ready? (d) Should there be price indexation of annuities? (e) How should we deal with the main challenges?

WHAT TYPE OF PROVIDERS SHOULD BE ALLOWED TO OFFER ANNUITIES?

Because of the insurance nature of annuity products, the insurance sector is bound to represent the largest set of annuity providers in any country. Pension funds (occupational and individual) may also provide annuities, especially if they provide defined benefits. Among insurance companies, there is an issue whether general life insurance companies should be allowed to sell annuities or whether specialized annuity companies should be licensed under the regulation (as in Mexico, for instance). On the one hand, life insurance companies may "hedge" the longevity and mortality risks when selling annuities and (say) term life products. On the other hand, information disclosure in the insurance industry is poor in practically all jurisdictions. Accounting standards are mostly opaque, and, from the point of view of consumer protection and transparency, an argument can be made for specialized annuity companies, especially to provide annuities from mandatory schemes.

WHAT KINDS OF PRODUCTS SHOULD BE ALLOWED?

Annuity markets are characterized by large asymmetric information between suppliers and demanders. This results in adverse selection and a difference between an actuarially fair price for an average individual and the typically insured of some 10 to 15 percent even in well-developed markets. This also results in complex products that compete on price as well as many other characteristics. It also results in differences in prices between deferred annuities (for example, where individuals pay premiums periodically through their active life) and annuities bought at retirement. Last, but not least, it results in price differences between individual and group insurance. To address the issue from a public policy perspective, a few needs stand out: (a) the need for comprehensive consumer information and protection for all products, (b) the need for standardized products as benchmarks for consumers, (c) the need for employers to be included in the selection of products, and (d) the need for innovative solutions (such as the auctioning of whole pension cohorts in a mandated pillar).

WHEN MUST A PRIVATE ANNUITY MARKET BE READY?

At the inception of pension reform in client countries, a functioning life insurance sector typically is not available and need not be so. These reforms concentrate initially on the accumulation phase, with the payout phase some 10 or more years away. But can a reform be launched without a view to the insurance sector? For example, the choice of individuals to join the second pillar may depend on available products and their characteristics (such as indexation and joint annuities). Our take is that if a financial sector fulfills the minimum requirements for launching such a reform, the insurance sector can (and must) be built over a period of five or so years. Major contributions to its development would be the adoption of a modern law establishing an operationally independent regulatory and supervisory authority, encouraging actuarial training, promoting reinsurance arrangements with highly reputable reinsurers, and opening up to well-established foreign life insurance companies from reputable jurisdictions, either in the form of joint ventures or the privatization of existing public institutions. For very small jurisdictions, considerations need to be made about unification or integration of several supervisory authorities, especially securities, insurance, and pensions (Impavido, Musalem, and Vittas 2002).

SHOULD THERE BE PRICE INDEXATION OF ANNUITIES?

For annuities to provide real consumption smoothing to individuals, they need to be price indexed; otherwise, even moderate inflation over a lengthy period of retirement will lead to a major fall in the real value of the annuity. For insurance companies to provide indexed annuities at reasonable prices (if at all) requires access to price-indexed assets, preferably in the form of price-indexed government bonds. Various countries have started to provide such bonds (Chile, Sweden, the United Kingdom, and the United States), but they are far from universal and often not long term. Even if indexed government bonds are available, insurance companies offering indexed annuities must forgo other more profitable investments and must therefore charge a higher price to annuitants than they would for nominal annuities. Therefore, indexation involves a difficult tradeoff between the higher financial security of older pensioners and the lower payouts they will receive when young. This tradeoff needs to be taken into account by governments when projecting the replacement rates that the new system will generate (Impavido, Thorburn, and Wadsworth 2004). Moreover, if governments want to ensure (or mandate) the availability of price-indexed annuities, they will need to issue the appropriate inflation-indexed or other specialized instruments to enable this market to develop. This, however, potentially imposes significant distributional tradeoffs because in nearly all developing (and many developed) countries the beneficiaries of indexed annuities are higher-income groups, while all will bear the costs of providing the financial instruments to enable them to develop.

HOW SHOULD WE DEAL WITH THE MAIN CHALLENGES?

Two issues are addressed around the question of who should bear the risk. The first concerns *rating or differential underwriting of survival probabilities* (such as genetic testing, for instance). One of the disadvantages of pooling risks is that good types (in the case of annuities, those who die early) subsidize bad types, giving rise to the pooling premium. For some groups of pensioners—for example, those with health impairments or those with poorer socioeconomic backgrounds—the terms on which pooling takes place may mean a high probability of subsidizing other parties to the pool because of the lack of homogeneity of lives.

Disallowing access by insurance companies to this information increases asymmetric information, adverse selection, and the danger of a breakdown of the market. Providing this information for both sides of the market leads to segmented risk pooling and the exclusion of some groups (those with identified high survival rates), for which public provisions may have to be established. The introduction of rating would eliminate the nonstochastic component (that is, those elements that would induce strong adverse selection) from the pooling equilibrium. In other words, types systematically better than the average (that is, who die earlier) would be better off, while types systematically worse than the average would be worse off.

The other main issue concerns the question of who should bear the risk of rising life expectancy and uncertain future investment income. Some demographers have been predicting large increases in life expectancy due to scientific breakthroughs. Some economists have been predicting prolonged drops in stock prices or bond interest rates due to aging populations who cash in their stocks and use them to buy more stable bonds. Evidence from many countries indicates that these companies now return the government bond rate to annuitants over their expected lifetime; that is, the "money's worth ratio," discounted at the government term structure, is close to 100 percent (see, for example, James, Vittas, and Song 2001). A large increase in longevity or a decrease in investment income may bring losses to these companies, including the possibility of insolvency and failure to keep their promises to annuitants.

How should we deal with these risks? Who is best equipped to deal with them? At least three approaches are relevant here. In the first approach, insurance companies continue to bear the risks, but with careful government regulation to ensure that their reserves are large enough to cover unexpected shocks. Such reserves and regulations have significant costs, so we would expect them to be factored into the prices (or money's worth ratios) offered annuitants.

The second method explicitly shares these risks with annuitants by allowing and possibly encouraging variable annuities whose value varies annually depending on actual longevity and investment outcomes. Annuitants get a higher expected return than they would under fixed-rate annuities, but they also bear some of the risk, which may be difficult for low-income pensioners. Also, they may not understand the complex terms of the variable annuity, and companies may take advantage of their lack of information. Obviously, if this approach is taken, government has a large responsibility for providing consumer information and for standardizing the terms of payout variation to facilitate comprehension and comparability.

The third method of assigning risk places a heavier burden on government, which might offer a minimum pension guarantee, sell longevity-indexed bonds, or provide the annuities directly. This enables the broadest possible intergenerational risk sharing, but it also creates the danger that government will be faced with a large contingent liability many years in the future. The "best" solution for the annuity dilemma remains an unresolved and controversial issue.

Readiness and Regulatory and Supervisory Financial Market Issues

The introduction of a mandated funded pension pillar has given rise to considerable debate inside and outside the Bank, and it will take many more years before a clear consensus is reached. This section addresses four issues that are at the core of the debate: (a) Can funded pensions be introduced in a rudimentary financial market environment, and, if so, what are the minimum conditions? (b) What are the good or best regulatory practices that typical client countries should follow? (c) What are the good or best supervisory practices to be applied? (d) What are the options for countries with small open systems?

Readiness, Minimum Conditions, and Synergies

Bank staff take the position that not all countries are ready to introduce a funded pillar and should not do so. Nevertheless, the introduction of a funded pillar does not need perfect conditions, with all financial products available from the very beginning, since the pillar is introduced gradually and creates synergies for moving toward improved financial markets. Hence, minimum conditions need to be satisfied, and these can be highlighted when discussing three types of countries and their financial market readiness (Impavido, Musalem, and Vittas 2002).

There are three main types of financial markets: (a) those that are incomplete but the segments that operate are sound, are associated with high per capita income, have a credible macroeconomic policy framework, and have open capital accounts (but domestic and international financial instruments are not perfect substitutes); (b) those that are incomplete and the segments that operate are predominantly unsound, are associated with low per capita income, have a long history of macroeconomic policy imbalances, and have closed capital accounts; and (c) those that have an intermediate position between the two.

Countries with incomplete but sound financial systems that have relatively high per capita income, credible macroeconomic policies, and free capital movements offer the best case for funded pension and annuity systems. This is true for several reasons. First, (voluntary) funded pension and annuity products are luxury financial services. They are demanded at high rather than low per capita income (that is, at high per capita income, the time preference or discount rate is lower, which increases the valuation of purchasing coverage for future contingencies, and family ties are weaker, which reduces self-insurance within the family). Second, credible macroeconomic policy provides an enabling environment for the development of long-term financial instruments (for example, pension savings and annuities). Third, even under incomplete financial markets (for example, embryonic capital markets), but where sound banks are operating, they provide a vehicle for channeling long-term savings into long-term loans to borrowers (government, enterprises, and individuals). Finally, open capital accounts do not constrain pension funds from investing in the local market.

The second type of countries—those with chronic macroeconomic imbalances and other limitations—provide little room for the development of funded pensions and annuities. Long-term savings instruments cannot prosper in a macroeconomic environment with high and volatile inflation, and pensions and annuities are not affordable at low per capita income. Furthermore, the financial systems of these countries are essentially limited to the banking sector, which usually is weak. Although it would be possible to invest abroad, these countries, by having weak domestic financial institutions, should have closed capital accounts. Hence, before trying to develop these instruments, the authorities should focus on establishing a credible long-term macroeconomic framework and strengthening prudential regulation and supervision of banks. These two conditions are necessary for the successful development of funded pensions and annuities.

In the third and intermediary category of financial systems, there are a variety of cases. There are countries with a credible macroeconomic policy, a relatively sound banking system, and an open capital account. However, they have incomplete financial markets (underdeveloped securities markets, insurance, pensions, and mortgages) and relatively low per capita income. These countries have the preconditions for developing funded pensions and annuities, although their relatively low per capita income imposes a barrier to the scale of the market. Initially, the portfolios of these funds would be composed primarily of government bonds and banks' long-term certificates of deposit. In addition, they could have small fractions in shares, foreign securities, and possibly leasing companies. As financial markets develop, investment regulations should allow more diversified portfolios by allowing higher investments in shares, foreign securities, corporate bonds, and asset-backed securities and small investments in venture capital companies.

These countries will obtain the benefits from the development of funded pensions and annuities. Gains from financial sector development will initially be concentrated in development of the government bond market and long-term lending through banks. In a second stage, benefits will come from development of the corporate bond market, asset-backed securities, and, in a later stage, the stock market. The development of funded pensions and annuities will encourage financial market innovation through development of the fund management industry and improved financial regulations, including stronger minority shareholder rights, transparency, and corporate governance. They also will provide competition to the banking system and foster efficiency and innovation in financial markets.

In summary, instead of a full-fledged financial system with a full array of efficient institutions and financial instruments, the following minimum conditions are needed for the successful introduction of a funded pillar (Vittas 2000): (a) the presence of a solid core of sound banks and insurance companies, (b) a long-term commitment by government to pursue sound macroeconomic policies, and (c) a long-term commitment to financial sector reform through the establishment of a sound regulatory and supervisory framework for pensions and insurance products and providers.

What Regulatory Practice to Follow?

Seasoned development practitioners respond to the call for best-practice application in developing countries by posing a question: If the countries could apply these practices, would they still be World Bank clients? Applied to contractual savings, the question implies that the best OECD-type practices may be beyond low- and middle-income countries for some time (OECD 2004b). Nevertheless, the many pension reform pilots in middle-income countries in Latin America and Central and Eastern Europe have created a rich body of experience. This subsection presents the main lessons from this experience (Carmichael and Pomerleano 2002; Hinz and Rao 2003; Rocha, Hinz, and Gutiérrez 2001; Vittas 1998a, 1998b).

For a country following the open-end fund concept (as in Chile), the Bank strongly suggests initially applying strict regulations and relaxing them gradually as sound financial markets develop. The strict initial rules include a limited choice for participants, the licensing of specialized providers under the rule of one fund–one account, uniform pricing and limited forms of fees, detailed investment limits, extensive disclosure, minimum return rules and state guarantees, and proactive supervision. The reason for the initial "Draconian rule" is essentially twofold. On the one hand, the new compulsory system starts with a weak capital market, limited traditions, and a lack of familiarity. On the other hand, strict regulations offer safeguards, control moral hazard, overcome opposition to the funded scheme, and are better able to prevent early failures. It is imperative to relax the rules as the market develops and the system matures.

The *less controversial regulations* should be applied to mandated, funded schemes from the very beginning. These include (a) appropriate licensing and capital requirements for providers; (b) full segregation of assets, sponsors, management firm, and custodian and the use of external custodian banks; (c) asset diversification and the rules of asset management (the qualifications and licensing of internal or external managers); (d) asset valuation rules (mark-to-market) and rate-of-return calculations (the mutual fund instead of the savings account model); (e) periodic actuarial reviews and financial audits; (f) transparency and information disclosure; and (g) effective supervision and consistent application of sanctions.

The *more controversial regulations,* for which there remains uncertainty regarding whether and when they should be applied, include (a) controls on market structure and choice (should only special institutions and products be permitted, and is there a tradeoff between choice and costs?); (b) funding, investment, and portability rules; (c) legal investment limits versus the prudent-man principle (can the latter be applied in a less sophisticated market?); (d) limits on commissions and switching; and (e) profitability rules and guarantees.

What Supervisory Practice to Apply?

Again, many rules are not controversial and should be applied early on. A few others are still uncertain, and the verdict is still out about what works best and under what conditions.

The *less controversial rules* and tasks for the supervisory body include (a) the need for a politically independent, proactive, well-financed, and professional staff; (b) the vetting of the application for licensing; (c) the undertaking of off-site surveillance and on-site inspection; (d) the elaboration and issuance of regulations; (e) the consistent and timely application of sanctions to rectify problems and establish a credible deterrent to abusive practices; (f) the publication of reports and statistics; and (g) collaboration with other regulators.

The *more controversial rules* and questions for supervision include (a) creation of a single-purpose or dedicated supervisory agency; (b) establishment of effective collaboration with other regulators and supervisors for the many institutions offering retirement-income products; (c) the best way to guarantee the independence of the supervisory body in a weak political environment; and (d) oversight and accountability of the supervisor.

Often the threshold decision related to the supervision of funded pensions is whether to establish this as an independent authority (as in Chile and most Latin American countries) or to integrate these functions with the supervision of similar financial entities, such as banks and insurance companies (as in Australia, Hungary, and the United Kingdom, among others). Both models have proven to be effective in achieving the objective of sound and reliable supervision, so there is no simple answer to the organizational question. The appropriate approach is likely to be a function of the design of the system and effectiveness of existing supervisory bodies. Pension funds that operate in a highly specialized manner as very distinctive financial institutions can be effectively supervised by independent authorities, while those that function as adjuncts to existing financial institutions are best addressed by an agency with integrated authority. The form of the institution is secondary to the independence, adequacy of resources, quality of staff, and clarity of mandate. The most compelling impetus for an integrated supervisor is the need for consistency and coordination of oversight across similar financial institutions, which are much better facilitated in a single authority. A central counterargument is that an integrated supervisor with a weak governance structure will face conflicts of interest in controlling the activities of institutions within its authority that compete or play multiple roles in a pension system (for example, asset managers, banks, and insurance companies) or be weakened in its ability to protect the system in the face of competing priorities.

Options for Countries with Small Financial Systems

Various small and open economies, such as in Central America, Central Europe, Mauritius, and Senegal, are starting pension reforms that include the development of a funded pillar. Undertaking such a reform in an environment with a limited financial sector creates both opportunities and challenges. The challenges include the resource-intensive development of country-specific regulations and the buildup of supervisory capacity, a potentially small number of pension funds given the small size of the country and the existence of significant economies of scale, and a limited range of financial instruments through which to diversify investment portfolios. These issues raise a number of questions. Would these countries be better off by developing their pension funds in a regional setting? If the regional option is not feasible, how can the costs be contained? How much international diversification should be undertaken, and how does one deal with the exchange rate issue?

There are many good arguments for regional development of financial systems, including institutions for providing funded retirement income. Bank research has found that countries with small financial systems tend to have smaller and shallower financial markets, to be poorer, to have a smaller population, and to be more open (Glaessner and Valdés-Prieto 1998; Impavido, Musalem, and Vittas 2002). Small countries cannot fully exploit the economies of scale and scope in the provision of financial services. The smaller population limits the amount and quality of human capital available. The lack of resources limits the scope for the development of financial infrastructure, such as payment systems, organized markets, supervision, and regulation. The fixed costs of establishing these basic systems may simply be too high for small or poorer countries. As a consequence, small financial markets are generally shallow, incomplete, poorly regulated, illiquid, prone to lack of competition and to concentration in the provision of services, inefficient, and characterized by relatively high transaction costs. Small economies are also more volatile. In fact, their median standard deviation of private consumption, terms of trade, inflation, GDP growth, and capital flows per GDP is between 1.5 and 4.0 times higher than in larger countries (Bossone, Honohan, and Long 2001).

Despite these potential advantages, little cooperation has taken place so far in client countries and elsewhere to exploit the economies of scale and to use pension reforms in regions to push for more integrated financial markets. Regions that could join such a collaborative for joint development include the Caribbean, Central and Eastern Europe, Central and South America, and Central as well as Western Africa (which both have a common currency and a common regulatory framework). This lack of integration is puzzling and requires research to ascertain the hidden technical reasons or explanations of political economy. Taken as a fact, this calls for other approaches and the review of existing practice.

Different countries have experimented with different institutional setups, and the international experience can serve as a benchmark for the pros and cons of specific designs. As already mentioned, the *one-fund approach* in the form of a publicly managed fund has not been a good experience in most countries, and the recent initiatives in five OECD countries with centralized funds is too early to judge and may be difficult to transfer into a developing-country context (Palacios 2002). One country (Bolivia) has selected *two funds* in an international bidding process guaranteed for a limited number of years (von Gersdorff 1997). While successfully importing knowledge and skills and keeping costs and fees down, the two funds merged ownership at the level of the mother company and, in this stronger position, reportedly are able to resist the pressure of the regulator to open up to competition. The *Kotlikoff approach* of full international diversification in a world index fund (which uses an international asset manager instead of developing a local financial market) has yet to be adopted by any country for reasons that have to do with home bias, incomplete markets, fears of foreign exchange problems, and the absence of a true world index (Kotlikoff 1999). A current experiment in Kosovo plans to use a variant on this approach, so five years from now we will be able to report on how well this works. Most countries, however, have opted for policies between these two extremes.

Countries that have opted for *open, nonemployer funds* have witnessed consolidation and concentration (with Chile seeing a decrease in the number of pension funds—from well over 20 some 10 years ago to 7 or 6 in 2004). Concentration may have created economies of scale and reduced marketing costs, but it also has posed the policy challenge of how to ensure a continued supply of competitive and efficient services. One solution would be to enable employers to opt out of the open-end system by allowing employer-sponsored plans. Countries that have relied on *closed, employer-based funds* have a much larger number of funds; however, these funds do not compete, as each is tied to a particular employer. Since several employers may use the same asset managers, the number of competing asset managers may be much smaller than the number of funds. Closed funds limit marketing costs and enjoy some economies of scope (and scale for large employers), but their performance depends on the solvency and integrity of employers as the sponsors of pension plans. The record seems to be positive for the pension funds of large employers, but rather mixed for the plans of smaller firms.

Finally, the recent *Swedish approach* is the prime example of the clearinghouse strategy, which uses a central public agency for collecting contributions, maintaining individual account records, controlling fees, and paying benefits in conjunction with decentralized private asset management. Workers have the right to direct their funds to several hundred authorized mutual funds, most of which predate the start of the new pension system. The system is highly complex and requires the presence of an efficient central administrative agency in concert with robust and effective regulation and supervision of the participating mutual funds. It is a highly promising innovation for advanced countries with well-developed financial markets that moves in the direction of regulated, constrained choice.

As international experience suggests, there is no silver bullet to circumvent significant economies of scale or to find a solution in simply opening fully to the international financial markets. Countries may not be able to avoid all the costs of domestic institution building and may profit from foreign experience, but this needs to be done in a transparent manner.

Countries with small financial systems and few resources may, perhaps, avoid the sunk costs associated with the provision of pension services (from contribution collection to asset management) by attracting investments from highly reputable foreign companies, ideally operating in joint venture with local companies. By attracting reputable foreign companies, reforming countries may also reduce the costs of supervision, which, regardless of cost, takes time to develop. This could provide the host country with a transition period during which effective regulation and supervision are established, while effective oversight is provided through the home country (Impavido, Musalem, and Vittas 2002).

In countries with small financial sectors, the small dimension of institutional relationships, the relative scarcity of human capital, the greater concentration of wealth, and a relatively less independent civil service facilitate the concentration of functions, interference by third parties, and the potential for weak governance. Hence, great importance should be given to the responsibility of governments to create a regulatory environment capable of preserving pension assets. This means that direct government control of asset management and direct investment in target industries, housing, and failing banks should be avoided, while pension funds should be afforded some freedom to invest abroad.

Last, but not least, is the role of international investments and the advantages of portfolio diversification for pension funds and the economy as a whole. While these benefits seem unquestionable, worldwide experience strongly suggests that the necessary conditions for the openness of the capital account include a sufficiently developed domestic financial market; otherwise, the country is likely to suffer from volatile capital flows and major exchange rate fluctuations (Karacadag, Sundararajan, and Elliot 2003; Prasad and others 2003). For pension funds, the exchange rates of small countries pose an additional problem because long-term hedging instruments are not available. While a rule of thumb may suggest that the share of foreign investment of pension funds should be approximately the expected scope of tradable goods consumed by retirees, what is the best strategy of a small country such as Mauritius, which imports in dollars and exports in euros? The potential alternative to a fully open capital account is the use of swaps by pension funds. Although discussed for some time inside and outside the Bank, and first suggestions have been put on paper (Bodie and Merton 2001; Vittas 2003), the market has not yet developed and may be too thin.

In summary, in small economies the implementation of pension reforms that move toward funded provisions creates special challenges. While the resource requirements may be high, they may be reduced by linking up with neighbors and international firms to avoid or reduce sunk costs. However, developing a financial market, including regulations, has other beneficial results, as domestic financial market development cannot be imported and is a requirement for an open capital account and risk sharing with the rest of the world.

Political Economy and Organization of Pension Reforms

A successful and sustainable pension reform requires a deep understanding of the political economy of reform and its organization. While no dominant paradigm has been established, progress has been made in some, but not all, areas (Holzmann, Orenstein, and Rutkowski 2003).[24] This section highlights a useful conceptualization borrowed from Orenstein (2000) and adjusted based on country experiences; a proposed checklist, linked to the conceptualization and based on recent reform experiences; and a link between the type of pension system and its ability to insulate itself from future political risks.

A Proposed Conceptualization

Orenstein (2000) proposes three main phases of pension reform: commitment building, coalition building, and implementation. Although the length of the phases may differ depending on individual country circumstances, there are certain commonalities.

The *commitment-building phase* is commonly the longest of the three phases. In this phase, it is desirable to include many actors in the debate, even at the expense of consensus. At this stage, it also is important to expose to and share with the general public and key policy players the relevant experience of other countries that have undertaken a successful pension reform. Key players include the parliamentarians, trade unions, and the national press. The duration and coverage of the debate should not be limited in order to reach a quick but artificial agreement. Just the opposite applies: open disagreements at this stage help parties to reach agreement in subsequent phases.

The *coalition-building phase* starts at a time when the government decides to put forward a reform concept. Crucial for the move from the commitment-building to the coalition-building phase and its successful completion is the emergence of a champion who believes in the need for reform and links his or her political fate with the cause.

During the coalition-building phase, the government remains open to modifications of the reform concept, but not necessarily to wholesale changes. The quality of the concept is of critical importance: the concept should be based on cutting-edge knowledge and should bring in the experience of other countries. It should have strong long-term projections, including sensitivity analysis, and be linked with opinion polls and focus groups showing that the concept responds to genuine concerns of the population with the existing system.

Presentation of the concept requires a focus on key messages. Pension reforms may be viewed as intergenerational struggles in which potential losers, usually current or near-term pensioners, often attempt to block reforms, while potential winners, young workers, are inactive in the debate out of myopia or lack of interest and understanding. At this stage it is, therefore, important to focus key messages on young people. Common strategies are the following:

- Emphasize that the new system brings the net present value of future payments close to the level of current contributions paid;
- Convince young workers that the state will honor its future obligations;
- Activate young workers in the pension debate, turning the debate explicitly into an intergenerational discussion;
- Engage organized workers, pensioners, financial sector representatives, and other parties with a stake in the outcome because the more organized the actors are, the more likely they will be to take into account macroeconomic benefits that will result from the reform.

The following stage of concept dissemination is a complicated activity. The experience of reformers shows that several activities bring significant payoffs. These include using professional public relations firms, focusing on key actors, building a core group of journalists who understand the reform process and are sympathetic to its goals, and working with donor agencies and other international organizations to extend the technical development and analysis.

The concept has to be converted into a legislative proposal and ultimately a draft law in order to initiate legislative proceedings. At this point, the reform package and supporting justification and communications materials should be comprehensive. Optimal management and sequencing of the legislative process is highly specific to individual country conditions and legislative processes and heavily influenced by political considerations. Chile, for example, enacted the full reform at once. Poland, however, first legislated the second and third pillar of the package and moved to the first pillar a year later.

The passage of laws begins the most critical phase: *reform implementation*. Almost invariably, the administrative capacity to support the new system is lower than expected. In Mexico the reform had to be delayed for a year until the new institutions required for implementation (Consar to supervise and Procesar to process information related to the transfer of funds to individual accounts) were sufficiently developed to fulfill their respective roles. In Poland, the new system malfunctioned because the social insurance institution was unable to pass contributions accurately and on time to the pension funds. During the implementation phase, it is important to have clear communication with the population, so that flaws in implementation are not confused with flaws in the reform.

A main lesson for Bank staff advice to client countries emerges from the tension between political readiness and administrative preparation: decide on the reform law when the political opportunity emerges and expectations of continued commitment are sufficiently high but implement the reform only when the administrative preparation is sufficiently advanced and problems are expected to be manageable.

The Experience of Reforming Countries

The following criteria could be used as a checklist for judging whether the country is prepared to undertake the reform:

- Presence of a political mandate and organized advocacy groups;
- Empowerment of the reform technical group;
- Development of comprehensive and sound analysis;
- Quality of information about public opinions of the existing system and reform proposals;
- Clear strategy for communication with the affected public;
- Involvement of trade unions and other stakeholder organizations;
- Fully formulated strategy and effective management of implementation;
- Evidence of potential for political consensus.

Overall, the experience of reforms leads to the following conclusions with respect to the organization of the process:

- Policy legacies influence the present choice of reform, and the design of a reform builds on the legacy of existing institutions.

- Establishing an office solely responsible for managing the reform process is very helpful. The burden of day-to-day management crowds out reformist thinking and acting for entities with other responsibilities.
- A well-thought-out public relations strategy and easily understood message are crucial to success.
- The choice of groups engaged in the reform dialogue systematically influences the outcome of reform because certain groups empower certain types of actors. Excluding actors from one forum often causes them to be more active in another.

Isolation from Political Risks

From a political economy perspective, a primary objective of reforms is to move to a system that is more robust to diverse kinds of shocks, which includes better isolation from the risks of political interventions that create adverse consequences for short-term political gains (Diamond 1997). From that point of view, both the nonfinancial and funded defined-contribution type of pillars are improvements relative to pay-as-you-go, defined-benefit systems that mix redistribution and insurance in a nontransparent manner. New structures either (a) move retirement incomes outside the government budget (a funded pillar) or (b) require the identification of an explicit source of financing for the benefits of any group of individuals or (c) make the benefits strictly and exclusively dependent on contributions (notional defined-contribution and funded pillar). It remains to be seen whether these will effectively preclude the political system from appropriating these resources for government revenue or accessing them for redistribution in other ways. Violating nonfinancial defined-contribution principles or requiring investment in government debt, particularly debt paying less than market rates, is the obvious route for the former. Redistributing part of the return on portfolios to "needier" accounts (which may have an age component) is one route for the latter. A central question is whether protection can be achieved by identifying individual accounts (in the nonfinancial defined-contribution as well as the funded form) as private property entitled to the same protection as other assets.

The recent example of Argentina illustrates the challenges in protecting the assets of funded pension systems under catastrophic macroeconomic conditions. The experience of Argentina indicates that simply placing assets in private control cannot guarantee their full protection, as all three pillars of the pension system suffered, along with depositors, insurance policyholders, bondholders, and shareholders. The experience in Argentina also indicates that the outcome for retirees may still be better under the funded pillar than under the potential alternatives.

Examples of Reform Dilemmas and Questions

This section presents some of the reform dilemmas in client countries where we do not yet know how best to proceed and what solutions to propose. While we face substantial uncertainty, we strongly believe that doing nothing is not a solution either. Consequently, we propose to substantiate our knowledge with analytical work, while working with clients on innovative solutions and joint learning.

What approach can be effective when the public sector is not delivering and the private sector cannot do so either, a situation frequently encountered in the least-developed countries? On the one hand, the public scheme does not deliver on its promises, is insolvent, and needs to be reformed, but any reform attempt fails. On the other hand, the financial sector does not meet the minimum conditions necessary even to think about replacing the public unfunded scheme with a funded scheme. Should one close down the public earnings-related scheme and provide minimum benefits (the zero pillar) only? Can even minimum benefits be delivered under current conditions? Should one establish a parallel institution, as is being discussed with regard to providing access to basic health and education in the low-performing countries? Should one follow the Kotlikoff (1999) proposal and park all the resources for a new funded scheme outside the country (as is being attempted in Kosovo)? Or should one simply engage in damage control until reform of the public sector makes progress before thinking about systemic reform?

Various client countries with Anglo-Saxon traditions run provident funds, which are defined-contribution systems that are formally funded. Two main problems surround these funds—one, in principle, is manageable; the other is less so. The manageable problem concerns poor performance as a result of poor governance and weak regulations and supervision, an issue for which solutions are, in principle, available if the political will exists. The less manageable problem concerns the pseudo funding of these provident funds because the portfolio consists essentially of government bonds. Diversifying to private assets may be possible, depending on the availability of market instruments, but not feasible for the government regarding access to financing. These are essentially unfunded schemes in which the government debt is implicit. Should the systems be transformed into explicitly unfunded schemes (say, of the notional defined-contribution type)? Should an effort be made to change the form of funding (and hence pay for the transition deficit)? Should these provident funds be phased out and replaced by a truly funded and privately managed system?

Many social insurance systems in client countries are far from maturation and therefore have accumulated some reserve funds. These funds pale
in comparison with the accumulated liabilities but nevertheless constitute
5 percent or more of GDP. They are poorly managed, generally earning
low rates of returns. There remains uncertainty about the true size of assets
(due to lack of auditing and accepted valuation techniques) and large-scale
corruption. In addition, individuals take out loans against many of these
funds prior to retirement. While improving fund governance and management would be the best solution, current administrative systems and staff
remain entrenched, and progress has been limited. Nevertheless, as asset
levels have risen, pressure has intensified to improve benefits, lower retirement ages, and lower eligibility requirements. Would it be better in these
circumstances not to accumulate funds at all? What are the possibilities for
the Bank and other international institutions to pressure for improved
fund management? Is the environment conducive to private sector solutions, or does reform of the existing public institutions offer the most realistic opportunity for improvement?

Chapter 7

Regional Experiences: Developments and First Evaluation of Reform

THE FIRST PART OF THIS CHAPTER REVIEWS THE REFORM EXPERIENCE in the two regions with the most reform activities since the beginning of the 1990s: Latin America and Europe and Central Asia.[25] While the transition economies in Europe and Central Asia were somewhat influenced by the early experience in Latin America, the process of reform developed quite differently in the two regions, including some innovative approaches to design and implementation of multipillar pension reform. The second part of this chapter briefly reviews the development of reform in the four other Bank regions—South Asia, Sub-Saharan Africa, Middle East and North Africa, and East Asia and the Pacific. While in these regions actual and comprehensive country reforms are still limited, the policy discussion about the need for reform and the direction it should take is occurring in many more countries.

Latin America and the Caribbean

Structural reform of retirement-income security systems in Latin America and the Caribbean began with the move to a funded plan of mandatory individual retirement accounts in Chile in 1981 and to date includes 12 countries.[26] A thirteenth country, Brazil, has made substantial changes to its national pay-as-you-go systems and introduced measures to strengthen and extend the private provision of voluntary retirement savings and insurance products but has not explicitly mandated individual savings accounts.

While Latin America's structural reforms can be grouped broadly together as "multipillar," since all of the 12 include a mandatory funded pillar of individual accounts administered by private pension providers, each of the reforms is unique in the balance between the pillars, the inclusion of current contributors within the reform, the degree of competition among providers, the arrangements for disability and survivor insurance, and institutional arrangements, among other features. Tables 7.1 and 7.2 compare structural reforms in the region during two periods.[27]

Table 7.1. Principal Features of Structural Reforms to Social Security Systems (Old-Age Disability and Death) in Latin America, 1980s and 1990s

Feature	Chile	Peru	Colombia	Argentina	Uruguay	Mexico	Bolivia	El Salvador
Year of reform	1981	1992–3	1994	1994	1996	1997	1997	1998
Contribution-related, pay-as-you-go system?	Closed	Remains	Remains	Remains	Remains	Closed	Closed	Closed
Total payroll tax rate (percent)								
Prereform	33	18	17.8	42	40	20	19	11.8
Postreform	20	20.5/22[a]	33.8	46[b]	40	26	24	13.5
Participation of new workers	Mandatory	Voluntary	Voluntary	Voluntary[c]	Voluntary[d]	Mandatory	Mandatory	Mandatory
Participation of self-employed?	Voluntary	Voluntary	Voluntary	Mandatory	Mandatory	Voluntary	Voluntary	Voluntary
Remaining separate system for civil servants?	No	No[e]	Yes	No[e]	No	Yes	No	No
Dedicated fund managers	AFP	AFP	AFP	AFJP	AFAP	AFORE	AFP	AFP
Contribution to individual retirement account (percent)[f]	10	8	10	7.72	12.27	12.07	10	10
Fees and insurance premiums (percent of wage)	2.31	3.73	3.49	3.28	2.68	4.48	2.50	3
Switching between fund managers?	Twice annually	Once annually	Twice annually	Twice annually	Twice annually	Once annually	Once annually	Twice annually

142

Payout options	Annuity or scheduled withdrawal	Annuity or scheduled withdrawal	Annuity or scheduled withdrawal	Annuity only	Annuity or scheduled withdrawal	Annuity only	Annuity or scheduled withdrawal
Minimum return on investment?	Relative to average	Relative to average	Relative to average	Relative to average	Unregulated	Unregulated[g]	Relative to average
Minimum contributory pension?	Yes	Yes (only for affiliates born before 1945)	Yes	Yes	Yes	No	Yes
Social assistance pension?	Yes	No	Yes	Yes	No	Yes	No

Sources: Gill, Packard, and Yermo (2004), based on AIOS (2003) and country case studies.

Note: AFP (Administradora de Fondos de Pensiones); AFAP (Administradora de Fondos de Ahorro Provisional); AFJP (Administradora de Fondos de Jubilaciones y Pensiones); AFORE (Administradora de Fondos para el Retiro).

a. 20.5 percent for private pension plans; 22 percent for the national system. Maximum taxable earning for disability and survivorship insurance: S/6,130.88 or US$1,751. Peru's currency is the nuevo sol.

b. Maximum allowed by law. The effective tax rate has been falling since the reform and varies by sector and region. The current rate is less than 30 percent.

c. Although new affiliates can choose, up to 80 percent in each year fail to make an explicit choice. The private second pillar is the default option.

d. Participation in individual accounts in Uruguay is determined by income level. Workers below a threshold level choose to split contributions between pay-as-you-go or individual retirement accounts.

e. Exceptions exist for some subnational systems.

f. At the time of publication.

g. Guarantees required from the fund managers.

Table 7.2. Principal Features of Structural Reforms to Social Security Systems (Old-Age Disability and Death) in Latin America, 1990s and 2000s

Feature	Costa Rica	Nicaragua	Ecuador	Dominican Republic
Year of reform	1995–2000[a]	2000, as yet unimplemented	2001, as yet unimplemented	2001[b]
Contribution-related, public pay-as-you-go system?	Remains	Closed	Remains	Closed
Total payroll tax rate (percent)				
Prereform	22	17	—	9.25
Postreform	26	21.5	Varies, but no more than 20	20
Participation of new workers?	Mandatory	Mandatory	Mandatory	Mandatory
Participation of self-employed?	Voluntary	Voluntary	Mandatory	Mandatory
Remaining separate system for civil servants?	—	No	—	No
Dedicated fund managers	OPC	AFP	EDAP	AFP
Contribution to individual retirement account (percent)	4.25	7.5	8.33	8
Fees and insurance premiums (percent of wage)	[c]	2.5	4.0	2.0
Switching between fund managers?	Once annually	Once annually	—	Once annually
Payout options	Annuity or scheduled withdrawal	Annuity or scheduled withdrawal	—	Annuity or scheduled withdrawal
Minimum return on investment?	Unregulated	Unregulated	Relative to average	Relative to average
Minimum contributory pension?	Yes	Yes	—	Yes
Social assistance pension?	Yes	Yes	Yes	Yes

Sources: Gill, Packard, and Yermo (2004), based on AIOS (2003) and country case studies.

Note: AFP (Administradora de Fondos de Pensiones); EDAP (Entidades Depositarias del Ahorro Provisional); OPC (Operadora de Pensiones Complementarios).

— Not available.

a. Costa Rica introduced voluntary retirement accounts in 1996 but made private individual retirement saving mandatory as a complement to the defined-benefit system in 2000.

b. Implemented in 2003.

c. Fees are charged as a percentage of returns from investment and capped at a maximum.

144

A critical feature of the reforms in Latin America, with the exception of Mexico and to some degree Argentina and Colombia, has been the creation of a single, unified national pension system from previously fragmented elements.[28] Across the region, the military is still not included in the reformed national systems, and other select groups in each country receive pensions from special plans that have not been integrated. The self-employed are not always required to participate.

The general unification brought by structural reforms has positive implications for labor market flexibility, equity, and redistribution and has led to long-term fiscal savings. Notably, in countries where structural reforms have not yet taken place, retirement security arrangements remain fragmented, constraining the functioning of the formal labor market, aggravating inequity, and posing a risk for the public fiscal stance.

A Preliminary Assessment of Multipillar Reforms

The stated goals of reform presented earlier in this report—namely, adequacy, affordability, sustainability, and robustness—provide a useful set of criteria with which to assess what has been achieved with structural reforms to retirement-income security systems in Latin America. However, a truly conclusive evaluation of reforms can only be made when the first cohort of workers who entered the labor market under the reformed systems begins to retire. In Chile, this will not take place until 2020 or so. This said, it is not too early for preliminary stock taking.[29]

ADEQUACY

Adequacy is defined as providing benefits to the full breadth of the population that will be sufficient to prevent old-age poverty as well as provide a means to smooth lifetime consumption. Most of Latin America's new multipillar pension systems provide reasonable benefits for those who contribute throughout their working life. Some countries, such as Costa Rica and Uruguay, implicitly target very high replacement rates, while others, including Chile, Dominican Republic, El Salvador, and Peru, have structured the parameters of their reformed systems to provide lower average benefit levels relative to wages.[30] The countries that rely heavily on defined-contribution plans also provide higher effective replacement rates to lower-income workers through minimum pension guarantees, for which workers with a certain minimum history of contribution to the systems are eligible.[31]

However, almost all of Latin America's reformed pension systems fall far short of covering the population, with the exception of Uruguay. This was also a shortcoming of single-pillar pay-as-you-go systems and, in many countries, was a prime motivation and political selling point for structural reforms. Using an ex ante concept of coverage as "participation"—that is, the share of the economically active population contributing (and thus acquiring rights or building savings) toward a pension—reveals widely varying levels of participation. At the low end, participation in Bolivia, El Salvador, and Peru ranges from 10 to 15 percent of the workforce, while at the higher end, participation in Argentina, Chile, and Uruguay ranges between 30 and 80 percent. Although the share of the economically active population contributing to the formal pension system is likely to increase with development and growth in per capita income, significant differences exist between countries with similar income levels. The available empirical evidence on changes in worker participation brought by structural reforms is mixed, with some authors claiming expanded coverage and others finding little evidence of increased participation.[32]

As a safety net to mitigate vulnerability to poverty in old age aggravated by low rates of worker participation in formal pension systems, most of the wealthier middle-income countries in the region (notably, those that have had social security systems for the longest time) include some mechanism to provide income support for the elderly with either an insufficient history of contributions or no record of prior participation in the covered sector of the economy. Financing and coverage of these "noncontributory" arrangements vary significantly. The most extensive coverage of a noncontributory scheme is found in Brazil, which has opted to provide all rural workers with a pension equivalent to 100 percent of the national minimum wage. However, even in Brazil, elderly men and women living in urban areas do not receive the same benefits, and poverty rates among this group are still substantial.[33]

The impact of structural reforms on adequacy is somewhat mixed and will almost certainly vary across countries. In countries where pensions were high and unsustainable before the reforms, generosity has been reduced. Simulations of likely outcomes show that the combined effects of parametric reforms and the shift to funded accounts have been very different, depending on the age cohort, income level, and even the gender of the individual.[34] The complexities involved in conducting credible simulations are daunting, and the results are sensitive to assumptions regarding what would have occurred if reforms had not taken place as well as assumptions regarding the (risk-adjusted) returns expected from investment of workers' savings in the coming decades, taking into account the level of administrative fees, which reduce the worker's effective rate of return.

Given current low rates of worker participation and short contribution histories, even among formal sector workers affiliated with national pension systems, in the medium and long run government resources will be devoted primarily to providing minimum pension guarantees to prevent poverty in old age. This outcome, however, should be considered in the context of the likely result without reform: government would have financed the growing deficits of pay-as-you-go programs, which tended to benefit workers at the higher end of the income distribution. After the initial transition period—the length of which can vary widely from 20 to 40 years—all of the reformed systems are expected to generate savings relative to the prereform systems (see Zviniene and Packard 2003), potentially freeing up resources for other types of social expenditures to meet the objective of adequacy, including pensions for the noncovered elderly. During the transition, however, the savings impact depends crucially on how the remaining liabilities of the prereform systems are financed, a point taken up in greater depth in the sections that follow.

AFFORDABILITY

Affordability is defined as being within the financing capacity of individuals and the government. Again, the countries in Latin America that have undertaken structural reforms cover the spectrum of potential results. The Dominican Republic and Peru have a relatively low contribution rate for pensions, while Argentina and Uruguay have a relatively high contribution rate. One expects that, on average, countries need a wage contribution rate of about 15 percent to fund pensions in the long run, although actual financing rates are both above and below this level. Contribution rates are based largely on historical experience, with the demographically "older" countries imposing higher contribution rates and the "younger" countries imposing lower rates.

Reforms lowered contribution rates in some cases and raised them in others. Tables 7.1 and 7.2 show the change in total payroll taxes (not just the change in the payroll taxes for pensions). Since social security reforms were frequently comprehensive, covering changes in health, unemployment insurance, housing, and other benefits, the increases shown refer to all of the changes, not just those in pensions.

Turning to affordability from the government's perspective, structural reforms in the region have frequently introduced or retained some type of minimum pension guarantee (again, the exception is Peru). In a few countries, such as Colombia, Dominican Republic, and Nicaragua, the minimum pension guarantees are quite large relative to the expected average pension and are likely to involve significant government financing in addition to payroll taxes. However, even in countries, such as Chile, where the contributory minimum guaranteed pension is set at a modest level, relative to the minimum or average covered wages or to the average pension, public spending on minimum benefits is likely to be substantial given the low rates of participation. Finally, the additional future cost of noncontributory benefits to cover the risk of old-age poverty among the majority of workers who will not be eligible for minimum benefit guarantees must also be considered in assessing affordability.

Sustainability is defined as the financial soundness of the pension system, both in the short run and over the long term. It is with regard to sustainability that the reforms have achieved the greatest gains. The reformed pension systems are based on a far more sustainable social contract than that which obtained prior to reforms; the consumption-smoothing goal of national pension systems is "individualized" among a large set of social security institutions (in some countries more than in others). The reformed systems rest largely on savings plans in individual retirement accounts where benefits are based on workers' contributions. The costs of financing the increases in life expectancy are, therefore, passed on to each generation rather than pooled in a discretionary way, as was the case under single-pillar, pay-as-you-go, defined-benefit plans.

As documented in Zviniene and Packard (2003), after initially raising deficits, the reforms are expected to lower deficits dramatically over the long run. Simulations show that in Bolivia, the deficit projected for 2050 will fall from 8.5 percent of GDP without reform to 0.9 percent with reform. In Mexico, the deficit will fall from 2.3 percent of GDP without reform to 0.6 percent with reform. Similarly, the implicit pension debt in Peru in 2050 will fall from 118 percent of GDP without reform to only 15 percent with reform. In the case of El Salvador and Chile, the long-run implicit pension debt is expected to be zero instead of 148 and 210 percent of GDP, respectively.[35]

Despite the somewhat rosy picture of fiscal sustainability, there are several areas of concern. In the short run, governments' pension cash deficits are likely to rise, as individuals divert their contributions to private pension accounts and away from public systems still paying benefits to current pensioners. This is an expected outcome of structural reforms, but one that governments in the region have had a mixed track record of managing effectively. A critical factor in Chile's success with structural reforms was the long period of fiscal preparation prior to implementation of individual accounts in 1981. Some countries, such as El Salvador, Mexico, and Uruguay, have chosen to finance the bulk of their transition costs from single-pillar to multipillar arrangements by issuing public debt. Much of this public debt is then held by the new private pension funds.

The rise in explicit government debt could outweigh savings in the implicit pension debt. Furthermore, during the transition period, higher deficits can make fiscal management exceedingly difficult.[36] Indeed, for countries that embark on structural reforms from a weak fiscal position, the transition costs can severely constrain governments. This has become a critical fiscal issue in Argentina and Bolivia and bodes against undertaking reforms without careful consideration of short- and middle-term fiscal implications, as the transition can last as long as 20 or 40 years.

ROBUSTNESS

Robustness refers to the capacity of the retirement security system to with-stand major shocks. A core objective of multipillar structural reforms is to diversify the risks—demographic, macroeconomic, political, financial—to retirement income. In the multipillar model, some portion or the majority of pensions is financed from the private investment of individual savings and, in theory, is less prone to government manipulation, while the public system provides at least a minimum pension guarantee and perhaps some part of the pension in addition.

In the longer-running reformed systems, such as that in Chile, there has been reasonable diversification. Mexico appears to be gradually following suit. However, the experience of Argentina in 2001 and 2002 shows that when the government becomes truly desperate in a financial crisis and the economy becomes virtually dysfunctional, no system of financing pensions is robust, whether public nor private. Indeed, a situation in which the portfolios of private pension funds are highly concentrated in government debt can re-create the conditions for government intervention that existed prior to structural reforms. The countries that have chosen to finance the transition costs by issuing government bonds to be held by pension funds are not really diversifying the risks to pension income and thus are forgoing one of the core benefits of the multipillar approach. In these countries, workers' pensions still depend on the solvency of the government, both to provide the explicit public guaranteed minimum and to service the debt that builds the privately financed portion of retirement benefits.

Another important matter that is still being debated is the extent to which the reforms generate growth through net additions to savings and through greater efficiency of labor and capital markets. By removing capital and labor distortions and improving the economic environment for growth, reforms are expected to have a positive impact on robustness and sustainability of the pension system. With regard to financial benefits, reforms have led to rapid growth of a new form of saving in the region.[37] Although it is not obvious how much of this growth in pension fund assets has taken place at the expense of other institutional investors, such as mutual funds, there should be little doubt that the importance placed on mandatory individual savings has encouraged financial sector development. However, with respect to the expected link between savings and growth, as noted by Corbo and Schmidt-Hebbel (2003), the increased growth effects arise largely from the choice of financing of the transition, with tax-financed transitions providing more impetus to growth than debt-financed transitions.

Challenges and Prospects

The first set of challenges is posed by the very structure of the reformed pension systems. Several countries in the region that adopted the multipillar model maintain large defined-benefit, pay-as-you-go programs that offer earnings-related pensions.[38] These earnings-related, defined-benefit systems will become increasingly costly to finance as life expectancy increases, unless policy makers are able to raise the retirement age or introduce longevity factors into the benefit formulas of these plans.

The second set of challenges arises from the performance of the new private components of the multipillar systems. Policy risk remains present in the private funded systems, as demonstrated by the Argentine experience. Reforms have also created complex and sophisticated new private pension systems that require strong regulation and challenge the ability of government to withstand industry pressures. Administrative costs are high, although they have generally declined from initial levels, and significantly reduce the workers' benefits from the new system. Risk management considerations are also a cause for concern in Latin America's new private pension systems, as international diversification of pension fund portfolios is often heavily constrained or even prohibited.

Finally, and perhaps most important, in many of the countries where pension systems have undergone structural reforms, coverage has stagnated at low levels and has become the single most important concern of policy makers in this area. A large portion of affiliates may not qualify for the minimum pension guarantee, and together with those who are not affiliated with any system, can only expect to receive rationed social assistance benefits in old age. Hence, the real challenge for policy makers who want to cover the risk of poverty in old age will be in establishing sustainable noncontributory, minimum-benefit programs.

Central and Eastern Europe and Central Asia

During the early transition period (1990–5), all of the countries of Europe and Central Asia had to react to pressures arising from a shrinking base of contributions and a growing population of beneficiaries, both of which were the result of contractions in economic activity.[39] In many countries, growing noncompliance exacerbated the fiscal and policy challenges. Such was the depth of the economic shocks in all countries that the ongoing pay-as-you-go mono pillar had to be changed to some degree, with some of the burden of adjustment borne by retirees and older workers. All countries had to modify indexing rules for some period to control costs, usually away from a preexisting norm of adjusting benefits in pay status according to nominal wage growth and toward price indexing (or, more radically, toward what the available resources would allow, even if this was less than price growth).

The other key variable was the retirement age, which initially was low and in some cases declined even further in the early 1990s. A few countries, such as the Czech Republic and Lithuania, were able to raise the effective retirement age gradually. In some others, like Georgia, where the retirement age was raised precipitously to 65 for both men and women, the pace was much faster. In the late 1990s and early 2000s, most of the countries managed to start increasing the retirement age and reducing early-retirement privileges.

In the 1990s some countries changed benefit formulas, including increasing the reference period on which benefits are based, in order both to lower future promises and to introduce more horizontal equity. To begin reforming the pension system, some countries embarked on an expansion of voluntary private pension alternatives (typically with favorable tax treatment, as in Slovenia, or through matching payments from the national budget, as in the Czech Republic). These voluntary schemes were designed to allow and encourage households to achieve more consumption smoothing than can now be provided in the public pension schemes and to diversify the risks in their retirement portfolio.

Despite a common heritage, two groups have emerged within the Europe and Central Asia region (for a detailed description of both groups, see Lindeman, Rutkowski, and Sluchynskyy 2001). Some countries in the region, especially those in Central Asia and the Caucasus, had to compromise the consumption-smoothing objective in light of insufficient resources; maintaining a minimally adequate income floor became the overriding objective. Therefore, as of early 2000, Albania, Azerbaijan, Armenia, Georgia, and Tajikistan, among others, effectively had systems in which there was little or small differentiation among recipients according to earnings or years worked. In Georgia, this happened as the result of legislation; more typically, it occurred as the result of a convergence between minimum pension floors and maximum pension ceilings.

The other group of countries, facing the prospects of a worsening dependency ratio, adopted a multipillar benchmark (for an overview of the movement toward multipillar systems in transition economies, see Rutkowski 1998, 2002; von Gersdorff and Rutkowski 2004). They shifted a portion of the mandatory contribution from the public pension system to private institutions that establish individual defined-contribution accounts for each worker. An individual's eventual pension portfolio will consist of a benefit from a downsized public pension scheme (mostly pay-as-you-go, financed) plus a benefit purchased with accumulated funds from the second pillar. The reforms were similar to those in Latin America but generally were less radical in their scope.

In 10 countries in Central and Eastern Europe, reforms already have resulted in the introduction of second pillars. In Hungary, legislation passed in 1997 was implemented in 1998. All entrants to the labor market were required to join the reformed system, with others given the option to switch. By 1999, 2.1 million workers—about half of the workforce (mostly under age 40)—had diverted part of their pension contributions (6 percent of payroll) to private pension fund managers (for a detailed description, see Palacios and Rocha 1998). In 1999, workers in Poland between the ages of 30 and 50 were given the choice of diverting one-fifth of their overall pension contribution (7.2 percent of payroll) to newly licensed pension funds and their managers (for a detailed description, see Chlon, Góra, and Rutkowski 1999; Góra and Rutkowski 1998). Workers under 30 years of age automatically joined the new scheme. More than 8 million people are now covered by the new multipillar pension system in Poland.

In Latvia, a smaller funded pillar (2 percent of payroll) was introduced in July 2001 (with a plan to increase the contribution rate to 9 percent of payroll eventually). In Bulgaria, a 2 percent mandatory second pillar started operating in January 2002 (with a plan to increase the contributions to 5 percent of payroll), building on voluntary pension funds and funds that manage resources built in the process of financing early-retirement sector privileges (previously unfunded). Also in 2002, a 5 percent mandatory funded pillar was established in Croatia (January) and a 6 percent pillar in Estonia (July). In January 2002 Russia began to accumulate funds for the second pillar; however, the funds are still controlled by the public pay-as-you-go pension fund, which has entrusted another public agency with investment of the funds. Two countries—Kazakhstan and Kosovo—have introduced a shift to a large funded pillar (in Kazakhstan, managed by competing pension funds, while in Kosovo, managed by international asset managers) and have moved the public pillar to a basic one of using means testing to cope with the risks of poverty in old age or disability. In January 2003 the Ukraine legislated a 2 percent second pillar (to grow to 7 percent) that will be implemented once the macroeconomic conditions are in place. A year later, in January 2004, Lithuania introduced a 2.5 percent second pillar that is already in operation. Slovakia passed all the legislation to start a sizable 9 percent second pillar that will begin operating in January 2005. In FYR Macedonia, a second pillar funded with a contribution of 7 percent of earnings has been legislated and implementation is being prepared, and in Romania, adoption of the second pillar with a contribution of 8 percent of earnings has been decided in principle and needs to be legislated again (a previous law was derogated). Overall, leaving aside Central Asia and the Caucasus, the Czech Republic, Moldova, Slovenia, and Turkey are the only countries not actively pursuing work on the second pillar. However, the Czech Republic and Slovenia have established voluntary third pillars with fairly broad participation, and Turkey introduced a new third pillar in 2003 that appears to be expanding rapidly.

While there was a general trend toward a multipillar structure in the region, the accompanying changes in the first pillar differed significantly. Some countries, such as Bulgaria, Croatia, Estonia, Hungary, and Slovakia, have sought to improve the microeconomic aspects of their pension systems by improving the traditional defined-benefit formulas (including point systems in some cases). Another, more fundamental, approach has been to recharacterize the ongoing pay-as-you-go promise in terms of what occurs in a funded, defined-contribution account by introducing a notional defined-contribution model. Latvia and Poland followed the notional defined-contribution or notional account approach, including a funded, defined-contribution component as part of the reforms. It is now part of Russia's reform package. In addition, the notional account approach is gaining interest among Commonwealth of Independent States countries that are not yet in a position to consider adopting a multipillar system. The Kyrgyz Republic introduced a notional account formula with respect to new accruals, and Moldova has the legislated objective to move toward use of a notional account formula in the future.

Table 7.3 compares some of the key parameters of the reforms in countries that introduced or fully legislated the introduction of the multipillar system. It is too early to make a full assessment of multipillar systems in Europe and Central Asia. The movement clearly is widespread, and, when given a choice, workers elect to take part in a funded pillar. The initial rates of return in the funds are encouraging and are a good starting point to achieve the relevant lifetime rate of return that will achieve the intended benefit target levels.

This trend toward substantial reforms in Central and Eastern Europe may well be explained by the countries' willingness to pursue the benefits of a funded pillar, their expectation of increased savings and growth, and, after a profound ideological crisis, their willingness to emphasize personal accountability and private savings. Although there is not yet sufficient analysis, the depth of the financial sector appears to have deepened, and this could, in part, be attributable to the growth of pension funds, which are large institutional investors.

Reform Issues

Introduction of a multipillar pension system with a mandatory funded component in Europe and Central Asia has posed complex challenges, including the need for financial market development and the establishment of administrative and supervisory capacities. In addition, countries must have a feasible fiscal strategy to deal with the financing requirements of the transition to the new pension system. The transition typically imposes initial welfare losses on some parts of the population; countries may not be prepared to assume such losses because of limits on how much of the shift to funding can be financed by debt to enable those losses to be offset over time through broader economic gains. The World Bank was active in articulating those challenges and assisting European and Central Asian countries in making individual choices that vary significantly by country (Rutkowski 2004).

Table 7.3. Characteristics of Pension Reforms Moving to a Multipillar System in Transition Economies in Europe and Central Asia, as of April 2004

Country and status of system	Starting date	First pillar	Size of second pillar as a percent of payroll	Projected pension fund assets in 2020 as a percent of GDP	Share of workforce in funded pillar in 2003	Switching strategy to new system by age of employee
Hungary, operating	January 1998	Pay-as-you-go defined benefit	6	31	45	Mandatory for new entrants; voluntary for others
Kazakhstan, operating	January 1998	Guaranteed minimum	10	30	100	Mandatory
Poland, operating	January 1999	Notional defined contribution[a]	7.2	33	70	Mandatory for < 30; voluntary for 30–50
Latvia, operating	July 2001 (notional defined contribution, January 1996)	Notional defined contribution	2, growing to 9	20	72	Mandatory for < 30; voluntary for 30–50
Croatia, operating	January 2002	Pay-as-you-go defined benefit	5	25–30	60–70	Mandatory for < 40; voluntary for 40–50
Bulgaria, operating	January 2002	Pay-as-you-go defined benefit	2, growing to 5	—	—	Mandatory for < 42

Slovakia, legislated	January 2005	Pay-as-you-go defined benefit	9	—	—	Mandatory for new entrants
Estonia, operating	July 2002	Pay-as-you-go defined benefit	6	20	60	Voluntary (opt-out + 2 percent)
Lithuania, operating	January 2004	Pay-as-you-go defined benefit	2.5	—	—	Voluntary
Romania, partially legislated then questioned	January 2003	Pay-as-you-go defined benefit	8	30	—	Mandatory for > 20 years from retirement
Macedonia, legislated	January 2005	Pay-as-you-go defined benefit	7	26	—	Mandatory for new entrants
Russia, partially legislated and operating	January 2002	Notional defined contribution	2 (< 35) to 6 (36–50)	—	—	Mandatory for < 50
Ukraine, partially legislated	January 2003	Pay-as-you-go defined benefit	2, growing to 7	—	—	Mandatory for new entrants
Kosovo, partially legislated and operating	January 2002	Minimum	10	—	—	Mandatory

Sources: Diverse World Bank documents and Pension Reform Database.

— Not available.

a. A notional defined-contribution system has the same features as a typical defined-contribution system but is not funded.

Reform efforts in the region have experienced a range of problems with implementation. In Poland, the administrative apparatus of the social security institution was unable to deal with a timely transfer of contributions to private pension funds, and a debt (now being cleared) to the funds was accumulated. In Hungary, the government reversed the decision to increase the size of the funded pillar and allowed the participants to move back to the pay-as-you-go system, creating uncertainty as to the fiscal liability of government and undermining credibility of the new system. Dividing contributions among several pension funds also proved difficult and costly to small employers in Hungary (where, in contrast to Poland, the social security institution is not involved). Regulatory institutions were inexperienced with the requirements for the transfer of individual contributions to the funds and in some cases introduced unnecessarily burdensome requirements on the funds. Most of the countries are increasingly concerned about the administrative costs of the second pillar (Murthi 2003) and are analyzing measures that could generate competition in the fees of the system to reduce these costs. Some countries (for example, Latvia) are concerned about the impact of the minimum pension guarantee, which reduces the incentives for individuals to contribute to a notional defined-contribution or funded pillar and could result in a substantial fiscal burden. Old pension systems (still operating, as reforms have a long phase-in period) continue to constitute a serious fiscal burden, especially with the reversal of pay-as-you-go policy reform, as in Croatia (where indexation was being moved back from prices to wages and additional pension "supplements" were introduced). These clearly constitute an even greater burden in countries, such as the Czech Republic and Slovenia, that have not adopted the multipillar approach.

In light of these difficulties, there is some increase in the skepticism toward the new systems. Administrative costs are high, current pensions have fallen as a part of fiscal adjustment, and the full benefits of the new system are not yet evident. Although rates of return are higher than those of other types of investment funds, or other reasonable benchmarks, it is doubtful whether these high returns can be sustained, as fiscal adjustment lowers the spreads on government debt, and foreign investments are heavily limited (except for Kazakhstan, Kosovo, and Russia). A greater diversification of domestic private and foreign assets is needed. European and Central Asian governments are not yet willing to allow this, although countries like Slovakia are legislating that a minimum as low as 30 percent of assets be domiciled in the country. Falling returns and high administrative costs risk becoming a serious concern for the level of future pensions. In addition, Maastricht criteria, binding for EU accession countries, count explicit debt, but not the reduction in the implicit pension debt, which means that reforms adversely affect countries' position vis-à-vis the criteria.

Overall Assessment of Reform

Although many of these reforms are even more recent than the Latin American ones, making it too early to judge their full impact, the reforms appear to have made positive progress, as measured by increased adequacy, affordability, sustainability, and robustness. However, a large agenda of outstanding first-pillar reforms is required to address the fiscal issues reemerging in many countries.

ADEQUACY

In the majority of cases, particularly in the Central European countries, the pensions provided are adequate to prevent old-age poverty. While the benefits relative to contributions paid are still generous and potentially unaffordable in many cases, in the face of rapidly expanding wage growth, they can appear inadequate. However, in many of the Central Asian countries, the benefits have not kept up with inflation and are basically flat payments, which may not be sufficient to prevent poverty. Attempts to link contributions with benefits in conjunction with fundamental change in labor markets have left some individuals in all countries with inadequate pensions and relying on social safety nets, which are not always sufficient to fulfill the new role to which they have been assigned. Further adjustments to the first pillar, such as increases in retirement age, will be required to provide adequate pensions in the reformed systems. For example, to provide a replacement rate of 40 percent in Poland, the retirement age needs to be 65 years or replacement rates will fall to 30 percent for women.

A key additional step in the reform process will be further specification of the payout phase for the funded part of the pension system. A wide array of options is being considered, but many countries, like Poland, Russia, and Slovakia, among others, have not completed this part of the design. In the end, the best-designed accumulation phase will not deliver adequate pensions if the rules for payout of benefits are not effectively structured to protect beneficiaries from high costs. Another outstanding issue is the reform of disability and survivorship insurance. In most cases, the beneficiaries of the system remain insured in the first pillar, and, in the case of a contingency, their saved funds revert to the provider of the benefit: the public pay-as-you-go pension fund. Some experiences in Latin America could be used, but the European countries have a much higher level of expenditures for disability pensions, and this could impair the fiscal viability of using the experiences of Latin America.

In terms of coverage, most of the elderly in this region are receiving some type of pension, although in all countries there are pockets of elderly who, for one reason or another, are not receiving any benefits. The concern with regards to coverage, however, is primarily for the future. Contributors as a percentage of the labor force vary from a low of 32 percent in Albania to a high of 97 percent in Belarus. While extreme, the example of Albania, where coverage fell from 81 percent in 1991 to 32 percent in 1995, is indicative of what has happened in all of the countries where the transition to a market economy has resulted in informalization of the labor force as well as higher unemployment. Countries with lower degrees of transition, like Belarus, have maintained high coverage rates. A few countries, such as the Czech Republic and Slovenia, have maintained high coverage rates during the transition to a market economy. The challenge in all of these countries is to provide an adequate safety net for those who cannot contribute, while linking the contributions tightly to benefits, as most of the reforms have done.

AFFORDABILITY

Contribution rates in most of these countries are extremely high relative to those in other countries in the world, ranging from 20 to 45 percent of wages (only for the mandated pension system). While some of the reforms have envisaged a future decline in contribution rates to improve the competitiveness of the economy and make local labor competitive, the necessity of financing the transition to a multipillar system and fiscal constraints have precluded immediate reductions in the contribution rate. Russia carried out some reductions and is now facing a deficit in 2005 that will require new sources of funds and could lead to some reversals in the reform. In countries that expected to reduce their contribution rates, the rapidly growing wage rates have led to strong political pressures for higher indexation of the existing pensions of an already large retired population in lieu of lower contribution rates. However, the lower wage rates in Central and Eastern Europe more than compensate for the negative impact that higher contribution rates have on competitiveness. As wage rates continue to rise, the higher contribution rates will begin to affect relative labor costs to the extent that they will not be competitive with other countries, and at that point, a sharper tradeoff will appear between continuing to raise pensions and lowering contribution rates.

SUSTAINABILITY

Sustainability has improved in all of the countries that have implemented substantial reforms to the pay-as-you-go systems. This has been achieved by raising the retirement age, changing benefit formulas, and changing indexation as well as by introducing the structure of notional accounts. However, the Central European countries face both a rapidly aging population and a very low fertility rate. Many of the countries will have to address unresolved or new fiscal issues in a second round of reforms to the first pillar. Further parametric reforms may be needed in almost all cases, particularly the need to adjust retirement ages as life expectancy increases.

ROBUSTNESS

By introducing a funded pillar, the reforms have attempted to increase the robustness of old-age support. Particularly with an aging population and low fertility, the pay-as-you-go systems are unable to support significant pensions. The developing financial markets are more likely to provide rates of return that are higher than the rate of growth in the wage base. This has not always been the case, as in countries with resource-based economic booms, like Kazakhstan. However, in order to take advantage of this potential, countries have to allow more diversification in the investment of these assets.

South Asia

With the exception of Sri Lanka, where fertility rates are currently below replacement level, South Asia is still at the beginning of its demographic transition.[40] The schemes that cover private sector workers are either provident funds (Nepal, Sri Lanka) or immature defined-benefit schemes with a high ratio of workers to pensioners (India, Pakistan). These schemes continue to experience positive cash flows and are a convenient form of government financing through their purchase of government bonds. These state monopolies are not without problems, including poor service to members and manipulated rates of return. Also, the newer defined-benefit schemes have amassed dangerous long-term liabilities. The long-term sustainability of these programs in their current form is in question, but none of these programs appears to face financial collapse in the next few years.

In contrast, the pension schemes covering public sector workers have always been financed directly from the budget. With the exception of Bhutan, the entire region maintained the inherited British noncontributory defined-benefit schemes that were completely unfunded. As these schemes began to mature, the magnitude of the hidden pension debt became increasingly obvious. Along with wages and interest payments, pension spending threatened to tie the hands of policy makers facing real budget constraints. While pension reform was probably justified for other reasons, pensions are now becoming a priority in several countries because the growth of spending on civil service pensions has become a fiscal threat. Although the schemes share a common colonial ancestor, they have evolved differently over the past 50 years. Accordingly, the extent of the problem varies across countries and even among states (India) and provinces (Pakistan) that have their own schemes.

Coverage of formal pension schemes that seek to smooth consumption is about one-third of the labor force in the Maldives and Sri Lanka and less than one-fifth in the rest of the region. This is partly the result of the large fraction of the labor force working in agriculture and partly the result of the size of the urban informal sector. In Afghanistan, Bangladesh, and Bhutan, there is no mandatory retirement-savings scheme for the private sector.

It is unlikely that current attempts to increase coverage will succeed among the poorer parts of the population due to various factors, including the most obvious one, namely, the inability of the poorest to save for old age. At the same time, several governments already sponsor noncontributory pension programs directed at the elderly poor. In India means-tested schemes administered by states and supplemented with federal funds reach 1 out of every 10 elderly Indians. Bangladesh has a similar scheme, and in Sri Lanka the massive social assistance programs sponsored by the state reach many households with elderly members. In Nepal, an innovative demogrant program is designed to provide a pension to all Nepali citizens age 75 and older. The Maldives is considering introducing its own demogrant system.

The potential for these programs to mitigate poverty among the elderly is limited, however. Administrative complexity and the potential for corruption can divert funds from deserving beneficiaries in means-tested programs, and there is evidence that this is often the case. While simpler to administer, even the demogrant program may not reach some of the poorest elderly (Palacios and Rajan 2004). Most important, however, budget allocations for these programs (just as for other areas of social assistance) are unreliable and relatively small.

Policy makers have expressed concern about low coverage as well as a desire to improve the way long-term savings generated in the provident funds and young defined-benefit schemes are channeled to the financial sector. Progress in both areas has been slow, however. Extension of formal coverage to the "unorganized sector," as it is known, has been attempted in Sri Lanka with very limited results and, most recently, in India, where two parallel experiments are under way along with an Asian Development Bank technical assistance project.

Regarding investment policy, the Employee Pension Fund Office in India has undertaken a review of asset allocation, which historically has been concentrated in government-backed securities. With the exception of Bhutan and to some extent Nepal, however, the vast majority of public pension reserves in the region is invested in government bonds. Bhutan is the only country with significant foreign investment, although concerns with its own capacity to manage reserves led to a request for an Investment Development Fund grant supported by the World Bank. Institutional capacity and governance in these institutions are a key area where improvements are needed.

The most important reforms in the region are driven by the fiscal burden of civil service pensions (Palacios 2004). The most ambitious effort to date is the systemic reform in India. State and federal outlays on pensions now consume around 15 percent of tax revenues after doubling over the course of the 1990s.

From January 1, 2004, all new federal government hires contribute 10 percent of their salary to a defined-contribution scheme, with a matching contribution from the government as employer. The mandate applies only to new entrants, but the possibility that those already covered by the old defined-benefit scheme may be given the choice to switch is being discussed. Several state governments, including Andra Pradesh, Karnataka, and Tamil Nadu, have announced that they intend to join the new scheme, and other states seem likely to follow. Regardless of the speed of the transition, the Indian reform represents a fundamental policy shift in the long run, with a noncontributory, unfunded defined-benefit scheme being replaced by a fully funded defined-contribution scheme. While many details of the design have yet to be spelled out (for example, the process for selecting asset managers and the central record keeper, structure of charges, and so forth), the reform stands out because it does not retain an unfunded defined-benefit scheme in the long run.

Meanwhile, Sri Lanka has thus far opted for a gradual parametric reform that went into effect in 2003 and included adjustments to contributions and benefits. A contribution of 8 percent for employees and 12 percent for the government as employer was required from all new entrants to the civil service. The benefit formula was changed such that a 70 percent replacement rate would be generated after 32 years of service. In other words, the accrual rate was reduced from 3 to 2.1875. The lump-sum payment of 24 months remained, as did other key parameters, including the earnings base and the lack of automatic indexation.

In addition to these important initiatives, task forces have been set up in Afghanistan, the Maldives, Nepal, and Pakistan and are considering reform options as of September 2004.[41] In the Maldives and Pakistan, reforms are being considered in the context of the periodic process of adjusting civil servants' remuneration. Bhutan is seeking to improve its institutional capacity, especially with regard to investment policy. More reforms are likely in the next few years.

Although formal pension schemes cover a relatively small fraction of the population in South Asia at present, they are an important source of social protection for millions in the region and will undoubtedly expand in the coming decades. This would be sufficient reason for reforms that ensure long-term sustainability and improve the "deal" for those contributing. Perhaps the major reason for concern about these schemes, however, is their disproportionate impact on the rest of the economy and the uncovered population. This impact takes place through the direct fiscal impact of schemes for civil servants, indirect subsidies to formal sector workers, and even the opportunity cost of efficiently using this important source of long-term savings. Finally, improvements in the administration and financing of existing noncontributory schemes could contribute to reducing poverty among the elderly long before mandated savings schemes can reach the majority of South Asians.

Sub-Saharan Africa

This section presents stylized facts about the region's pension policy.[42] It also highlights key issues for pension policy and reviews early reform experience.

Pension reform has only recently found its way onto the agenda in Sub-Saharan Africa. Current policy around the region reflects a colonial legacy of defined-benefit schemes and provident funds and, in a few countries, the significant presence of private pension funds organized along occupational lines. Generally, coverage is limited to less than one-fifth of the labor force, with the rest of the population relying on its own resources and informal old-age support. Noncontributory schemes, financed by general revenues that reach most of the elderly, including the poor, are found only in Southern Africa (Botswana, Mauritius, Namibia, and South Africa).

With the exception of occupational schemes in Namibia, South Africa, and to a lesser extent Kenya, pension promises in the region are largely unfunded. This is clearly the case for the civil service schemes but is also true for the partially funded defined-benefit schemes that cover the relatively small proportion of the private sector labor force that participates in the formal sector.

The defined-benefit schemes covering private sector workers have run surpluses during the postindependence era. Poor investment and unrealistic parameters have forced countries to increase contribution rates over time. In Francophone Africa, these funds are managed by tripartite boards with representatives from unions, government, and employers. These institutions belong to the Conférence Interafricaine de la Prévoyance Sociale, a regional organization that is supposed to set standards for administration and investment policy and serve as a policy forum. Based in Lomé, Togo, and with a small operating budget, it has limited influence over the national schemes in the 14 member countries.[43]

A few Anglophone countries have retained the provident fund model that was inherited from British rule. Although similar to defined-contribution schemes in principle, the tendency to use administered returns that do not reflect the market value of the assets of the institutions has led to the appearance of liabilities.

Both the more common partially funded defined schemes and the provident funds have had perennial problems in two important areas: administration and investment of reserves. Administrative costs are higher in Africa than in any other region and can consume more than one-third of contribution revenues in some cases. Even relatively low-cost countries spend around 10 percent of revenues, a figure that is 10 times higher than European countries of similar size. Partly, this has to do with limited coverage, which reduces the base and prevents economies of scale. It is also related to overstaffing and inefficiency, however, and the poor quality of service to the client is a common complaint. Costs of this magnitude make it difficult to provide a reasonable rate of return regardless of the type of scheme or form of financing.

Investment performance has also compromised attempts to prefund pension obligations and to avoid the need to raise contribution rates. This has been due sometimes to direct political interference in investment policy, but just as often to the fact that the mechanisms to channel long-term savings efficiently in the domestic economy are largely absent in most countries. In Francophone Africa, the CFA franc devaluation crisis of the mid-1990s even wiped out bank deposits in countries like Cameroon and Senegal. Returns documented in Kenya, Tanzania, Zambia, and other countries have been negative in real terms over large periods of time. For provident fund members, the impact has translated directly into paltry balances at retirement.

Although the problems of the schemes that cover private sector workers have become increasingly evident, the motivation for reform has come more frequently from the fiscal pressures of civil service pensions. This phenomenon is not exclusive to Africa, but in this region it reflects a widespread pattern of government expansion over several decades following independence and a subsequent stabilization or even contraction. The cohorts hired during the expansionary period are retiring with full benefits, and the formula used to calculate the pension for civil servants tends to be more generous than for private sector workers. The impact of a more generous formula and a more mature system along with a lack of reserves results in the crowding out of other important expenditures. In some countries, spending on the pensions of civil servants doubled during the 1990s.

In several countries, the need to address this short-term fiscal issue has led policy makers to reconsider overall pension policy. In particular, the alternatives to the current arrangements for civil servants include a new system that replaces the dualism with one in which all formal sector workers participate. Motivations include the desire to increase labor mobility, impose fiscal discipline, and address inequities that arise when parallel schemes are used. In several smaller countries, there may also be advantages, as economies of scale might reduce high administrative costs.

A fourth area of concern is the stagnant level of coverage of the formal sector schemes in the region. Rationalizing existing schemes (for example, lowering administrative costs, providing more stable benefits, and improving fund management) may encourage participation, but the determinants of formal sector participation go beyond the pension system.

Based on international patterns of income and coverage, it appears that contributory schemes will not cover the majority of the labor force in the coming few decades. The extent of the old-age security problem depends on the viability of informal arrangements, mostly family support. Yet neither this support nor the evolving status of the elderly in Africa has been the subject of much study, and little is known. In some countries, particularly those stricken by the HIV/AIDS epidemic, the problem appears to be more acute. A possible policy response is the introduction of noncontributory pensions. This approach, however, requires fiscal resources to be diverted from other areas and is complicated by the fact that most elderly live in multigenerational households, making it more difficult to ascertain need. Moreover, early research suggests heterogeneity with regard to the poverty among households with elderly members (Kakwani and Subbarao 2005).

Most of the reform initiatives under way in the region retain the existing structure of the pension system. We are aware of only one country—Nigeria—where a systemic reform has been seriously proposed. However, parametric reforms are under way in a handful of countries (such as Kenya, Senegal, and Uganda). These involve changes to the benefit formula of schemes covering civil servants, private sector workers, or both. Another area of reform within the existing structure is the management of pension reserves. Here again, a few efforts are under way to increase transparency and professionalism, but little progress has been made to date. Meanwhile, proposals to integrate civil servants and private sector workers into the same scheme are rare and face political difficulty. In Zambia, for example, new civil servants have been contributing to the scheme covering private sector workers since 2000. Ghana unified its schemes decades ago, but civil servants have recently lobbied to reverse the integration and reintroduce a separate scheme.

The challenges of systemic reform, where there is a shift from unfunded to funded schemes and possibly the introduction of private management of assets, are particularly great in Sub-Saharan Africa. Reformers face three major obstacles: first and foremost, any diversion of contributions to a new funded scheme will force governments to find resources to cover the resulting gap. Since most of the countries depend heavily on foreign aid to supplement their budgets, there is little scope for financing the transition, at least not a rapid transition. Second, existing public pension institutions are generally not equipped to meet the record-keeping requirements of a funded individual accounts scheme. Finally, few of the conditions that make a privately managed, funded system viable—investment opportunities, solid regulatory institutions, and potential participants in the private pension sector—are present in most of the region.

There is, however, growing awareness of the need for pension reform in Africa. In 2003, for example, nine countries established the Africa Pension

Forum with the intention of serving as a catalyst for reform in the region. A partnership between the World Bank Institute and the Kenyan Retirement Benefit Authority was recently established as that country seeks to improve supervision of its large private pension market (exceptional in the region). Requests to the World Bank for assistance in this area have increased in the last few years, and at least half a dozen operations are under way with significant pension components. None of them involves systemic reforms, including the introduction of a second funded pillar.

Middle East and North Africa

All countries in the region have put in place defined-benefit pension systems essentially financed on a pay-as-you-go basis.[44] Only a few countries—Egypt, Iran, and Libya—have developed noncontributory pension schemes. In most cases, there is more than one mandatory scheme, albeit sometimes managed by a single fund. In countries like Egypt, Morocco, and Tunisia the fragmentation is considerable and severely constrains the mobility of the labor force. In Tunisia, for instance, there are separate schemes for civil servants, private sector workers in the industrial and service sectors, two schemes for agricultural sector workers, and a scheme for the self-employed. Countries like Iran and Jordan are also characterized by the proliferation of occupational plans—usually associated with public companies—that act as substitutes, not complements, to the public system.

The coverage of the public pension system varies between 10 and 75 percent of the labor force. This large variation is explained largely by two factors. First, different institutional arrangements exist for pension provision, particularly the extent to which different labor market groups are covered by the mandate. The pension system in Egypt, for example, is able to cover 70 percent of the labor force because a scheme for casual workers enrolls 24 percent of the labor force. Second, the level of employment and its distribution vary between different sectors of the economy. For instance, the highest coverage rate (75 percent) is observed in Libya, where the large majority of the employed population (77 percent) works in the public sector or state-owned enterprises. In contrast, Morocco and Yemen, where more than half of the labor force operates in the agricultural sector, have low coverage rates: 21 and 10 percent, respectively. In the other countries, coverage rates range between 25 and 40 percent of the labor force.

In general, the mandatory schemes have received large mandates regarding income replacement. In the majority of cases, gross replacement rates for the average full-career worker, in the schemes for both public sector and private sector workers, surpass 80 percent of the last salary. In the schemes for private sector workers in Iran and Yemen, gross replacement rates surpass 100 percent of the last salary. Moreover, most schemes do not enforce ceilings on the covered wage and offer generous minimum pensions—in excess of 35 percent of the average wage. This large mandate of the pension system is not affordable and also reduces the incentives for private providers of pensions to participate in the market. In fact, the highest level of activity of private providers of pension products is observed in Egypt and Morocco, where the mandatory pension system has a more modest mandate (gross replacement rates below 60 percent), and Lebanon, where there is no mandatory pension system for private sector workers. In Jordan, in contrast, where there is a similar level of development of the financial sector but where the public pension system still has a large mandate (an 80 percent gross replacement rate for the average full-career worker), the role of private pensions is marginal.

Pension systems in the region are capturing growing shares of the economy, and, despite favorable demographics, their financial sustainability is a cause for concern. Pension expenditures range between 0.5 percent (Yemen) and 5 percent (Tunisia) of GDP, with a median of 3 percent of GDP for the region. In all cases, expenditures are higher than the level that would be expected, given international trends, for the current age structure of the population. While most schemes are still generating operational surpluses, the financial situation is deteriorating rapidly. The main reason is the misalignment among the targeted level of income replacement, the contribution rate, and the retirement ages, which are low across-the-board, particularly for women (55 years in many cases). Hence, accrued-to-date liabilities in all the schemes reviewed already represent between 30 and 100 percent of GDP, well above the current level of financial reserves. [45] All countries in the region are only entering the second stage of the demographic transition, characterized by falling fertility rates. Thus population growth rates remain among the highest in the world, and old-age dependency ratios are well below world averages. But even if this situation were to continue indefinitely, the financial situation of most pension schemes would not be sustainable.

Another challenge facing pension systems in the region is related to inappropriate governance structures and weak institutional capacity to design and implement policies. All schemes are governed by tripartite boards that are not appropriately insulated from political influences and lack proper accountability. Hence, while several of the schemes still own reserves, these are not being managed in the best interest of plan members. Weak institutional capacity also explains the proliferation of complex and ad hoc benefit formulas and eligibility conditions that distort incentives and open the schemes to adverse distributional transfers between and within generations. For instance, in the majority of schemes, there are multiple, often nontransparent, conditions for retirement, only the last few salaries are used to compute pensions, there are no actuarially fair penalties for early retirement, and indexation mechanisms are ad hoc.

Many schemes are still struggling to keep information systems up to date and to implement basic administrative functions, such as the tracking and collection of contributions.

On the positive side, there is growing awareness in the region of the challenges facing the pension system. Today, in all countries, pension reform is part of the agenda of the governments, albeit with different degrees of visibility.[46] There are also important differences in the mechanisms used to engage in the policy dialogue. For instance, in Morocco, policy discussions are taking place with civil society at-large. In Jordan, most of the debate is taking place within the government. Finally, there are marked differences in the reform initiatives.

Jordan has opted to preserve a defined-benefit pension system financed on a pay-as-you-go basis. The reform has focused on the integration and rationalization of this system. Hence, the schemes for civil servants and military personnel have been closed to new entrants, who now join the Social Security Corporation—the scheme for private sector workers. The goals are to review the mandate of the Social Security Corporation to allow middle- and high-income workers to diversify their source of savings for retirement and to bring benefit formulas and eligibility conditions up to the standards. Jordan has also made important progress toward improving management of the reserves. A new, more independent investment unit was created and staffed with professionals in the area of pension fund management through a competitive process. The new investment unit has issued a statement of investment policies that follows internationally accepted principles and practices regarding investments. Djibouti is following a similar strategy.

Morocco, on the contrary, is considering moving to a multipillar system, but without aiming for full integration of the pension system. The country plans to have a dual first pillar (defined benefit), with separate schemes for civil servants and private sector workers, but with more modest mandates. At the same time, it plans to transform the current defined-benefit scheme for contractual workers and state-owned enterprise employees into the core of a second pillar for all workers (a fully funded defined-contribution scheme). The country is exploiting the fact that this scheme is basically already managed as a funded scheme with individual accounts. Morocco is also leading reforms in the banking and insurance sectors.

Lebanon has drafted legislation to replace the end-of-service indemnity program for the private sector with a fully funded defined-contribution system. The goal is to integrate into the new system the schemes for civil servants and the military. Basically, Lebanon is proposing moving to an integrated, funded single-pillar system (West Bank and Gaza is following a similar approach). Because the public sector lacks the expertise necessary to manage a defined-contribution system with individual accounts, the proposal is to outsource various functions, including the management of part of the funds, to the private sector. This is possible in Lebanon because the insurance sector is relatively well developed.

Most of the other countries are still in a diagnosis phase and have yet to develop an integrated multiyear reform program. Several have made efforts to improve administration, and there have been sporadic initiatives to adjust benefit formulas and eligibility conditions, unfortunately, not always with positive results.

East Asia

This section presents stylized facts about the region's pension systems.[47] It captures issues under the status quo and highlights recent directions of reform.

The countries of the East Asia region demonstrate considerable variation in both demographic and economic indicators. At the same time, most of them are experiencing aging populations, lower fertility, rapid urbanization, and low pension coverage. Pension systems in the region fall into three main groups: national provident fund systems, social security–type systems in market economies, and social security–type systems in transition economies. Apart from these national schemes, almost all of the economies in East Asia operate separate pension schemes for public and private sector workers, except for Hong Kong, China, where civil servants hired since 2001 participate in a mandatory provident fund with a top-up arrangement.

With the exception of Hong Kong (China), the provident fund systems in Indonesia, Malaysia, Papua New Guinea, and Singapore operate at the national level under public administration. Provident funds, which operate on the basis of defined contribution, enjoy full funding and, in principle, provide a strong benefit-contribution link, which allows them to avert the financial unsustainability and distortions in pay-as-you-go social insurance schemes. Typically, these centralized provident funds have suffered from low returns, nontransparent investment decisions, management practices that overemphasize social and economic policy objectives, mismatch between short-term assets and long-term liabilities, as well as inadequate benefit levels and low labor force coverage.

Three countries (Philippines, Korea, and Thailand) have relatively immature OECD-style defined-benefit pension schemes. These systems, by and large, were not designed with proper linkage between contributions and benefits. Although these systems are in a strong financial position when measured in cash terms, the high implicit pension debt will manifest itself within the next 15 or 20 years if reform is not undertaken soon. Policy makers in Korea and Thailand have long recognized the problems with the current design and have attempted to reduce the benefit level and increase the contribution rate. However, these measures fall short of reaching a balanced contribution-benefit link. Given the recent stagnant growth and perverse incentive to drop out early (with just 10 years of contributory service), the Philippine system is particularly in need of a strategy that permits better risk management to restore financial sustainability and the ability to withstand shocks, be they economic, demographic, or political.

China, Mongolia, and Vietnam have been undergoing a major transformation from planned to market economies. In these economies, income levels are low, while the informal sector is large. Agriculture accounts for a significant share of the economy and the labor force. As a result, their transition to a market economy is often compounded by the urbanization and industrialization process.

China, Mongolia, and Vietnam all inherited some form of old-age pension system designed primarily for urban public sector employees. They were invariably defined-benefit, pay-as-you-go systems. Contributions were mostly or exclusively the responsibility of the employer (state-owned enterprises). The pension policies were characterized by low statutory and effective retirement age, generous benefits that were not closely linked to the individual's contribution, and limited coverage of the labor force overall. In China, the pension program is highly fragmented, inhibiting labor mobility. Contribution rates, benefit levels, and eligibility requirements vary significantly geographically, across ownership types, and among industries.

Public pension programs have become increasingly unsustainable in both China and Mongolia. Expenditure has risen significantly, partly due to the use of early retirement as a mechanism to deal with redundancies of state-owned enterprises. Meanwhile, contribution collections have been weakened due to the poor performance of state-owned enterprises, rising unemployment, significant informal sector, and lack of effective collection apparatus.

Regardless of the type of pension system and the economy in which it operates, a common reform initiative currently under way in the region is to improve the investment outcome of the reserve funds. There is also a clear trend for reserve funds holding primarily government debt in-house to move toward investing in liquid, market-priced assets as well as toward outsourcing the asset management function to the private sector. However, introducing funded defined-contribution provisions as a means to limit the long-term fiscal problem and to diversify social risk has not been adopted generally, with Thailand being the potential exception. While there is growing awareness of the merits of strengthening governance to insulate managers from political pressures and prevent conflicts of interest, few have taken any steps to move closer to best practice. Nevertheless, a number of countries (China and Thailand) have decided to expand coverage through the introduction of voluntary pension schemes, but mechanisms that facilitate prudential regulation and supervision for such schemes are slow to emerge.

Most of the reform initiatives in the region retain the existing structure of the pension system. Indonesia is the one exception, having introduced a bill to Parliament extending comprehensive social security coverage to all Indonesians. Not much detail is known at this point.

Systemic reforms are under way in a few countries. These involve the shift from an unfunded to a funded scheme for civil servants (Hong Kong, China) and from an unfunded to a partially funded scheme for state-owned enterprise workers in three pilot provinces in China. Mongolia has introduced a notional defined-contribution setup as a means to manage its transition costs and move gradually toward partial funding. However, further policy development is needed in both China and Mongolia to achieve the intended policy objectives. For reform to succeed in these countries, additional measures are needed, for example, increasing the retirement age and eliminating special early-retirement provisions. Various fragmented programs need to be unified gradually, and overall coverage needs to be expanded to enhance equity and labor mobility.

With the exception of low-income economies, where few mechanisms for formal social protection exist, most of the emerging-market and transition economies have been engaged in pension reform in one way or another. Requests to the World Bank for assistance in this area have generally been in the form of policy notes or technical assistance and only occasionally have lending programs been involved.

Chapter 8

Final Remarks

THIS REPORT PROVIDES AN OVERVIEW OF THE WORLD BANK'S POLICIES and perspectives on pension reform. It articulates the reasons why pension reform is a key development issue for client countries and sets forth a policy framework that guides work in this area. This framework is founded on the view that pensions represent a key element of both social and economic policy and that many existing systems are unsustainable and represent a significant impediment to long-term growth and stability.

The approach proposed for implementing pension reforms is based on the concept that pension systems should be designed in accordance with the characteristics of the social and economic risks of old-age security and are best organized in a manner that is focused on the management of risks through diversification and some prefunding of benefit obligations. The potential for funding to contribute to economic efficiency and growth is central to the support for this aspect of pension design. The World Bank's approach to pension reform explicitly recognizes the need for the design of systems and the path of reform to reflect the conditions and context of individual countries but also to adhere to a basic set of common goals and criteria.

For these reasons, the Bank uses a multipillar "benchmark" as a framework for evaluating pension reforms. The multipillar approach includes a noncontributory basic pillar for the lifetime poor and a reasonably sized universal contributory system to alleviate poverty and provide basic income maintenance and longevity insurance, access to a funded pillar that provides flexibility and an appropriate incentive structure, and the development of voluntary savings arrangements to supplement mandatory public systems.

The report is intended to reassure client countries that the Bank, rather than promote only a funded defined-contribution model, considers the unique nature of each reform against a set of outcome-oriented goals and process criteria in making decisions about lending its support. The record of World Bank lending associated with pension reforms reflects both the priority assigned to pensions and the diversity of reforms that have been supported.

The report notes that there is a range of possible options and that many aspects of the implementation of pension reforms will depend on the circumstances. It also provides insights into common challenges and approaches that will guide client countries in resolving these issues. Through this discussion, the Bank seeks to demonstrate that the best approach is a continuous reevaluation of principles, positions, and experience so that all countries can learn from the experience of those that precede them.

The World Bank's involvement in pension reform over the past decade has shown that successful reforms require not only the best available technical design but also attention to the political economy of reform and the readiness and capacity of implementation. This experience strongly supports a continuing role for the Bank in developing and sharing this knowledge as broadly as possible in the future.

Appendix

Tables on Old-Age
Income Poverty

Table A.1. Poverty Gap in Select African Countries,
by Type of Household, Various Years

Country and year	No elderly persons	Elderly persons only	Elderly and children only	Mixed household	Not headed by elderly	Headed by elderly	All persons
Burkina Faso, 1998	14.6	12.2	18.8	18.3	15.4	18.6	16.7
Burundi, 1998	26.2	27.0	33.6	23.1	26.2	24.3	25.9
Cameroon, 1996	22.6	23.8	21.1	25.3	22.5	27.3	23.4
Côte d'Ivoire, 1998	10.0	16.0	25.1	14.3	10.5	13.9	11.1
Ethiopia, 2000	9.9	12.1	10.7	11.0	9.9	11.4	10.2
Gambia, The, 1998	20.9	24.7	11.8	31.0	23.7	30.6	25.6
Ghana, 1998	14.4	12.0	22.3	19.8	14.9	18.9	15.7
Guinea, 1994	10.2	13.0	21.7	14.0	10.9	14.3	11.8
Kenya, 1997	17.1	15.9	21.6	21.0	17.1	21.2	17.7
Madagascar, 2001	27.1	17.6	25.1	26.1	27.1	25.1	26.9
Malawi, 1997	26.5	25.6	33.7	29.6	26.5	30.5	27.1
Mozambique, 1996	29.4	19.2	31.9	29.8	29.2	31.3	29.4
Nigeria, 1996	28.3	12.1	26.8	38.1	29.0	34.1	29.9
Uganda, 1999	16.7	20.1	22.9	15.9	16.6	17.2	16.7
Zambia, 1998	32.8	41.6	59.3	44.1	33.0	46.5	34.7

Source: Kakwani and Subbarao 2005.

Table A.2. Inventory of Noncontributory Pension Programs in Developing Countries

Country	Recent law	Type	Administration	Age of eligibility	65 + population share in 2002	Number of beneficiaries and year	Means of finance	Monthly pension (US$)[c]	Expenditure as a percent of GDP[d]
Argentina	1993	Means test	Ministry of Social Development	70	13	113,006 (2000)	Government	153	0.23
Bangladesh	1998	Means test	Ministry of Social Welfare	57	5	403,110 (2002)	Government	2	—
Bolivia[a]	1993	Universal but cohort restricted	Ministry of Economic Development	65	6	—	Government	20	0.90
Botswana	1996	Universal	Department of Labor and Social Security	65	5	71,000 (1999)	Government	24	0.40
Brazil									
Social assistance [b]	(1974) 1993	Means test	National Social Security Institute	67	8	1,215,988 (2000)	Government	87	0.30
Rural pension	1992	Means test, basic contributory record		60 for men, 55 for women	—	6,024,328 (2000)	91.6 percent government; 8.4 percent tax on first sale of produce	87	1.00
Chile	1980 and 1981	Means test	Ministry of Development and Planning	70	11	163,338 (2001)	Government	60	0.38
Costa Rica	1995	Means test	Costa Rican Social Insurance Fund	65	8	41,620 (2000)	Government	30 39	0.30
India	1995	Means test	Ministry of Labor	65	8	2,200,000 (2000)	Government	2	0.01

Country									
Mauritius	1976	Universal	Ministry of Social Security and National Solidarity	60	9	112,000 (2001)	Government	58 (age 60–89) 220 (age 90–99) 252 (age 100+)	2.00
Namibia	1990	Universal	Government Pension Fund	60	6	82,000 (1999)	Government	26	0.7
Nepal	1995–6	Universal	Ministry of Local Development	75	6	191,953 (2001–2)	Government	2	—
South Africa	1992 (amended in 1997)	Means test	National and Provincial Departments of Social Development	65 for men, 60 for women	6	2,002,320 (2003)	Government	93 (2003)	1.4 (2002)
Sri Lanka	1939	Means test	Provincial Department of Social Services	—	10	425,477 (2000)	Government	1.25 (4 maximum per household)	—
Uruguay	1995	Means test	Ministry of Labor and Social Security and Social Welfare Fund	70	17	64,600 (2001)	Government	90	0.62
Western Samoa	1990	Universal	Labor Department and Accident Compensation Board	65	—	—	Government	30	—

Sources: Barrientos and Lloyd-Sherlock 2002; Bertranou 2002; Delgado and Cardoso 2000; ISSA 1999; Rajan 2003; Rajan, Perera, and Begum 2002; South Africa, Department of Social Development 2002, 2003; United Nations Population Division 2002; Willmore 2003; World Bank 2001g.

Note: The information is for the pension program as a whole. In some cases, the figures include disability and survivor pensions in addition to old-age pensions.

— Not available.

a. Bolivia's program was intended to provide an annuity payment to all persons 20 years of age and over in 1995. It began operating in 1997, was discontinued in 1998, and reinstated in 2002.

b. The RMV (*renda mensual vitalicia*) is being replaced by the BPC (*beneficio de prestação continuada*).

c. These values are in current U.S. dollars but for different years, so data are not strictly comparable, especially where exchange rates fluctuate significantly.

d. Figures are from different sources and for different years.

Table A.3. Money as a Percentage of GDP Required to Eliminate the Poverty Gap in Select African Countries, by Type of Household, Various Years

Country and year	No elderly persons	Elderly persons only	Elderly and children only	Mixed households	Not headed by elderly	Headed by elderly
Burkina Faso, 1998	1.90	0.01	0.02	1.28	2.40	0.81
Burundi, 1998	23.44	0.24	0.51	3.24	23.71	3.72
Cameroon, 1996	6.56	0.06	0.05	2.89	7.53	2.02
Côte d'Ivoire, 1998	2.89	0.04	0.04	1.21	3.26	0.90
Ethiopia, 2000	8.43	0.09	0.11	2.24	8.82	2.05
Gambia, The, 1998	8.08	0.03	0.01	9.10	11.71	5.51
Ghana, 1998	7.44	0.16	0.21	3.01	8.36	2.39
Guinea, 1994	3.43	0.04	0.13	2.85	4.44	2.01
Kenya, 1997	8.05	0.18	0.14	1.83	8.27	1.92
Madagascar, 2001	9.04	0.07	0.07	1.39	9.39	1.14
Malawi, 1997	20.85	0.28	0.46	3.90	21.53	3.97
Mozambique, 1996	21.91	0.19	0.27	4.49	22.94	3.92
Nigeria, 1996	9.70	0.09	0.10	2.83	10.34	2.39
Uganda, 1999	7.16	0.15	0.19	1.73	7.52	1.71
Zambia, 1998	18.91	0.19	0.17	4.49	19.77	3.99

Source: Kakwani and Subbarao 2005.

Table A.4. Cost of Social Pensions (0.70 Percent of the Poverty Threshold) as a Percentage of GDP in Select African Countries, Various Years

Country and year	All elderly		Poor elderly	
	60 years +	65 years +	60 years +	65 years +
Burkina Faso, 1998	2.11	1.39	1.19	0.79
Burundi, 1998	3.05	2.09	1.81	1.26
Cameroon, 1996	1.55	0.96	0.97	0.63
Côte d'Ivoire, 1998	1.11	0.69	0.52	0.33
Ethiopia, 2000	3.74	2.36	1.63	1.03
Gambia, The, 1998	2.83	1.89	1.93	1.24
Ghana, 1998	3.30	2.29	1.50	1.04
Guinea, 1994	2.66	1.62	1.17	0.72
Kenya, 1997	2.06	1.42	1.11	0.76
Madagascar, 2001	1.15	0.72	0.64	0.40
Malawi, 1997	3.13	2.18	2.24	1.55
Mozambique, 1996	2.92	1.75	1.93	1.15
Nigeria, 1996	1.68	0.99	1.00	0.55
Uganda, 1999	1.86	1.27	0.97	0.69
Zambia, 1998	1.68	1.06	1.33	0.84

Source: Kakwani and Subbarao 2005.

Endnotes

1. A demogrant is the same as a universal flat benefit, where individuals receive an amount of money based solely on age and residency. A glossary at the end of the report defines this and other terms.

2. The need for reform of pension systems in developed countries, in particular to address their fiscal unsustainability, has been documented for at least two decades in early publications by international organizations, including the International Monetary Fund (Heller, Hemming, and Kohnert 1986) and the Organisation for Economic Co-operation and Development (OECD 1988). A research publication by the World Bank (1994) was one of the first to look in a comprehensive manner at the situation in developing countries, and by now the need for reform and approaches adopted by Latin American countries and the transition economies in Central and Eastern Europe have been well covered in many publications. For the regions of the Middle East and North Africa, South and East Asia, and Sub-Saharan Africa, our knowledge is much more limited but has improved in recent years (for the main references pertaining to all regions, see the notes in chapter 7). Cross-country papers and books on pension issues in developing countries are still an exception (such as that by Charlton and McKinnon 2001).

3. A full country-by-country assessment of existing pension schemes among World Bank clients in the low- and middle-income countries is beyond the scope of this report. For detailed assessments, see the regional reviews, individual country reports, and case studies that form part of our policy dialogue and reform support (http://www.worldbank.org/pensions).

4. For the beginnings of the concept, see Holzmann and Jorgensen (2000, 2001); for the application, see World Bank (2000b); and for the use of

the Bank's Social Protection Sector Strategy Paper as a conceptual envelope, see World Bank (2001f). For further developments and more recent
use in the developing-country context, including in risk and vulnerability
assessments, see the social risk management Web site (www1.worldbank
.org/sp/risk_management).

5. The multipillar reform proposal gained prominence with publication
of the Bank's research report *Averting the Old-Age Crisis* (World Bank
1994), which proposed a specific three-pillar system. Other Bank proposals have also focused on the basic elements of a multipillar system. See
Vittas (1993).

6. See the glossary at the end of this report for a definition of
demogrant and other terms.

7. On interest rate volatility, see Alier and Vittas (2001); Burtless (2000).
On the capacity to manage mortality risk, see James and others (1999);
James, Smalhout, and Vittas (2001); James, Martínez, and Iglesias (2003);
Mitchell, Myers, and Young (2000).

8. The role of financial systems in economic growth is an area where
Nobel Prize laureates and other influential economists disagree sharply
(Levine 2003). One can add the academic dispute about the role of funded
pension systems in the development of financial markets. As a development institution, the Bank has always focused on the nexus between
financial sector development and economic growth and, more recently, on
the nexus between contractual saving and financial sector development.
The main Bank contributions to the latter research are quoted throughout
the report. Other important references include the reader by Bodie and
Davis (2000); Corbo and Schmidt-Hebbel (2003); Davis and Steil (2003);
Reisen (2000).

9. The literature on the first question is reviewed and summarized in
Congressional Budget Office (1998); for the second question, see Bosworth
and Burtless (2003).

10. If more productive projects are less liquid, an increase in the availability of long-term capital should, on average, increase the return of projects.

11. The replacement rate of 40 percent is in line with International
Labour Office (ILO) Convention 102 of 1952—the basic convention for
social security benefits—which suggests that the periodic payments to
standard beneficiaries in old age for a man of pensionable age with a wife
should be at this level. The convention allows a lot of leeway with regard
to the definition of replacement rate, such as gross or net of tax and social
security or last income versus lifetime income. The more ambitious ILO
Convention 128 of 1967 raises this rate to 45 percent, and ILO Recommen-
dation 131 raises it even higher to 55 percent, but these higher rates
should be applied only by more developed economies (which are not
defined). For a presentation of the ILO's standards, see ILO (2002b) and

the ILO Web site: http://www.ilo.org/. The Bank believes that prescribing these higher standards of mandated minimum benefits for more developed economies makes little sense. With a higher level of income and financial sector development, individuals have more opportunities, not fewer, to adjust their retirement savings to their individual replacement rate goal.

12. A special view of robust pension design emerges when one takes into account the vulnerability of benefit and revenue design to political changes and anticipates this in how programs are developed and implemented. In other words, one moves immediately to a second- or third-best world to ensure the survival of the program design in the face of a variety of political and other shocks. Such an approach opens the traditional bilateral tradeoff between equity and efficiency to include robustness in design and implementation.

13. Because the identification of pension reform components in Bank lending is not as straightforward as one may think, the data presented may change slightly over time as new projects are identified in Bank documents and included. Yet the overall picture and message are unlikely to change. These figures include only loans approved through the end of fiscal 2004, which ended on July 1, 2004. Subsequent analysis may indicate slightly higher numbers if they include loans that were approved after this date. Small differences in the period of analysis, however, will not have any material effect on the general pattern of lending.

14. A billion is 1,000 million. All dollars are U.S. dollars.

15. Options for the reform of pension systems and their assessment are greatly influenced by the international academic and political discussion in OECD countries. The discussion in the United States about the reform of social security (the public pension system) attracts considerable attention internationally but has little practical relevance for typical Bank clients because the conditions for reform are so different elsewhere. The European reform experience is more relevant, as those systems exhibit more need for reform and are more diverse in structure and reform experience. Similarly, the most recent reforms in other high-income economies, such as Australia and Hong Kong, China, provide interesting lessons for reform options and implementation. Still, the underlying conceptual discussion in these high-income countries makes their experience relevant for other parts of the world. A selective list of recent publications includes Bateman, Kingston, and Piggott (2001); Diamond (2004); Feldstein and Siebert (2002); Feldstein 2005; Mitchell 1999; Takayama (2003); Thompson (1998); and Valdés-Prieto (1998, 2002).

16. What constitutes an ideal notional defined-contribution system and how it fares compared with other benefit options (such as nonfinancial defined-benefit or financial defined-contribution schemes) or how it performs

in reality and under political stress are still very much open to discussion (see, for example, Disney 1999; Valdés-Prieto 2000; Williamson and Williams 2003). For this reason, the World Bank and the Swedish Social Insurance Board organized a defined-contribution conference that took place in Sandhamn, Sweden, on September 28–30, 2003. For the agenda and the revised papers, see http://www.rfv.se/konferens/index.htm. The conference volume will be published in early 2005 as Holzmann and Palmer (2005). The papers in the conference volume cover conceptual and analytical issues and the experience of countries that have introduced notional defined-contribution systems and those that are thinking about introducing them. It also provides papers and written-up thoughts of a high-powered ad hoc panel comprising Nick Barr, Axel Boersch-Supan, Peter Diamond, Assar Lindbeck, and Salvador Valdés-Prieto (all 2005).

17. Funded schemes, even when they are fully invested in government bonds, will have positive market effects relative to purely unfunded schemes. They will stimulate the debt market because the development of contractual savings creates a demand for long-term public debt—which is matched by the issuance of bonds—instead of short-term instruments, and this eventually helps to build the yield curve. If government debt is issued, the debt market will develop even more, particularly in response to an extended yield curve. Of course, this may come at the expense of the equity and corporate bond markets (Musalem and Tressel 2003).

18. The enhanced focus on basic pension provisions in the Bank's client countries was launched with preparation of a Social Protection Strategy Paper (see World Bank 2001b) and received major emphasis during the United Nations "World Conference on Ageing" in 2002. Various international organizations and nongovernmental organizations have taken on the issue of income support for the elderly in advocacy and increasingly also in analytical and empirical work. For a first empirical analysis of the relative policy status of the elderly in 15 African countries, see Kakwani and Subbarao (2005); for a first outline of analytical and empirical issues, see Schwarz (2004). The experience with basic pension schemes in (joint) client countries is now documented on the Web sites of the International Labour Office and the World Bank. A United Nations conference in autumn 2003 was devoted to a discussion of poverty among the elderly, and a joint workshop of HelpAge and the World Bank held in New Delhi in early 2004 was devoted to taking stock of basic pension provisions in India. Visit http://www.worldbank.org/pensions for cross-links to all of these Web sites.

19. While there are still different views among the ILO, IMF, and World Bank about the importance of implicit pension debt (compare Gillion and others 2000; Holzmann 1999; Mackenzie and others 2001), or at least the best way to measure it, there is strong agreement about the need to

improve financial governance of pension institutions, including improved actuarial capacity and oversight of social insurance bodies. To this end, in early 2004 the ILO, IMF, and World Bank together with the International Association of Actuaries created an informal working group to strengthen and sponsor better actuarial training and financial management of social security institutions (covering pensions, health, unemployment benefits, and beyond).

20. A limited but growing literature underlines the importance of governance for the performance of public pension funds, including Carmichael and Palacios (2004); Iglesias and Palacios (2001); Impavido (2002); Mitchell and Hsin (1997); Useem and Mitchell (2000). The empirical literature on the relationship of governance and public pension fund performance is based largely on U.S. data, and its findings clearly indicate that the governance structure determines the investment strategy, which in turn affects investment performance. Hess and Impavido (2004) provide a survey of the governance practices of public pension funds in 26 developing countries. Their results indicate a very heterogeneous governance practice, which is consistent with the diversity of investment outcomes. Palacios (2002) reviews five recent initiatives by OECD countries aimed at improving the governance of public pension funds. Since 2002 an annual international conference on public pension funds at the World Bank has served to discuss country experiences as well as conceptual and empirical work on this issue. The most recent conference took place in September 20–25, 2004; for papers presented at the conference, see http://www1.worldbank.org/finance/html/ppfm2004.html.

21. For detailed discussion, see Carmichael and Palacios (2004); Hess and Impavido (2004); Impavido (2004).

22. However, record keeping is subsidized to some extent through the administrative structures of government agencies that separate and forward payroll deductions.

23. See, for example, Blake (1999); Davidoff, Brown, and Diamond (2003); Davis (2002); Impavido, Thorburn, and Wadsworth (2004); James, Martínez, and Iglesias (2003); James, Vittas, and Song (2001); Walliser (2001).

24. The literature consists of three main areas. The first provides the conceptual underpinnings of the political economy of policy reform coming from political science or economics. Main references include Rodrik (1996) and Williamson (1994) for policy reforms in general and Pierson (1994, 1996) for pension reform in particular. The second provides insights into policy reform through cross-regional comparison, such as the reform processes in Latin America and Central and Eastern Europe. Main references in this area include Gillion and others (2000), James and Brooks (2001), and Müller (2000, 2001, 2003a, 2003b). Finally, country case studies

of pension reform try to distill lessons or apply a conceptual framework to countries for verification. Examples of the latter include Mesa-Lago (2002), Müller (2000, 2001), Piñera (1991), and Queisser (1998a 1998b) on Latin America; Müller (1999, 2003a, 2003b), Nelson (2001), Orenstein (2000), and Orenstein and Haas (2000) on Central and Eastern Europe; Bonoli (2000), Hinrichs (2001), and Reynaud (2000) on Western Europe; and the contributions and papers quoted in Holzmann, Orenstein, and Rutkowski (2003).

25. A more formal and comprehensive evaluation of the Bank's pension work and advice is currently being undertaken by OED, the Bank's independent evaluation unit, which reports only to the Bank's Board of Directors rather than to Bank management. The evaluation involves two main and closely interrelated components. The first major component consists of assessing the effectiveness of the Bank's direct assistance to member countries in the pension area, involving policy dialogue, country-specific studies, and projects, and focuses on Latin America and the Caribbean and Europe and Central Asia. The second component consists of an assessment of the Bank's three-pillar paradigm and its evolution over time. The review is expected to be delivered to the board in the first half of 2005. A first assessment of pension reform issues five years after publication of *Averting the Old-Age Crisis* (World Bank 1994) was undertaken as an international Bank conference in autumn 1999, and the revised papers are published in Holzmann and Stiglitz (2001). Broad assessments of worldwide trends in pension reform by Bank staff include Fox and Palmer (2001) and Schwarz and Demirgüç-Kunt (1999).

26. This section was prepared by Anita Schwarz, Indermit Gill, Truman Packard, and Todd Pugatch, drawing from several recent assessments of pension reforms in Latin America. Guillermo Perry and Helena Ribe provided helpful feedback and guidance. At the time of preparing this report, the implementation of structural reforms had stalled in Ecuador and Nicaragua.

27. In view of the Chilean pension reform more than 23 years ago and the many reforms in Latin America since the early 1990s, there is an extensive literature describing and assessing the reforms. A small subset of recent references includes De Ferranti, Leipziger, and Srinivas (2002); Gill, Packard, and Yermo (2004); Hujo, Mesa-Lago, and Nitsch (2004); IFPFA (2003); Mesa-Lago (2002); Palacios (2003); Queisser (1998a, 1998b); and Valdés-Prieto (2002). Case studies of individual countries can be found in the Bank's Pension Reform Primer series, including case studies of Argentina, Dominican Republic, El Salvador, Mexico, and Peru.

28. Mexico has drafted legislation that brings federal civil servants into the national system, and Colombia has integrated some, but not all, of its pension plans. Separate pension plans remain for provincial or state pub-

lic sector workers. Argentina integrated about half of its provincial civil servant pension regimes and all of its federal civil servants into the national system, but some of the largest provincial plans—the provinces of Buenos Aires and Córdoba, for example—remain separate from the reformed national system.

29. The Office of the Chief Economist for the World Bank's Latin America Regional Department recently completed a critical assessment of structural reforms to retirement security systems (Gill, Packard, and Yermo 2004). Background papers are available on the chief economist's Web page: http://www.worldbank.org/lcrce.

30. This has led to important distributional benefits. Besides allowing countries to spend more on public education, health, and social assistance, in all the reforming countries the regressivity of public pension expenditures has been markedly reduced for those who participate in the programs, when measured using (gross of commission and fee) rates of return obtained by wealthier and poorer workers (Zviniene and Packard 2003).

31. A notable exception is the reformed pension system in Peru. The majority of affiliates to the new funded pillar of individual retirement accounts do not enjoy the protection of a minimum pension guarantee. The vulnerability of affiliates to Peru's AFP (Administradora de Fondos de Pensiones) system, and indeed of the wider population, to old-age poverty is compounded by the lack of any noncontributory pension arrangements.

32. Corbo and Schmidt-Hebbel (2003), Edwards and Cox-Edwards (2002), and Packard (2002) find some positive impact on the share of workers contributing to formal pension systems with reforms, while Mesa-Lago (2002) claims that worker participation has fallen due to reforms.

33. This translates into 400 percent of their earnings before retirement in many cases. Strictly speaking, rural pensions in Brazil are "contributory," but eligibility requirements are generous and hardly enforced. A truly noncontributory program does exist, but only for elderly individuals in urban households. The urban noncontributory pension is targeted to the poor; however, the amount of the benefit is the same as the seemingly noncontributory rural pension and the same as the minimum contributory pension. For a review of noncontributory schemes in four Latin American countries, see Bertranou, van Ginneken, and Solorio (2004). For a comparison of the arrangements in Brazil and South Africa, see HelpAge International (2003).

34. See Bucheli (1998) for a thorough analysis of intergenerational and intragenerational effects of the reforms in Uruguay.

35. The unification of systems has also led to substantial fiscal savings, above those estimated in Zviniene and Packard (2003), who assume that all currently covered individuals were covered in the less generous

national system prior to reforms. As a result, many of their numbers on pension debt before reform underestimate the true extent of fiscal problems at that time.

36. To the extent that debt financing is used to cover the transition, estimates become extremely sensitive to interest rate assumptions.

37. Just between 1998 and 2002, the ratio of pension fund assets to GDP rose from 3.3 to 11.3 percent in Argentina, from 3.9 to 15.5 percent in Bolivia, from 40 to 56 percent in Chile, from 2.7 to 7.7 percent in Colombia, from 0.4 to 7.4 percent in El Salvador, from 2.7 to 5.3 percent in Mexico, from 2.5 to 8.1 percent in Peru, and from 1.3 to 5.7 percent in Uruguay. Further, reforms created a new financial industry in which regulatory oversight has been a role model for other industries in the region. The funded systems have achieved high standards in asset valuation, risk rating, and disclosure. Furthermore, insurance companies have flourished in their auxiliary role as providers of disability, survivor, and longevity insurance in the new systems. So whereas the direct role of pension reform in increasing national saving is still being debated, improved financial sector functioning is likely to have had an indirect positive effect on saving (Gill, Packard, and Yermo 2004).

38. In Costa Rica and Uruguay the pay-as-you-go plan is mandatory, while in Argentina, Colombia, and Peru workers can choose between defined-benefit, pay-as-you-go plans and individual accounts.

39. With eight countries in (Central and Eastern) Europe and Central Asia having so far moved toward a multipillar structure and with many other countries in the region considering or even implementing reforms, the number of studies describing or evaluating pension reforms in the regions has become quite sizable. The Bank's Pension Reform Primer series includes country case studies on Hungary (Palacios and Rocha 1998), Kazakhstan (Andrews 2001), Latvia (Fox and Palmer 1999), and Poland (Chlon, Góra, and Rutkowski 1999). More recent cross-country assessments of reform include Barr and Rutkowski (2004); Chlon (2003); Fultz and Ruck (2000); Lindeman, Rutkowski, and Sluchynskyy (2001); Müller (1999, 2003a, 2003b, 2004); OECD (2004a); Schmähl and Horstmann (2002); and von Gersdorff and Rutkowski (2004). This section draws on the last three publications and was prepared by Hermann von Gersdorff, Michal Rutkowski, and Anita Schwarz.

40. A review of the pension reform needs of and options for the region is currently being prepared by World Bank staff and should be finished by summer 2005. A comprehensive review of India's pension scheme is found in World Bank (2001c). A study of the Nepalese demogrant scheme is found in Palacios (2004) and Palacios and Rajan (2004). A review of civil service schemes in the region is found in Palacios (2004). This section was prepared by Robert Palacios.

41. The World Bank is providing technical assistance to the task forces in the Maldives, Nepal, and Pakistan, and an Investment Development Fund grant is supporting pension reform in Nepal.

42. An attempt to take stock of existing programs in Africa can be found in Barbone and Sánchez (1999) and Bonnerjee, Pallares-Miralles, and Schwarz (2002). Relevant country case studies include World Bank (2002a) for Senegal and Devereaux (2001) for Namibia. Several published studies have examined South Africa's social pension scheme, including Case and Deaton (1998). This section was prepared by Robert Palacios.

43. For further information, see their Web site: http://www.izf.net/izf/Institutions/Integration/Zone/CIPRES.htm.

44. For a recent overview of pension systems in the Middle East and North Africa region, see Robalino (2005). Other relevant documents are the various country reports on pensions, in particular, World Bank (2002b) for Algeria; World Bank (2001e) for Djibouti; World Bank (2003c) for Iran; World Bank (2003b) for Jordan; World Bank (2004d) for Lebanon; World Bank (2001d, 2004c) for Morocco; World Bank (2003e) for Tunisia; World Bank (2002c) for West Bank and Gaza. Lebanon is a special case. There is no public pension system for private sector workers. The country only has access to an end-of-service indemnity scheme. This section was prepared by David Robolins.

45. Among non-gulf countries, these reserves range between 4.2 percent of GDP in Djibouti to 47 percent of GDP in Egypt. The average for the region is close to 14 percent of GDP.

46. The Bank currently has technical assistance programs in Algeria, Bahrain, Djibouti, Egypt, Iran, Iraq, Jordan, Lebanon, Libya, Morocco, West Bank Gaza, and Yemen.

47. Reviews of pension systems and reforms of the region include studies by the World Bank (Holzmann, MacArthur, and Sin 2000; World Bank 2004b) and Asian Development Bank (2000). Other relevant documents are the various country case studies, including World Bank (2000a, 2001a, 2004a) for China; World Bank (2003d) for Mongolia; World Bank (1999) for the Philippines; and World Bank (1998) for Thailand. This section was prepared by Yvonne Sin.

Glossary

Accrual rate. The rate at which pension entitlement is built up relative to earnings per year of service in earnings-related schemes—for example, one-sixtieth of final salary.

Accrued pension. The value of the pension to a member at any point prior to retirement, which can be calculated on the basis of current earnings or also include projections of future increases in earnings.

Actuarial fairness. A method of setting insurance premiums according to the true risks involved.

Additional voluntary contributions. Contributions to an occupational pension scheme over and above the employee's normal contribution rate.

Adverse selection. A problem stemming from an insurer's inability to distinguish between high- and low-risk individuals. The price for insurance then reflects the average risk level, which leads low-risk individuals to opt out and drives the price of insurance still higher until insurance markets break down.

Agency slack. A situation in which individuals are unable to monitor the efforts of their agents comprehensively. Agency slack occurs when the agent is averse to effort and so underperforms. In the case of pensions, for example, investors may not be able to monitor fund managers, who, as a consequence, may not do their best for the investors. See also moral hazard.

Annuity. A stream of payments at a specified rate, which may have some provision for inflation proofing, payable until some contingency occurs, usually the death of the beneficiary or a surviving dependent.

Annuity factor. The net present value of a stream of pension or annuity benefits.

Annuity rate. The value of the annuity payment relative to its lump-sum cost.

Average effective retirement age. The actual average retirement age, taking into account early retirement and special regimes.

Basic state pension. The flat-rate state pension paid to all persons of pensionable age meeting the national insurance contribution test and their surviving dependents.

Benefit rate. The ratio of the average pension to the average wage, which could be expressed as relative to the economywide average wage or to the individual's specific average or final wage.

Ceiling. A limit on the amount of earnings subject to contributions.

Commutation. Exchange of part of the annuity component of a pension for an immediate lump sum.

Comprehensive income tax. A tax on all incomes, whether from earnings or investments and whether used for savings or consumption. A pure comprehensive income tax allows the component of investment returns compensating for inflation and so only taxes real returns.

Contracting out. The right of employers or employees to use private pension fund managers instead of participating in the publicly managed scheme.

Contracting-out rebate. The amount by which employers' and employees' national insurance contributions are reduced for contracting out of the state earnings-related pension scheme and the minimum contribution to a personal pension plan.

Deferred annuity. A stream of benefits commencing at some future date.

Defined benefit. A pension plan with a guarantee by the insurer or pension agency that a benefit based on a prescribed formula will be paid. Can be fully funded or unfunded and notional.

Defined contribution. A pension plan in which the periodic contribution is prescribed and the benefit depends on the contribution plus the investment return. Can be fully funded or notional and nonfinancial.

Demogrant. Same as a universal flat benefit, where individuals receive an amount of money based solely on age and residency.

Demographic transition. The historical process of changing demographic structure that takes place as fertility and mortality rates decline, resulting in an increasing ratio of older to younger persons.

Disclosure. Statutory regulations requiring the communication of information regarding pension schemes, funds, and benefits to pensioners and employees.

Discretionary increase. An increase in a pension payment not specified by the pension scheme rules.

Early leaver. A person who leaves an occupational pension scheme without receiving an immediate benefit.

Early retirement. Retirement before reaching an occupational scheme's normal retirement age or, in the state scheme, before reaching the state's pensionable age.

Earnings cap (ceiling). A limit on the amount of earnings subject to contributions.

Full funding. The accumulation of pension reserves that total 100 percent of the present value of all pension liabilities owed to current members.

Funding. Accumulation of assets in advance to meet future pension liabilities.

Implicit pension debt (net). The value of outstanding pension claims on the public sector minus accumulated pension reserves.

Indexation (uprating). Increases in benefits by reference to an index, usually of prices, although in some cases of average earnings.

Intergenerational distribution. Income transfers between different age cohorts of persons.

Intragenerational distribution. Income transfers within a certain age cohort of persons.

Legal retirement age. The normal retirement age written into pension statutes.

Marginal pension. The change in the accrued pension between two periods.

Means-tested benefit. A benefit that is paid only if the recipient's income falls below a certain level.

Minimum pension guarantee. A guarantee provided by the government to bring pensions to some minimum level, possibly by "topping up" the capital accumulation needed to fund the pensions.

Moral hazard. A situation in which insured people do not protect themselves from risk as much as they would have if they were not insured. For example, in the case of old-age risk, people might not save sufficiently for themselves if they expect the public system to come to their aid.

Nonfinancial (or notional) defined-benefit (plan). A defined-benefit pension plan that is unfunded (except for a potential reserve fund).

Nonfinancial (or notional) defined-contribution (plan). A defined-benefit pension plan that mimics the structure of (funded) defined-contribution plans but remains unfunded (except for a potential reserve fund).

Normal retirement age. The usual age at which employees become eligible for occupational pension benefits, excluding early-retirement provisions.

Notional (or nonfinancial) accounts. Individual accounts where the notional contributions plus interest rates accrued are credited and determine the notional capital (that is, the liability to society).

Notional (or nonfinancial) capital. The value of an individual account at a given moment that determines the value of annuity at retirement or the transfer value in case of mobility to another scheme or country.

Notional or nonfinancial interest rate. The rate at which the notional accounts of notional defined-contribution plans are annually credited. It should be consistent with the financial sustainability of the unfunded scheme (potentially the growth rate of the contribution base).

Occupational pension scheme. An arrangement by which an employer provides retirement benefits to employees.

Old-age dependency ratio. The ratio of older persons to working-age individuals. The old-age dependency ratio may refer to the number of persons over 60 divided by, for example, the number of persons ages 15–59, the number of persons over 60 divided by the number of persons ages 20–59, and so forth.

Overannuitization. A situation in which a compulsory pension forces an individual to save more in pension than he or she would in the absence of the compulsory provision.

Pay-as-you-go. In its strictest sense, a method of financing whereby current outlays on pension benefits are paid out of current revenues from an earmarked tax, often a payroll tax.

Pension coverage rate. The number of workers actively contributing to a publicly mandated contributory or retirement scheme, divided by the estimated labor force or by the working-age population.

Pension lump sum. A cash withdrawal from a pension plan, which in the case of some occupational pension schemes is provided in addition to an annuity. Also available from personal pension plans.

Pension spending. Usually defined as old-age retirement, survivor, death, and invalidity-disability payments based on past contribution records plus noncontributory, flat universal, or means-tested programs specifically targeting the old.

Pensionable earnings. The portion of remuneration on which pension benefits and contributions are calculated.

Portability. The ability to transfer accrued pension rights between plans.

Provident fund. A fully funded, defined-contribution scheme in which funds are managed by the public sector.

Replacement rate. The value of a pension as a proportion of a worker's wage during a base period, such as the last year or two before retirement or the entire lifetime average wage. Also denotes the average pension of a group of pensioners as a proportion of the average wage of the group.

Supplementary pensions. Pension provision beyond the basic state pension on a voluntary basis.

Support ratio. The opposite of the system dependency ratio: the number of workers required to support each pensioner.

System dependency ratio. The ratio of persons receiving pensions from a certain pension scheme divided by the number of workers contributing to the same scheme in the same period.

System maturation. The process by which a pension system moves from being immature, with young workers contributing to the system, but with few benefits being paid out since the initial elderly have not contributed and thus are not eligible for benefits, to being mature, with the proportion of elderly receiving pensions relatively equivalent to their proportion of the population.

Universal flat benefit. Pensions paid solely on the basis of age and citizenship, without regard to work or contribution records.

Valorization of earnings. A method of revaluing earnings by predetermined factors such as total or average wage growth to adjust for changes in prices, wage levels, or economic growth. In pay-as-you-go systems, pensions are usually based on some percentage of average wage. This average wage is calculated over some period of time, ranging from full-career average to last salary. If the period for which earnings history enters into the benefit formula is longer than the last salary, the actual wages earned are usually revalued to adjust for these types of changes.

Vesting period. The minimum amount of time required to qualify for full and irrevocable ownership of pension benefits.

References

Abel, Andrew, N. Gregory Mankiw, Larry Summers, and Richard Zeckhauser. 1989. "Assessing Dynamic Efficiency." *Review of Economic Studies* 56 (1): 1–20.

AIOS (Asociación Internacional de Organismos de Supervisión de Fondos de Pensiones [International Association of Pension Funds Supervisory Organizations]). 2003. *Boletín Estadísticos* (various issues). Available at www.aiosfp.org.

Alier, Max, and Dimitri Vittas. 2001. "Personal Pension Plans and Stock Market Volatility." In *New Ideas about Old-Age Security*, ed. Robert Holzmann and Joseph Stiglitz. Washington, DC: World Bank.

Andrews, Emily. 1999. "Disability Insurance: Programs and Practice." Social Protection, World Bank, Washington, DC.

———. 2001. "Kazakhstan: An Ambitious Pension Reform." Social Protection Discussion Paper 0104, World Bank, Washington, DC.

Antolin, Pablo, Allain de Serres, and Christine de la Maisonneuve. 2004. "Long-Term Budgetary Implications of Tax-favoured Retirement Saving Plans." OECD Working Paper 393, Economic Department, OECD, Paris.

Asher, Mukul. 2002. "The Role of the Global Economy in Financing Old Age: The Case of Singapore." Research Paper 37, Asian Development Bank Institute, Tokyo.

Asian Development Bank. 2000. "Social Protection Systems in the Asia and Pacific Region." Asian Development Bank, Manilla. http://www.adb.org.

Bailliu, Jeanine, and Helmut Reisen. 1997. "Do Funded Pensions Contribute to Higher Aggregate Savings? A Cross-Country Analysis." In *Pensions, Savings, and Capital Flows: From Ageing to Emerging Markets,* ed. Helmut Reisen, 113–31. Paris: Organisation for Economic Co-operation and Development.

Barbone, Luca, and Luis-Alvaro Sánchez. 1999. "Pensions and Social Security in Sub-Saharan Africa: Issues and Options." Africa Region Working Paper Series 4, World Bank, Washington, DC.

Barr, Nicholas. 2000. "Reforming Pensions: Myths, Truths, and Policy Choices." IMF Working Paper WP/00/139, International Monetary Fund, Washington, DC.

———. 2001. "The Truth about Pension Reform." *Finance and Development* 38 (3): 6–9.

———. 2005. "Notional Defined Contribution Pensions: Mapping the Terrain." In *Pension Reform through NDCs: Issues and Prospects for Non-Financial Defined Contribution Schemes,* ed. Robert Holzmann and Edward Palmer. Washington, DC: World Bank. In print.

Barr, Nicholas, and Michal Rutkowski. 2004. "Pensions." In *Labor Markets and Social Policy in Central and Eastern Europe: The Accession and Beyond,* ed. Nicholas Barr. Washington, DC: World Bank.

Barrientos, Armando, and Peter Lloyd-Sherlock. 2002. *Noncontributory Pensions and Social Protection.* Geneva: ILO.

Bateman, Hazel, Geoffrey Kingston, and John Piggott. 2001. *Forced Saving: Mandating Private Retirement Incomes.* Cambridge, U.K.: Cambridge University Press.

Beattie, Roger, and Warren McGillivray. 1995. "A Risky Strategy: Reflections on the World Bank Report *Averting the Old-Age Crisis.*" *International Social Security Review* 48 (3–4): 5–23.

Beck, Thorsten, Ross Levine, and Norman Loayza. 2000. "Finance and the Sources of Growth." *Journal of Financial Economics* 58 (1–2): 261–300.

Bertranou, Fabio. 2002. "Filling the Protection Gap: The Role of Minimum Pensions and Welfare Benefits; Noncontributory and Social Assistance Pensions in Argentina, Brazil, Chile, Costa Rica, and Uruguay." Paper presented at the "Seminar on Financial and Actuarial Bases of Pension Schemes," International Social Security Association, Santiago, Chile, November 21–22.

Bertranou, Fabio, Wouter van Ginneken, and Carmen Solorio. 2004. "The Impact of Tax-Financed Pensions on Poverty Reduction in Latin America: Evidence from Argentina, Brazil, Chile, Costa Rica, and Uruguay." *International Social Security Review* 57 (4): 3–18.

Blake, David. 1999. "Annuity Market: Problems and Solutions." *Geneva Papers on Risk and Insurance* 24 (July): 358–75.

Bodie, Zvi, and E. Philip Davis, eds. 2000. *The Foundations of Pension Finance.* 2 vols. Cheltenham, U.K.: Edward Elgar.

Bodie, Zvi, and Robert Merton. 2001. "International Pension Swaps." *Journal of Pension Economics and Finance* 1 (1): 77–83.

Boersch-Supan, Axel. 2005. "What Are NDC Pension Systems? What Do They Bring to Reform Strategies?" In *Pension Reform through NDCs: Issues and Prospect for Non-Financial Defined Contribution Schemes*, ed. Robert Holzmann and Edward Palmer. Washington, DC: World Bank. In print.

Boersch-Supan, Axel, Robert Palacios, and Patrizia Tumberello. 1999. *Pension Systems in the Middle East and North Africa: A Window of Opportunity*. Pension Reform Primer. Washington, DC: World Bank.

Bonnerjee, Aniruddha, Montserrat Pallares-Miralles, and Anita M. Schwarz. 2002. "Pensions in Sub-Saharan Africa." Social Protection, World Bank, Washington, DC.

Bonoli, Giuliano. 2000. *The Politics of Pension Reform: Institutions and Policy Change in Western Europe*. Cambridge, U.K.: Cambridge University Press.

Bossone, Biagio, Patrick Honohan, and Millard, Long. 2001. "Policy for Small Financial Systems." Financial Sector Discussion Paper 6, World Bank, Washington, DC.

Bosworth, Barry, and Gary Burtless. 2003. "Pension Reform and Saving." Brookings Institution, Washington, DC.

Bucheli, Marisa. 1998. "Los efectos de la reforma de la seguridad social sobre las cuentas generacionales." Working Paper 14/98, Departamento de Economía, Facultad de Ciencias Sociales, Universidad de la República, Uruguay, November.

Burtless, Gary. 2000. "Social Security Privatization and Financial Market Risk." Center on Social and Economic Dynamics Working Paper 10, Brookings Institution, Washington, DC.

Carmichael, Jeffrey, and Robert J. Palacios. 2004. "A Framework for Public Pension Fund Management." In *Public Pension Fund Management*, ed. Alberto R. Musalem and Robert J. Palacios. Washington, DC: World Bank.

Carmichael, Jeffrey, and Michael Pomerleano. 2002. *The Development and Regulation of Non-Bank Financial Institutions*. Washington, DC: World Bank.

Case, Anne, and Angus Deaton. 1998. "Large-Scale Transfers to the Elderly in South Africa." *Economic Journal* 108 (450): 1330–61.

Catalán, Mario, Gregorio Impavido, and Alberto R. Musalem. 2001. "Contractual Savings or Stock Market Development: Which Leads?" *Journal of Applied Social Science Studies* 120 (3): 445–87.

Chan-Lau, Jorge A. 2004. "Pension Funds and Emerging Markets." IMF Working Paper WP/04/181, International Monetary Fund, Washington, DC, September.

Charlton, Roger, and Roddy McKinnon. 2001. *Pensions in Development*. Aldershot: Ashgate.

Chlon, Agnieszka. 2003. "Evaluation of Reform Experiences in Eastern Europe." In *Pension Reforms: Results and Challenges,* ed. International Federation of Pension Fund Administrators, 145–237. Santiago, Chile: International Federation of Pension Fund Administrators.

Chlon, Agnieszka, Marek Góra, and Michal Rutkowski. 1999. "Shaping Pension Reform in Poland: Security through Diversity." Social Protection Discussion Paper 9923, World Bank, Washington, DC.

Cichon, Michael, Wolfgang Scholz, Arthur van de Meerendonk, Krzysztof Hagemejer, Fabio Bertranou, and Pirre Plamondon. 2004. "Financing Social Protection." International Labour Office and International Social Security Association, Geneva.

Coady, David, Margaret Grosh, and David Hoddinott. 2004. *Targeting of Transfers in Developing Countries: Review of Lessons and Experience.* Washington, DC: World Bank.

Coate, Stephen, and Martin Ravallion. 1993. "Reciprocity without Commitment: Characterisation and Performance of Informal Insurance Arrangements." *Journal of Development Economics* 40: 1–24.

Congressional Budget Office. 1998. "Social Security and Private Savings: A Review of the Empirical Evidence." Congressional Budget Office, Washington, DC. Memorandum.

Corbo, Vittorio, and Klaus Schmidt-Hebbel. 2003. "Macroeconomic Effects of the Pension Reform in Chile." In *Pension Reforms: Results and Challenges,* ed. International Federation of Pension Fund Administrators, 241–329. Santiago, Chile: International Federation of Pension Fund Administrators.

Corsetti, Giancarlo, and Klaus Schmidt-Hebbel. 1997. "Pension Reform and Growth." In *The Economics of Pensions: Principles, Policies, and International Experience,* ed. Salvador Valdés-Prieto. Cambridge, U.K.: Cambridge University Press.

CSIS (Center for Strategic and International Studies) and Watson Wyatt International. 1999. *Global Aging: The Challenge of the New Millennium.* Washington, DC: Center for Strategic and International Studies.

Davidoff, Thomas, Jeffrey Brown, and Peter Diamond. 2003. "Annuities and Individual Welfare." Working Paper 2003-11, Center for Retirement Research, Boston College.

Davis, E. Philip. 2002. "Issues in the Regulation of Annuities Markets." Paper prepared for the conference "Developing an Annuity Market in Europe," Turin, June 21–22.

Davis, E. Philip, and Yuwei Hu. 2004. "Is There a Link between Pension Funded Assets and Economic Growth? A Cross-Country Study." Brunnel University, London, December.

Davis, E. Philip, and Benn Steil. 2003. "Institutional Investors." *International Review of Economics and Finance* 12 (1): 145–7.

De Ferranti, David, Danny Leipziger, and P. S. Srinivas. 2002. "The Future of Pension Reform in Latin America." *Finance and Development* 39 (3): 39–43.

Deininger, Klaus, Marito García, and Kalanidhi Subbarao. 2003. "AIDS-Induced Orphanhood as a Systematic Shock: Magnitude, Impact, and Program Interventions in Africa." *World Development* 31 (7): 1201–20.

Delgado, Guilherme C., and José C. Cardoso, eds. 2000. *A universalização de direitos sociais no Brasil: a prêvidencia rural nos anos 90.* Brasilia: Instituto de Pesquisa Econômica Aplicada.

Demarco, Gustavo, and Rafael Rofman. 1999. "Collecting and Transferring Pension Contributions." Social Protection Discussion Paper 9907, World Bank, Washington, DC.

Dercon, Stefan. 2003. "Poverty Traps and Development: The Equity Efficiency Trade-Off Revisited." Oxford University, New York, September. Mimeo.

Devereaux, Stephan. 2001. "Namibia: Social Pensions in Namibia and South Africa." IDS Discussion Paper 379, Institute of Development Studies, Brighton, U.K., January.

Diamond, Peter. 1997. "Insulation of Pensions from Political Risk." In *The Economics of Pensions: Principals, Policies, and International Experience,* ed. Salvador Valdés-Prieto, 33–57. Cambridge, U.K.: Cambridge University Press.

———. 2003. *Taxation, Incomplete Markets, and Social Security: The 2000 Munich Lectures.* Cambridge, MA: MIT Press

———. 2004. "Social Security." *American Economic Review* 94 (1): 1–24.

———. 2005. "Panel Discussion: NDC versus NDB." In *Pension Reform through NDCs: Issues and Prospect for Non-Financial Defined Contribution Schemes,* ed. Robert Holzmann and Edward Palmer. Washington, DC: World Bank. In print.

Dilnot, Andrew, and Paul Johnson. 1993. *The Taxation of Private Pensions.* London: Institute for Fiscal Studies.

Disney, Richard. 1999. "Notional Accounts as a Pension Reform Strategy: An Evaluation." Social Protection Discussion Paper 9928, World Bank, Washington, DC.

Edwards, Sebastian. 1995. "Why Are Saving Rates So Different across Countries? An International Comparative Analysis." NBER Working Paper 5097, National Bureau of Economic Research, Cambridge, MA.

Edwards, Sebastian, and Alejandra Cox-Edwards. 2002. "Social Security Privatization Reform and Labor Markets: The Case of Chile." NBER Working Paper 8924, National Bureau of Economic Research, Cambridge, MA.

Feldstein, Martin. 2005. "Rethinking Social Insurance." The 2005 presidential address to the American Economic Association, forthcoming in the *American Economic Review* (March). Available at www.nber.org/feldstein.

Feldstein, Martin, and Horst Siebert, eds. 2002. *Social Security Pension Reform in Europe*. Chicago: National Bureau of Economic Research and University of Chicago Press.

Fox, Louise, and Eduard Palmer. 1999. "The Latvian Pension Reform." Social Protection Discussion Paper 9922, World Bank, Washington, DC.

———. 2001. "What in the World Is Going On?" In *New Ideas about Old-Age Security*, ed. Robert Holzmann and Joseph Stiglitz. Washington, DC: World Bank.

Fultz, Elaine, and Martin Ruck. 2000. *Pension Reform in Central and Eastern Europe: An Update on the Restructuring of National Pension Schemes in Selected Countries*. ILO-CEET Report 25. Budapest and Geneva: International Labour Office.

Gill, Indermit, Truman Packard, and Juan Yermo. 2004. *Keeping the Promise of Old-Age Income Security in Latin America*. Washington, DC: World Bank.

Gillion, Colin. 2000. "The Development and Reform of Social Security Pensions: The Approach of the International Labour Office." *International Social Security Review* 53 (1): 35–63.

Gillion, Colin, John Turner, Clive Baily, and Denis Latulippe, eds. 2000. *Social Security Pensions: Development and Reform*. Geneva: International Labour Organisation.

Glaessner, Thomas, and Salvador Valdés-Prieto. 1998. "Pension Reform in Small Developing Countries." Policy Research Working Paper 1983, Latin America and Caribbean Region, World Bank, Washington, DC.

Góra, Marek, and Edward Palmer. 2004. "Shifting Perspectives in Pension Reform." IZA Discussion Paper 1369, IZA, Warsaw and Stockholm, October.

Góra, Marek, and Michal Rutkowski. 1998. "The Quest for Pension Reform: Poland's Security through Diversity." Social Protection Discussion Paper 9815, World Bank, Washington, DC.

Gruber, Jonathan, and David A. Wise, eds. 1999. *Social Security and Retirement around the World*. Chicago: University of Chicago Press.

Grushka, Carlos, and Gustavo Demarco. 2003. "Disability Pensions and Social Security Reform: Analysis of the Latin American Experience." Social Protection Discussion Paper 0325, World Bank, Washington, DC.

Heller, Peter. 2003. *Who Will Pay? Coping with Aging Societies, Climate Changes, and Other Long-Term Fiscal Challenges*. Washington, DC: International Monetary Fund.

Heller, Peter, Richard Hemming, and Peter Kohnert. 1986. *Aging and Social Expenditure in Industrial Countries, 1980–2025*. IMF Occasional Paper 47. Washington, DC: International Monetary Fund.

HelpAge International. 2003. *Non-Contributory Pensions and Poverty Prevention: A Comparative Study of Brazil and South Africa.* London: HelpAge International.

——. 2004. *Age and Security: How Social Pensions Can Deliver Effective Aid to Poorer Older People and Their Families.* London: HelpAge International.

Hess, David, and Gregorio Impavido. 2004. "Governance of Public Pension Funds: Lessons from Corporate Governance and International Evidence." In *Public Pension Fund Management,* ed. Alberto R. Musalem and Robert J. Palacios. Washington DC: World Bank.

Hinrichs, Karl. 2001. "Aging and Public Pension Reforms in Western Europe and North America: Patterns and Politics." In *What Future for Social Security? Debates and Reforms in National and Cross-National Perspective,* ed. Jochen Clasen. The Hague: Kluwer Law International.

Hinz, Richard, and G. V. Nageswara Rao. 2003. "Approach to the Regulation of Private Pension Funds in India: Application of International Best Practice." In *Rethinking Pension Provision in India,* ed. Gautam Bhardwaj and Anand Bordia. Invest India/Tata McGraw-Hill Series. New Delhi, India: Tata McGraw-Hill.

Hofer, Helmut, and Reinhard Koman. 2001. *Social Security and Retirement in Austria.* Vienna: Institute for Advanced Studies.

Holzmann, Robert. 1990. "The Welfare Effects of Public Expenditure Programs Reconsidered." *IMF Staff Papers* 37 (2): 338–59.

——. 1997a. "On the Economic Benefits and Fiscal Requirements of Moving from Unfunded to Funded Pensions." In *The Future of the Welfare State: Challenges and Reforms,* ed. Commission of the European Union, 121–63. European Economy-Report and Studies 4. Brussels: Commission of the European Union.

——. 1997b. "Pension Reform, Financial Market Development, and Economic Growth: Preliminary Evidence from Chile." *IMF Staff Papers* 44 (2): 149–78.

——. 1999. *Financing the Transition to Multi-pillar.* Pension Reform Primer. SP Discussion Paper 9809. Washington, DC: World Bank.

——. 2000. "The World Bank Approach to Pension Reform." *International Social Security Review* 53 (1): 11–34.

——. 2002. "Can Investments in Emerging Markets Help to Solve the Aging Problem?" *Journal of Emerging Market Finance* 1 (2): 215–41.

——. 2003. "A Provocative Note on Coverage." In *The Three Pillars of Wisdom: A Reader on Globalisation; World Bank Pension Models and Welfare Society,* ed. Anton Tausch, 85–99. New York: Nova Science Publisher.

——. 2005 "Toward a Reformed and Coordinated Pension System in Europe: Rational and Potential Structure." In *Pension Reform through*

NDCs: Issues and Prospect for Non-Financial Defined Contribution Schemes, ed. Robert Holzmann and Edward Palmer. Washington, DC: World Bank. In print.

Holzmann, Robert, and Steen Jorgensen. 2000. "Social Protection as Social Risk Management: Conceptual Underpinnings for the Social Protection Sector Strategy Paper." Journal of International Development 11 (7): 1005–27.

————. 2001. "A New Conceptual Framework for Social Protection and Beyond." International Tax and Public Finance 8 (4): 529–56.

Holzmann, Robert, Ian W. MacArthur, and Yvonne Sin. 2000. "Pension Systems in East Asia and the Pacific: Challenges and Opportunities." Social Protection Discussion Paper 0014, World Bank, Washington, DC.

Holzmann, Robert, and Rainer Münz. 2004. Challenges and Opportunities of International Migration for the EU, Its Member States, Neighboring Countries, and Regions: A Policy Note. Stockholm: Institute for Future Studies.

Holzmann, Robert, Michael Orenstein, and Michal Rutkowski, eds. 2003. Pension Reform in Europe: Progress and Process. Washington, DC: World Bank.

Holzmann, Robert, Truman Packard, and José Cuesta. 2001. "Extending Coverage in Multi-Pillar Pension Systems: Constraints and Hypotheses, Preliminary Evidence, and Future Research Agenda." In New Ideas about Old-Age Security, ed. Robert Holzmann and Joseph Stiglitz. Washington, DC: World Bank.

Holzmann, Robert, Robert Palacios, and Asta Zviniene. 2004. Implicit Pension Debt: Issues, Measurement, and Scope in International Perspective. Pension Reform Primer. Washington, DC: World Bank.

Holzmann, Robert, and Edward Palmer, eds. 2005. Pension Reform through NDCs: Issues and Prospect for Non-Financial Defined Contribution Schemes. Washington, DC: World Bank. In print.

Holzmann, Robert, and Joseph Stiglitz, eds. 2001. New Ideas about Old-Age Security. Washington, DC: World Bank.

Holzmann, Robert, and Milan Vodopivec, eds. 2005. Mandated Severance Pay Programs: An International Perspective on Status, Concepts, and Reforms. Washington, DC: World Bank.

Hujo, Katja, Carmelo Mesa-Lago, and Manfred Nitsch, eds. 2004. ¿Público o privado? Los sistemas de pensiones en América Latina después de dos décadas de reformas. Caracas: Nueva Sociedad.

Hustead, Edwin C., and Toni Hustead. 2001. "Federal Civilian and Military Retirement Systems." In Pensions in the Public Sector, ed. Olivia S. Mitchell and Edwin C. Hustead, 66–104. Philadelphia: University of Pennsylvania Press.

IFPFA (International Federation of Pension Fund Administrators). 2003. *Pension Reforms: Results and Challenges.* Santiago, Chile: International Federation of Pension Fund Administrators.

Iglesias, Augusto, and Robert Palacios. 2001. "Managing Public Pension Reserves: Evidence from the International Experience." In *New Ideas about Old-Age Security,* ed. Robert Holzmann and Joseph Stiglitz. Washington, DC: World Bank.

ILO (International Labour Office). 2002a. *Social Security: A New Consensus.* Geneva: International Labour Office.

———. 2002b. *Standards for the XXIst Century: Social Security.* Geneva: International Labour Office.

IMF (International Monetary Fund). 2004. *World Economic Outlook: September 2004; The Global Demographic Transition.* Washington, DC: IMF.

Impavido, Gregorio. 2002. "On the Governance of Public Pension Fund Management." In *Financial Sector Governance: The Roles of Public and Private Sectors,* ed. Robert Litan, Michael Pomerleano, and V. Sundararajan. Washington, DC: Brookings Institution Press.

———. 2004. "Governance of Public Pension Plans: The Importance of Residual Claimants." World Bank, Washington, DC.

Impavido, Gregorio, Alberto R. Musalem, and Thierry Tressel. 2002a. "Contractual Savings Institutions and Banks' Stability and Efficiency." Policy Research Working Paper 2751, World Bank, Washington, DC.

———. 2002b. "Contractual Savings and Firms' Financing Choices." In *World Bank Economists' Forum,* vol. 2, ed. Shantayanan Devarajan and F. Halsey Rogers, 179–222. Washington, DC: World Bank.

———. 2003. "The Impact of Contractual Savings Institutions on Securities Markets." Policy Research Working Paper 2948, World Bank, Washington, DC.

Impavido, Gregorio, Alberto R. Musalem, and Dimitri Vittas. 2002. "Contractual Savings in Countries with a Small Financial System." In *Globalization and Financial Systems in Small Developing Countries,* ed. James Hanson, Patrick Honohan, and Giovanni Majnoni. Washington, DC: World Bank.

Impavido, Gregorio, Craig Thorburn, and Mike Wadsworth. 2004. "A Conceptual Framework for Retirement Product: Risk Sharing Arrangements between Providers and Annuitants." Policy Research Working Paper 3208, World Bank, Washington, DC.

ISSA (International Social Security Association). 1998. *The Future of Social Security.* Geneva: ISSA.

———. 1999. *Social Security Programs throughout the World.* Geneva: ISSA. http://www.ssa.gov/international.

———. 2004. *Guidelines for Investment of Social Security Funds.* Geneva: ISSA. http://www.issa.int.

James, Estelle. 2000. "Averting the Old-Age Crisis: Five Years After." *Spectrum* (Spring): 27–29. Social Protection. World Bank, Washington, DC.

———. 2002. "How Can China Solve Its Old-Age Security Problem? The Interaction between Pension, SOE, and Financial Market Reform." *Journal of Pension Economics and Finance* 1 (1): 53–75.

James, Estelle, and Sarah Brooks. 2001. "The Political Economy of Structural Pension Reform." In *New Ideas about Old-Age Security,* ed. Robert Holzmann and Joseph Stiglitz. Washington, DC: World Bank.

James, Estelle, Alejandra Cox-Edwards, and Rebeca Wong. 2003a. "The Gender Impact of Pension Reform." *Journal of Pension Economics and Finance* 2 (2): 181–219.

———. 2003b. "The Impact of Social Security Reform on Women in Three Countries." Policy Report 264, National Center for Policy Analysis, Washington, DC.

James, Estelle, Gary Ferrier, James Smalhout, and Dimitri Vittas. 1999. "Mutual Funds and Institutional Investments: What Is the Most Efficient Way to Set up Individual Accounts in a Social Security System?" Policy Research Working Paper 2099, World Bank, Washington, DC.

James, Estelle, Guillermo Martínez, and Augusto Iglesias. 2003. "Payout Choices by Retirees in Chile: What Are They and Why?" Michigan Retirement Research Center, University of Michigan.

James, Estelle, and Renuka Sane. 2003. "The Annuity Market in India: Do Consumers Get Their Money's Worth? What Are the Key Public Policy Issues?" In *Rethinking Pension Provision in India,* ed. Gautam Bhardwaj and Anand Bordia. Invest India/Tata McGraw-Hill Series. New Delhi: Tata McGraw-Hill.

James, Estelle, James Smalhout, and Dimitri Vittas. 2001. "Administrative Costs and Organization of Individual Accounts: A Comparative Perspective." In *New Ideas about Old-Age Security,* ed. Robert Holzmann and Joseph Stiglitz. Washington, DC: World Bank.

James, Estelle, and Dimitri Vittas. 2001. "Annuities Markets in Comparative Perspective: Do Consumers Get Their Money's Worth?" In *Private Pensions Systems: Administrative Costs and Reforms.* Paris: OECD.

James, Estelle, Dimitri Vittas, and Xue Song. 2001. "Annuities Markets around the World: Money's Worth and Risk Intermediation." CeRP Working Paper 16/01, Center for Research on Pensions and Welfare Policies, Moncalieri, Italy.

Kakwani, Nanak, and Kalanidhi Subbarao. 2005. "Ageing and Poverty in Africa and the Role of Social Pensions." Social Protection Discussion Paper, World Bank, Washington, DC. Forthcoming.

Karacadag, Cem, V. Sundararajan, and Jennifer Elliot. 2003. "Managing Risk in Financial Market Development: The Role of Sequencing." IMF Working Paper 03/116, International Monetary Fund, Washington, DC.

Kotlikoff, Laurence J. 1999. "The World Bank's Approach and the Right Approach to Pension Reform." Boston University, Boston, MA.

Legros, Florence. 2005. "Notional Defined Contribution: A Comparison of the French and the German Point Systems." In *Pension Reform through NDCs: Issues and Prospect for Non-Financial Defined Contribution Schemes*, ed. Robert Holzmann and Edward Palmer. Washington, DC: World Bank. In print.

Levine, Ross. 1997. "Financial Development and Economic Growth: Views and Agenda." *Journal of Economic Literature* 35 (2): 688–726.

———. 1999. "Law, Finance, and Economic Growth." *Journal of Financial Intermediation* 8 (1-2): 8–35.

———. 2003. "Finance and Growth: Theory, Evidence, and Mechanism." University of Minnesota and National Bureau of Economic Research, Cambridge, MA.

Lindbeck, Assar. 2005. "Panel Discussion: NDC vs. NDB." In *Pension Reform through NDCs: Issues and Prospect for Non-Financial Defined Contribution Schemes*, ed. Robert Holzmann and Edward Palmer. Washington, DC: World Bank. In print.

Lindbeck, Assar, and Mats Persson. 2003. "The Gains from Pension Reform." *Journal of Economic Literature* 41 (1): 74–112.

Lindeman, David, Michal Rutkowski, and Oleksiy Sluchynskyy. 2001. "The Evolution of Pension Systems in Eastern Europe and Central Asia: Opportunities, Constraints, Dilemmas, and Emerging Practices." *OECD Financial Market Trends* 80: 79–130. Paris: Organisation for Economic Co-operation and Development.

López-Murphy, Pablo, and Alberto R. Musalem. 2004. "Contractual Savings and National Saving." Policy Research Working Paper 3410, World Bank, Washington, DC.

Mackenzie, G. A., Philip Gerson, Alfredo Cuevas, and Peter Heller. 2001. "Pension Reform and Fiscal Policy Stance." IMF Working Paper WP/01/214, Fiscal Affairs and Western Hemisphere, International Monetary Fund, Washington, DC.

Mesa-Lago, Carmelo. 2002. "Myth and Reality of Pension Reform: The Latin American Experience." *World Development* 38 (8): 1309–21.

Mitchell, Olivia S. 1999. "The Role of Annuity Products in Financing Retirement." In *Aging, Financial Markets, and Monetary Policy*, ed. Alan J. Auerbach and Heinz Herrmann. Heidelberg: Springer.

Mitchell, Olivia S., and Ping-Lung Hsin. 1997. "Public Sector Pension Governance and Performance." In *The Economics of Pensions: Principles, Policies, and International Experience*, ed. Salvador Valdés-Prieto. Cambridge, MA: Cambridge University Press.

Mitchell, Olivia, and David McCarthy. 2002. "Annuities for an Ageing World." NBER Working Paper 9092, National Bureau of Economic Research, Cambridge, MA.

Mitchell, Olivia S., Robert J. Myers, and Howard Young, eds. 2000. *Prospects of Social Security Reform*. Pension Research Council Publications. Philadelphia: University of Pennsylvania Press.

Müller, Katharina. 1999. *The Political Economy of Pension Reform in Central-Eastern Europe*. Cheltenham, U.K.: Edward Elgar.

———. 2000. "Pension Privatization in Latin America." *Journal of International Development* 12: 507–18.

———. 2001. "Conquistando el este: Los modelos previsionales Latinoamericanos en los países ex socialistas." *Revista Latinoamericana de Políticas Sociales* 4 (March): 39–52.

———. 2003a. "The Making of Pension Privatization: Latin American and East European Cases." In *Pension Reform in Europe: Progress and Process*, ed. Robert Holzmann, Michael Orenstein, and Michal Rutkowski. Washington, DC: World Bank.

———. 2003b. *Privatising Old-Age Security: Latin America and Eastern Europe Compared*. Cheltenham, U.K.: Edward Elgar.

———. 2004. "The Political Economy of Pension Reform in Central and Eastern Europe." In *Reforming Public Pensions: Sharing the Experiences of Transition and OECD Countries*, 23–49. Paris: Organisation for Economic Co-operation and Development.

Murthi, Mamta. 2003. "Administrative Costs of Multipillar Systems in ECA." World Bank, Washington, DC.

Musalem, Alberto R., and Robert Palacios, eds. 2004. *Public Pension Fund Management*. Proceedings of the "Second Public Pension Fund Management Conference." Washington, DC: World Bank.

Musalem, Alberto R., and Thierry Tressel. 2003. "Institutional Savings and Financial Markets: The Role of Contractual Savings Institutions." In *The Future of Domestic Capital Markets in Developing Countries*, ed. Robert E. Litan, Michael Pomerleano, and V. Sundararajan. Washington, DC: Brookings Institution Press.

Nataraj, Sita, and John B. Shoven. 2003. "Comparing the Risks of Social Security with and without Individual Accounts." *American Economic Review* 93 (2): 348–53.

Nelson, Joan M. 2001. "The Politics of Pension and Health-Care Reforms in Hungary and Poland." In *Reforming the State: Fiscal and Welfare Reform in Post-Socialist Countries*, ed. János Kornai, Stephan Haggard, and Robert R. Kaufman, 235–66. Cambridge, U.K.: Cambridge University Press.

OECD (Organisation for Economic Co-operation and Development). 1988. *Reforming Public Pensions*. Paris: OECD.

———. 2001a. *Private Pension Systems: Administrative Costs and Reforms*. Private Pension Series 2. Paris: OECD.

———. 2001b. "A Proposal for Developing a Taxonomy of Private Pension Systems." Working Party on Private Pensions. DAFFE/

AS/PEN/DW(2001)5/Rev1,   November   26.   OECD,   Paris.
Restricted.

———. 2003. *Transforming Disability into Ability: Policies to Promote Work and Income Security for Disabled People.* Paris: OECD.

———. 2004a. *Reforming Public Pensions: Sharing the Experiences of Transition and OECD Countries.* Paris: OECD.

———. 2004b. *Supervising Private Pensions: Institutions and Methods.* Private Pension Series 6. Paris: OECD.

OED (Operations Evaluation Department). Forthcoming. "The Pension Reform Evaluation." World Bank, Washington, DC.

Ooghe, Erwin, Erik Schokkaert, and Jeff Flechet. 2003. "The Incidence of Social Security Contributions: An Empirical Analysis." *Empirica* 30 (2): 81–106.

Orenstein, Mitchell. 2000. "How Politics and Institutions Affect Pension Reform in Three Postcommunist Countries." Policy Research Working Paper 2310, Development Research Group, Macroeconomics and Growth, World Bank, Washington, DC.

Orenstein, Mitchell, and Martine Haas. 2000. "The Global Politics of Attention and Social Policy Transformation in East-Central Europe." Paper presented to the American Association for the Advancement of Slavic Studies "Annual Conference," Denver, November 9–12.

Orszag, Peter, and Joeseph Stiglitz. 2001. "Ten Myths of Pension Reform." In *New Ideas about Old-Age Security,* ed. Robert Holzmann and Joseph Stiglitz, 17–56. Washington, DC: World Bank.

Packard, Truman. 2001. "Is There a Positive Incentive Effect from Privatization of Social Security? A Panel Analysis of Pension Reforms in Latin America." Policy Research Working Paper 2719, World Bank, Washington, DC.

Packard, Truman G. 2002. "Is There a Positive Incentive Effect from Privatization Social Security? Panel Evidence from Latin America." *Journal of Pensions Economics and Finance* 1 (2, July): 89–109.

Palacios, Robert. 2002. "Managing Public Pension Reserves Part II: Lessons from Five OECD Initiatives." Social Protection Discussion Paper 0219, Washington, DC: World Bank.

———. 2003. "Pension Reform in Latin America: Design and Experiences." In *Pension Reforms: Results and Challenges,* 13–122. Santiago, Chile: International Federation of Pension Fund Administrators.

———. 2004. "Civil Service Schemes in South Asia: A Rising Tide of Reform." World Bank, Washington, DC. Revised draft.

Palacios, Robert, and Augusto Iglesias. 2001. "Managing Public Pension Reserves: Evidence from International Experience." In *New Ideas about Old-Age Security,* ed. Robert Holzmann and Joseph Stiglitz, 213–53. Washington, DC: World Bank.

Palacios, Robert, and S. Irudaya Rajan. 2004. *Safety Nets for the Elderly in Poor Countries: The Case of Nepal.* Pension Reform Primer. Washington, DC: World Bank, June.

Palacios, Robert, and Roberto Rocha. 1998. "The Hungarian Pension System in Transition." Social Protection Discussion Paper 9805, World Bank, Washington, DC.

Palacios, Robert, and Edward Whitehouse. 2004. *Civil Servants Pension Schemes around the World.* Pension Reform Primer. Washington, DC: World Bank, June.

Palmer, Edward. 2000. "The Swedish Pension Reform Model: Framework and Issues." Social Protection Discussion Paper 0012, Washington, DC: World Bank.

———. 2005. "Conversion to NDC: Issues and Models." In *Pension Reform through NDCs: Issues and Prospect for Non-Financial Defined Contribution Schemes,* ed. Robert Holzmann and Edward Palmer. Washington, DC: World Bank. In print.

Palmer, Edward. 2005a. "Conversion to NDC: Issues and Models." In *Pension Reform through NDCs: Issues and Prospect for Non-Financial Defined Contribution Schemes,* ed. Robert Holzmann and Edward Palmer. Washington, DC: World Bank. In print.

———. 2005b. "What Is NDC?" In *Pension Reform through NDCs: Issues and Prospect for Non-Financial Defined Contribution Schemes,* ed. Robert Holzmann and Edward Palmer. Washington, DC: World Bank. In print.

Pierson, Paul. 1994. *Dismantling the Welfare State? Reagan, Thatcher, and the Politics of Retrenchment.* Cambridge, U.K.: Cambridge University Press.

———. 1996. "The New Politics of the Welfare State." *World Politics* 48 (January): 143–79.

Piñera, José. 1991. *El cascabel al gato: La batalla por la reforma previsional.* Santiago de Chile: Zig-Zag.

Prasad, Eswar, Kenneth Rogoff, Shang-Jin Wei, and M. Ayhan Kose. 2003. "Effects of Financial Globalization on Developing Countries: Some Empirical Evidence." International Monetary Fund, Washington, DC.

Prescott, Edward. 2004. "Why Do Americans Work So Much More Than Europeans." *Federal Reserve Bank of Minneapolis Quarterly Review* 28 (1): 2–13.

Queisser, Monika. 1998a. *Pension Reform: Lessons from Latin America.* Policy Brief 15. Paris: OECD Center.

———. 1998b. *The Second-Generation Pension Reforms in Latin America.* Paris: OECD Center.

Rajan, S. Irudaya. 2003. "Old-Age Allowance Programme in Nepal." Paper presented at the "Chronic Poverty Research Conference," Institute for Development Policy and Management, Manchester, U.K.

Rajan, S. Irudaya, Myrtle Perera, and Sharifa Begum. 2002. "Economics of Pensions and Social Security in South Asia, with Special Focus on India, Sri Lanka, and Bangladesh." Paper presented at the "Fourth Annual Conference," South Asia Network of Economic Research Institutes (SANEI), Dhaka, Bangladesh, August 28–29.

Reisen, Helmut. 2000. *Pensions, Savings, and Capital Flows: From Ageing to Emerging Markets.* Cheltenham, U.K. and Northhampton, MA: Martin Edward Elgar.

Reynaud, Emmanuel, ed. 2000. *Social Dialogue and Pension Reform.* Geneva: International Labour Office.

Robalino, David A. 2005. *Pensions in the Middle East and North Africa: Time for Change.* Orientations in Development Series. Washington, DC: World Bank.

Rocha, Roberto. 2004. "The Chilean Pension System: An Evaluation of Its Performance and Current Challenge." World Bank, Washington, DC.

Rocha, Roberto, Richard Hinz, and Joaquín Gutiérrez. 2001. "Improving Regulation and Supervision of Pension Funds: Are There Lessons from the Banking Sector?" In *New Ideas about Old-Age Security,* ed. Robert Holzmann and Joseph Stiglitz. Washington, DC: World Bank.

Rodrik, Dani. 1996. "Understanding Economic Policy Reform." *Journal of Economic Literature* 34 (March): 9–41.

Rutkowski, Michal. 1998. "A New Generation of Pension Reforms Conquers the East: A Taxonomy in Transition Economies." *Transition* 9 (4, August): 16–19.

———. 2002. "Pensions in Europe: Paradigmatic and Parametric Reforms in EU Accession Countries in the Context of EU Pension System Changes." *Journal of Transforming Economies and Societies* (EMERGO) 9 (1): 2–26.

———. 2004. "Home-Made Pension Reforms in Central and Eastern Europe and the Evolution of the World Bank Approach to Modern Pension Systems." In *Rethinking the Welfare State: The Political Economy of Pension Reform,* ed. Martin Rein and Winfried Schmahl. Cheltenham, U.K., and Northhampton, MA: Martin Edward Elgar.

Schmähl, Winfried, and Sabine Horstmann, eds. 2002. *Transformation of Pension Systems in Central and Eastern Europe.* Cheltenham, U.K., and Northhampton, MA: Martin Edward Elgar.

Schwarz, Anita. 2004. "Non-Contributory Schemes for Low-Income Countries: Issues and Progress." Social Protection, World Bank, Washington, DC.

Schwarz, Anita, and Aslı Demirgüç-Kunt. 1999. "Taking Stock of Pension Reforms around the World." Social Protection Discussion Paper 9917, World Bank, Washington, DC.

Schwarz, Anita, and Ekta Vashakmadze. 2002. "Pension Expenditure and Other Social Expenditure: Cyclical and Structural Crowding Out." Social Protection, World Bank, Washington, DC.

Settergren, Ole, and Boguslaw D. Mikula. 2005. "The Rate of Return of Pay-As-You-Go Pension Systems." In *Pension Reform through NDCs: Issues and Prospect for Non-Financial Defined Contribution Schemes,* ed. Robert Holzmann and Edward Palmer. Washington, DC: World Bank. In print.

Shiller, Robert. 2003. "Social Security and Individual Accounts as Elements of Overall Risk-Sharing." *American Economic Review* 93 (2): 343–53.

Sinn, Hans-Werner. 2000. "Why a Funded Pension System Is Useful and Why It Is Not Useful." *International Tax and Public Finance* 7 (4): 389–410.

Smetters, Kent. 2002. "Controlling the Cost of Minimum Benefit Guarantees in Public Pension Conversions." *Journal of Pension Economics and Finance* 1 (1): 1–33.

———. 2004. "Is the Social Security Trust Fund a Store of Value?" *American Economic Review Papers and Proceedings* 94 (2): 176–81.

———. 2005. "Social Security Privatization with Elastic Labor Supply and Second-Best Taxes." NBER Working Paper 11101, National Bureau of Economic Research, Cambridge, MA.

Snyder, James M., Jr., and Irene Yackovlev. 2000. "Political and Economic Determinants of Changes in Government Spending on Social Protection Programs." Background paper for the "Securing Our Future Study." Massachusetts Institute of Technology, Cambridge, MA, and World Bank, Washington, DC.

South Africa, Department of Social Development. 2002. *National Report on the Status of Older Persons, 1994–2002.* Pretoria, South Africa: Department of Social Development.

———. 2003. "Fact Sheets: Social Grant Beneficiaries." Department of Social Development, Pretoria, South Africa. http://www.welfare.gov.za/Documents/2003/Fact%20Sheets/Beneficiaries.pdf.

Subbarao, Kalanidhi. 1999. "Financial Crisis and Poverty: Adequacy and Design of Safety Nets for the Old and New Poor in Korea." World Bank, Washington, DC. http://www1.worldbank.org/sp/safetynets/.

Takayama, Noriyuki. 2003. *Taste of Pie: Searching for Better Pension Provisions in Developing Countries.* Tokyo: Maruzen.

Thompson, Lawrence. 1998. *Older and Wiser: The Economics of Public Pensions.* Washington, DC: Urban Institute.

United Nations. 2004. "Follow-up to the Second World Assembly on Ageing: Report of the Secretary-General." New York: United Nations.

United Nations Population Division. 2002. *World Population Prospects: The 2002 Revision.* New York: United Nations, Population Division, Department of Economics and Social Affairs.

Useem, Michael, and Olivia S. Mitchell. 2000. "Holders of the Purse Strings: Governance and Performance of Public Retirement Systems." *Social Science Quarterly* 81 (2): 489–506.

Valdés-Prieto, Salvador. 2000. "The Financial Stability of Notional Account Pensions." *Scandinavian Journal of Economics* 102 (3): 395–417.

———. 2002. *Políticas y mercados de pensiones: Un texto universitario para América Latina.* Santiago: Ediciones Universidad Católica.

———. 2005. "Panel Discussion: NDC versus NDB." In *Pension Reform through NDCs: Issues and Prospect for Non-Financial Defined Contribution Schemes,* ed. Robert Holzmann and Edward Palmer. Washington, DC: World Bank. In print.

Valdés-Prieto, Salvador, ed. 1998. *The Economics of Pensions: Principals, Policies, and International Experience.* Cambridge, U.K.: Cambridge University Press.

Vittas, Dimitri. 1993. "Swiss Chilanpore: The Way Forwards for Pension Reform?" Policy Research Working Paper 1093, Financial Policy and Systems Division, Country Economics Department, World Bank, Washington, DC.

———. 1998a. "Institutional Investors and Securities Markets: Which Comes First?" Policy Research Working Paper 2032, World Bank, Finance, Development Research Group, Washington, DC.

———. 1998b. "The Role of Non-Bank Financial Intermediaries." Policy Research Working Paper 1892, Development Research Group-Finance, World Bank, Washington, DC.

———. 2000. "Pension Reform and Capital Market Development: 'Feasibility' and 'Impact' Preconditions." Policy Research Working Paper 2414, Development Research Group, Finance, World Bank, Washington, DC.

———. 2003. "The Role of Occupational Pension Funds in Mauritius." Policy Research Working Paper 3033, Development Research Group, Finance, World Bank, Washington, DC.

Vodopivec, Milan. 2004. "Income Support Systems for Unemployed: Issues and Options." World Bank, Washington, DC.

von Gersdorff, Hermann. 1997. "Pension Reform in Bolivia: Innovative Solutions to Common Problems." Policy Research Working Paper 1832, Private Sector Development Cluster, Private Sector, and Infrastructure Department, Finance, World Bank, Washington, DC.

von Gersdorff, Hermann, and Michal Rutkowski. 2004. "Pension Reforms: Security through Diversity." Social Protection, World Bank, Washington, DC.

Walker, Eduardo, and Fernando Lefort. 2001. "Pension Reforms and Capital Markets: Are There Any (Hard) Links?" Social Protection Discussion Paper 0201, World Bank, Washington, DC.

Walliser, Jan. 2001. "Regulation of Withdrawals in Individual Account Systems." In *New Ideas about Old-Age Security*, ed. Robert Holzmann and Joseph Stiglitz. Washington, DC: World Bank.

Whitehouse, Edward. 1999. "The Tax Treatment of Funded Pensions." Social Protection Discussion Paper 9910, World Bank, Washington, DC.

———. 2000. "Administrative Charges for Funded Pensions: An International Comparison and Assessment." Social Protection Discussion Paper 0016, World Bank, Washington, DC.

Williamson, John, ed. 1994. *The Political Economy of Policy Reform*. Washington, DC: Institute for International Economics.

Williamson, John, and Matthew Williams. 2003. "The Notional Defined-Contribution Model: As Assessment of the Strengths and Limitations of a New Approach to the Provision of Old Age Security." Working Paper 2003-18, Center for Retirement Research at Boston College, Chestnut Hill, MA.

Willmore, Larry. 2003. "Universal Pensions in Low-Income Countries." Discussion Paper IPD-01-05, Initiative for Policy Dialogue, Pensions and Social Insurance Section, Social Science Research Network. http://ssrn.com/abstract=381180.

World Bank. 1994. *Averting the Old-Age Crisis: Policies to Protect the Old and Promote Growth*. New York: Oxford University Press.

———. 1998. "The World Bank's Position Paper on the Proposed Pension Law under the Social Security Act of Thailand." World Bank, Washington, DC.

———. 1999. "The Retirement Income System: Strengths, Weaknesses, and Direction for Reform in the Philippines." World Bank, Washington, DC.

———. 2000a. "China: Social Security Reform: Technical Analysis of Strategic Options." World Bank, Washington, DC.

———. 2000b. *World Development Report 2000/01: Attacking Poverty*. Washington, DC: World Bank.

———. 2001a. "China: The Lagging Regions of China." World Bank, Washington, DC.

———. 2001b. *Demographic Projections*. Washington, DC: World Bank.

———. 2001c. "India: The Challenge of Old-Age Income Security." Report 22034-IN, Finance and Private Sector Development, World Bank, Washington, DC.

———. 2001d. "Kingdom of Morocco. Poverty Update." 2 vols. Report 21506-MOR, World Bank, Washington, DC.

————. 2001e. *Republic of Djibouti. Pension System Reform, Strategic Note.* Report 22087-DJI, Middle East and North Africa Region, World Bank, Washington, DC.

————. 2001f. *Social Protection Sector Strategy: From Safety Net to Springboard.* Washington, DC: World Bank.

————. 2001g. World Development Indicators Database. Washington, DC: World Bank.

————. 2002a. "Building a Secure, Sustainable and Modern Retirement Income System in Senegal." World Bank, Washington DC.

————. 2002b. "Democratic and Popular Republic of Algeria. Public Expenditure Review of the Social Sector." Report 22591-AL, Middle East and North Africa Region, World Bank, Washington, DC.

————. 2002c. "West Bank and Gaza. Pensions in Palestine: Reform in a Context of Unrest." Report 25046-GZ, Middle East and North Africa Region, World Bank, Washington, DC.

————. 2003a. "Administrative Charges in Second Pillar Pensions in ECA: A Case Study Approach." Human Sector Development Unit, Europe and Central Asia, World Bank, Washington, DC.

————. 2003b. "Hashemite Kingdom of Jordan. Pension Reform: Consolidating the Social Security Corporation as the National Pension System." Report 25948, Social and Human Development Group, Middle East and North Africa, World Bank, Washington, DC.

————. 2003c. "Islamic Republic of Iran: The Pension System in Iran; Challenges and Opportunities." Report 25174-IRN, Social and Human Development Group, Middle East and North Africa, World Bank, Washington, DC.

————. 2003d. "Mongolia: Social Security Sector Strategy Paper." World Bank, Washington, DC.

————. 2003e. "Pension Reform: Tunisia." World Bank, Washington, DC.

————. 2003f. *World Development Indicators (WDI).* Washington, DC: World Bank.

————. 2004a. "China: Pension Liabilities and Reform Options for Old-Age Insurance." World Bank, Washington, DC.

————. 2004b. "Individual Account System Comparison: Singapore, Thailand, Hong Kong, and PRC." World Bank, Washington, DC.

————. 2004c. "Kingdom of Morocco. Pensions in Morocco: Toward an Integrated Reform Strategy." Report 28605-MOR, Social and Human Development Group, Middle East and North Africa, World Bank, Washington DC.

————. 2004d. "Lebanon: Assessment Report." In *Public Debt Management and Government Securities Market Development, Insurance Control Commission for Lebanon.* Washington, DC: World Bank.

————. 2004e. *World Development Indicators (WDI).* Washington, DC: World Bank.

Yermo, Juan. 2002. "The Performance of Funded Pension Systems in Latin America." Paper prepared for the Office of the Chief Economist, LAC Regional Study on Social Security Reform, World Bank, Washington, DC.

Yoo, Kwang-Yeol, and Allain de Serres. 2004. "Tax Treatment of Private Pension Savings in OECD Countries and the Net Tax Costs per Unit of Contribution to Tax-Favoured Schemes." Working Paper 406, Economic Department, OECD, Paris.

Zviniene, Asta, and Truman Packard. 2003. "A Simulation of Social Security Reforms in Latin America: What Has Been Gained?" Background paper prepared for the Office of the Chief Economist, Latin AC Regional Study on Social Security Reform, World Bank, Washington, DC.

Contributors

Indermit Gill is a sector manager and economic adviser in the Poverty Reduction and Economic Management (PREM) Unit in the World Bank's East Asia and Pacific Regional Office. Before his current assignment, he was economic adviser to the PREM vice president and head of the Human Development Network. During the 1990s, he worked as a senior country economist in Brazil, leading the World Bank's policy dialogue on pension reform. On his return to Washington, he served as lead economist for human development in the Latin America and Caribbean Regional Office, during which time he authored, among other reports, regional studies on economic risk management and social security reforms. He has a PhD in economics from the University of Chicago. IGill@Worldbank.org

Richard Hinz is a pension policy adviser in the Social Protection Team of the Human Development Network at the World Bank, where his work focuses on the establishment, regulation, and supervision of funded pension arrangements in a broad range of settings throughout the world. Prior to joining the World Bank in January 2003, he was director of the Office of Policy and Research at what is now the Employee Benefits Security Administration of the U.S. Department of Labor. In this capacity, he was responsible for managing the research, economic, and legislative analysis of the agency responsible for the regulation and supervision of private employer-sponsored health insurance and pension programs. He has contributed to pension reforms in many countries around the world since 1991 through policy development and technical assistance programs of the International Organization of Pension Supervisors, the OECD, the World Bank, and the U.S. government. RHinz@worldbank.org

Robert Holzmann has been director of the Social Protection Department of the World Bank since 1997 and is a leading international authority on pensions. His department is in charge of the conceptual and strategic

Bank work in the area of social risk management, and it leads the Bank's work on pension reform. Before joining the Bank, he was professor of economics and director of the European Institute at the University of Saarland, Germany (1992–7), professor of economics at the University of Vienna, Austria (1990–2), senior economist at the IMF (1988–90), and principal administrator at the OECD (1985–7). His research on and operational involvement in pension reforms extend to all regions of the world, and he has published 22 books and more than 100 articles on social, fiscal, and financial policy issues. RHolzmann@worldbank.org

Gregorio Impavido is senior financial economist in the Financial Sector Operations and Policy Department of the World Bank. Since joining the Bank in 1998, he has been advising client countries on pension reform and the regulation and supervision of private and public pension plans. He has participated in more than a dozen Financial Sector Assessment Program missions on insurance and pensions. He has published extensively on the impact of contractual savings development on financial markets and the governance of public pension fund management. He organizes or co-organizes two annual conferences, one on public pension fund management and one on regulatory and supervisory issues for pension and insurance markets. He holds a PhD and an MSc in economics from Warwick University (United Kingdom) and a BSc in economics from Bocconi University (Italy). GImpavido@worldbank.org

Alberto R. Musalem has been deputy director and chief economist of the Financial Stability Center of Argentina since December 2004. From 1985 to November 2004, he was on the staff of the World Bank, where he led research on the effects of contractual savings on national saving and financial markets and the organization of conferences on contractual savings and public pension fund management. He held the positions of lead economist in the Middle East and North Africa Human Development Group and adviser to the Capital Markets Department. He also worked on structural reform programs in several countries. Before joining the Bank, he was a visiting professor at several universities in Latin America and the United States as a staff member of either the Ford Foundation or the Rockefeller Foundation. Finally, he was an economic adviser to the government of Colombia as a staff member of the Harvard Institute of International Development. He has published extensively in several countries. He holds a PhD in economics from the University of Chicago. AMusalem@cefargentina.org

Robert Palacios is senior pension economist in the South Asia Region of the World Bank. Between 1992 and 1994, he was a member of the research department team that produced the World Bank's influential volume on international pension systems, *Averting the Old-Age Crisis: Policies to Protect the Old and Promote Growth*. Since 1995, he has divided his time between operational work and applied research with work in more than a dozen countries in Africa, Asia, Eastern Europe, and Latin America. More recently, he led a team that produced a major report on India's pension system, "The Challenge of Old-Age Income Security" in 2001. He is currently working in India, the Maldives, Nepal, and Pakistan, and he has served since 1998 as editor and contributor to the applied research working paper series, the Pension Reform Primer (see http://www.worldbank.org/pensions). RPalacios@worldbank.org

David Robolino is senior economist in the Human Development Sector of the Middle East and North Africa (MNA) region of the World Bank. In this position he is involved in pension reform dialogue in essentially all countries from Morocco to Iran. He is the lead author of the recent key assessment of pension reform needs and options of the MNA region. DRobalino@worldbank.org

Michal Rutkowski has been director of the Human Development Department in the Middle East and North Africa Region since October 2004. He is a former director of the Office for Social Security Reform in the government of Poland (1996–7). Between 1998 and 2003, he worked as sector manager for social protection, where he led a team of professionals working on pensions, labor market, and social assistance reforms in 28 countries of Central and Eastern Europe, the former Soviet Union, and Turkey. He is the principal author of *World Development Report 1995: Workers in an Integrating World*, and he is the co-author of the first comprehensive summary of key welfare issues in transition economies: *Labor Markets and Social Policy in Central and Eastern Europe*. He holds a PhD in economics from the Warsaw School of Economics. MRutkowski@worldbank.org

Anita M. Schwarz is lead economist in the Human Development Department in the World Bank's Europe and Central Asia Region, specifically focused on pensions work. She is currently working on pension issues throughout the region, especially focused on Georgia, Serbia, Slovak Republic, and Turkey. Previous to her current appointment, she was lead economist in the Bank's Social Protection Department, where she was team leader for the Bank's pensions work. She worked on pension reforms in Argentina, Brazil, Costa Rica, Ecuador, Mexico, Morocco, Nicaragua, Malta, Romania, Thailand, and Uruguay. She was part of the research department team that produced *Averting the Old-Age Crisis*, the Bank's seminal initiation into the world of pension reform. She has subsequently published analytical pieces as well as country-specific work related to reforms in which she has worked. ASchwarz@worldbank.org

Yvonne Sin is lead specialist in the Social Protection Department of the World Bank. She heads the team responsible for coordinating the Bank's work on pension reform. Prior to joining the World Bank in 1993, she worked as a consulting actuary and practice leader in a number of international actuarial consulting firms, specializing in asset–liability management, investment risk mitigation, pension plan design, as well as human resource management. She is an associate of the Society of Actuaries and the Canadian Institute of Actuaries and a member of the American Academy of Actuaries and the International Actuarial Association. Over the years, she has provided policy advice and technical assistance to some 20 countries around the world, including China, Eritrea, India, Lebanon, Mauritius, Pakistan, Philippines, and Romania. YSin@worldbank.org

Kalanidhi Subbarao was until recently a lead economist in the Africa Region of the World Bank, responsible for social protection, poverty, and vulnerability. He is currently a consultant on social protection for the Africa Region. Prior to joining the Bank, he taught and conducted research at the Delhi School of Economics, the Institute of Economic Growth, Delhi, and the University of California, Berkeley. At the Bank, he has played a major role in analytical and policy work on poverty, particularly in the domain of safety nets and social protection. He has published extensively on the subject and is the lead author of "Safety Net Programs and Poverty Programs: Lessons from Cross-Country Experience." His recently completed work and current research interests include aging and poverty in Africa and the role of social pensions, risk and vulnerability assessments, and the framework for social protection policy for Africa's orphans and vulnerable children. KSubbarao@worldbank.org

Hermann von Gersdorff is sector manager for social protection in the World Bank's Europe and Central Asia Regional Office, where he leads a team of 40 professionals working on pensions, labor market, and social assistance reforms in 28 countries of Central and Eastern Europe, the former Soviet Union, and Turkey. In his previous work in the Bank from 1989 to 2002, he carried out analytical and project work on pension system reform, including complementary reforms of financial and capital markets in Bolivia, Bulgaria, Colombia, Costa Rica, the Czech Republic, Dominican Republic, Macedonia, Nicaragua, Poland, Romania, Russia, and Slovakia. Before joining the World Bank, he was an economist at the Economic Commission for Latin America and the Caribbean and the United Nations Industrial Development Organization. He was also professor of economics at Instituto Tecnológico Autónomo de México and the Universidad de Chile. He is a graduate of both the Universität Köln and the University of Chicago. HVongersdorff@worldbank.org

Index